DEADLY WORLDS

~

THE EMOTIONAL COSTS OF GLOBALIZATION

~

CHARLES LEMERT

and

ANTHONY ELLIOTT

ROWMAN & LITTLEFIELD PUBLISHERS, INC.

Lanham • Boulder • New York • Toronto • Oxford

ROWMAN & LITTLEFIELD PUBLISHERS, INC.

Published in the United States of America
by Rowman & Littlefield Publishers, Inc.
A wholly owned subsidary of The Rowman & Littlefield Publishing Group, Inc.
4501 Forbes Boulevard, Suite 200, Lanham, Maryland 20706
www.rowmanlittlefield.com
PO Box 317
Oxford
OX2 9RU, UK

British Library Cataloguing in Publication Information Available

Library of Congress Cataloging-in-Publication Data

Lemert, Charles C., 1937–
    Deadly worlds : the emotional costs of globalization / Charles Lemert
and Anthony Elliott.
        p. cm.
    Includes bibliographical references and index.
    ISBN 0-7425-4238-6 (cloth : alk. paper)—
    ISBN 0-7425-4239-4 (pbk. : alk. paper)
    1. Individualism. 2. Globalization. I. Elliott, Anthony. II. Title.
HM1276.L46 2006
302.5'4—dc22   2005016340

Printed in the United States of America

♾™ The paper used in this publication meets the minimum requirements
of American National Standard for Information Sciences—Permanence of
Paper for Printed Library Materials, ANSI/NISO Z39.48-1992.

To Noah and Oscar, brothers to Annie and Caoimhe,
who by the grace of life's chances are themselves
of different times and places
—and to Matthew, who left these dangerous worlds.

CONTENTS

～

ACKNOWLEDGMENTS

~

WE OWE THANKS to various institutions that provided support for the writing of this book. The British Academy, through the awards of various grants, made possible much of the travel that was necessary to complete the project, and we are grateful to the trustees of the academy for their support. In the United Kingdom, a good deal of the research underpinning the project was carried out at the Centre for Critical Theory at the University of the West of England, Bristol, and at the School of Social Policy, Sociology, and Social Research at the University of Kent at Canterbury; and in the United States at the Department of Sociology at Wesleyan University. Versions of some of these chapters were presented in recent years as lectures or seminars at the Tate Modern, the London School of Economics, and the Boston School of Psychoanalysis, as well as at the universities of Oxford, Aberdeen, Nottingham, Nottingham Trent, Calgary, Seoul, La Trobe, and Monash.

We are, for rather obvious reasons, very grateful to those who make up "the new individualism" for giving of their time during interviews and informal discussions. We also wish to thank those who assisted us in the interpretation of the psychoanalytic case studies and other secondary materials that we have drawn upon in the telling of these narratives.

Many individuals provided helpful comments, suggestions, or responses to our work, and we would especially like to thank Anthony Moran, Nick Stevenson, Larry Ray, Alison Assiter, Judith Brett, John B. Thompson, Paul Hoggett, David Held, Sean Watson, Sam Han, Daniel Chaffee, David Stein, Dan Reif, and Jem Thomas.

Gerhard Boomgaarden at Routledge has been marvelously helpful, providing just the right editorial suggestions at key junctures, and always at hand with suggestions for how to escape the pressures of looming deadlines at the necessary moments. Also at Routledge, thanks to Constance Sutherland and Mark McKenzie. At Rowman & Littlefield, our thanks to Alan McClare.

Also, special thanks are due to Norman Bishop, the very model of an individualist who will not cut himself off from the mass of men and women; and to the late Phyllis Meadow, who, even in death, reminds those who knew her that an individual can move mountains; and also to the many who come and go through the doors of Positive Solutions and other such places, leaving little behind as they go save for the collective ghosts of their readiness to face the risks of the deadly worlds.

Finally, special thanks to Nicola Geraghty as well as Caoimhe and Oscar Elliott. And, from Charles, the same warm thanks to Geri as to Annie and Noah.

INTRODUCTION

~

KELLY JUST KNEW that bigger breasts were the way to go. Not that she needed them: she was, after all, naturally curvaceous. Pretty too. Very feminine and fashionably polished—expensively dressed, blonde shoulder-length hair, manicured nails. No, necessity had nothing to do with it. Kelly's decision to go under the plastic surgeon's knife—with a breast enlargement from 30B to 30DD—was a matter of choice. It was a matter of desire: of her wish for an improved body and above all a new sense of self.

Although on the face of it Kelly's decision to undergo a breast enlargement procedure was entered into freely, a sense of personal autonomy was the last thing plastic surgery provided. For Kelly's operation, undergone when she was only eighteen, ended unsatisfactorily. Not happy with the size and shape of her reconstructed breasts, Kelly underwent further plastic surgery—in fact, several more times—in her search for physical perfection. These operations also failed to provide the desired outcomes, and indeed a third operation ended disastrously—the implants were deemed to sit too high and unnaturally. Paradoxically, the matter of beauty (or, at least, traditional notions of the beautiful) had begun to disappear as the issue. For Kelly had become absorbed by the possibilities of plastic surgery, of how far the process of self and bodily reconstruction might be taken. Seeking to have her latest bungled surgery reversed, Kelly underwent a fourth procedure. Finally, at the age of twenty-two and after having spent in excess of $50,000, she found a meaningful solution to her specific dilemmas of identity: plastic surgery provided Kelly with 30G breasts.

Kelly's search for bigger breasts as a means of redefining her sense of individualism can be seen as part and parcel of our plastic culture of celebrity, of image, of instant identity makeovers. Yet hers is not the world of LA glitz, film premieres, or globe-trotting. She works an unglamorous nine-to-five job in promotions, and her "story" appeared in a 2004 feature article in the UK's *Daily Mail*. Journalist Morag McKinnon tells the story of Kelly—and of countless others just like her—as typical of a new breed of attractive, educated women "who are having plastic surgery at the drop of a hat—'boob jobs', 'bum jobs', Botox injections, collagen fillers, liposuction." McKinnon notes that more than a quarter of all women seeking plastic surgery in the UK are under twenty-five. Just as sociologically revealing, she gleans from her interviews with these young women who comprise "the plastic generation" an unfaltering belief that "the body can be shaped and remoulded over and over again, regardless of the price (both financial, mental and physical)."

McKinnon rightly ties these women's belief in the transformative powers of plastic surgery to our culture of consumption. "The incredible buzz of a successful operation," comments one of McKinnon's interviewees, "is like the buzz I get when I go shopping. You get a dose of that high every morning." Bodily "improvements" are thus closely interwoven with our culture of shopping—endlessly available, quickly consumed, and with immediate results. And yet however insightful McKinnon's comments on the intricate connections between plastic surgery and consumerism are, it remains the case that a journalistic explanation like this may shift the focus away from the social context in which individuals struggle to define their individualism. That is, such popular accounts of current cultural trends often fail to critically probe the social conditions that shape, and are shaped by, the passionate attachments and emotional strategies of individuals. Whether or not contemporary Western women increasingly treat cosmetic surgery as casually as buying the latest fashions, it is evident that social pressures to redesign and instantly transform one's identity are becoming a common affliction. What all of us are increasingly called upon to do, in the frame of globalizing social processes, is reshape, reconstruct, reinvent, and transfigure ourselves. Ours is the age of the new individualism.

GLOBAL SPACES, INDIVIDUALIST LIVES

Consider the following paradox. In the kind of society we live in—that of the polished, expensive, globally networked cities of the West—the lures and seductions of individualism reign supreme. Everywhere in contemporary society, people desperately search for self-fulfillment and try to minimize as much as possible interpersonal obstacles to the attainment of their egocentric designs—as the culture of individualism has come to represent not just personal freedom but the essential shape of the social fabric itself. As British prime minister Margaret Thatcher famously summed up this individualist ethos, "There is no society, only individuals and families." In the so-called do-it-yourself society, we are now all entrepreneurs of our own lives. What is unmistakable about the rise of individualist culture, in which constant risk taking and an obsessive preoccupation with flexibility rule, is that individuals must continually strive to be more efficient, faster, leaner, and more inventive and self-actualizing than they were previously—not sporadically, but day in, day out. Meanwhile, both throughout the academy and in public political discourse, proclamations about the "end of individuality" and "death of the subject" are increasingly heard.

How are we to account for this massive contradiction between our individualist culture on the one hand and our reckoning (or, some would say, denial) of today's global realities on the other? Why should it be that at precisely the historical moment individualism is raised to the second power in institutional conditions of globalization and political conditions of neoliberalism, the very notion of individualism is claimed to be obsolete by much of the academy and also in public political debate?

The term "individualism" was coined by Alexis de Tocqueville in the early nineteenth century to describe an emerging sense of social isolation in American society. A denial of social connection, the individualist creed was premised on the assumption that people should leave it to others to deal with their own problems and to get on with the living of life on their own terms. Today, evidence suggests that this individualist impulse thrives, albeit as an individualism suitably modified and adjusted to fit the technological innovations and multinational financial transactions spawned by globalization. In a report that powerfully underlines the interweaving of individualism with our cultures of immediacy, the United Nations Development Programme points to the enormous demand around the world for individual services and consumer products. "Demand" in this instance means desire for instant gratification, a desire that, as it happens, not only bolsters the sense of social isolation Tocqueville first noted when studying individualism but also carries potentially disastrous global consequences. As regards inequitable consumption, for example, the UN notes that while basic education for all who live in developing countries would cost somewhere in the region of $6 billion a year to provide, the United States alone already spends a staggering $8 billion annually on cosmetics. This inequality is not just a product of a cultural obsession with youth, beauty, and attractiveness; it derives from a more thoroughgoing individualist emphasis on the satisfaction of individual desires and the cultivation of individual needs. UN figures provide ample illustration of this, but in the interests of brevity let us selectively summarize. While the UN calculates that it would cost $13 billion to provide basic health care and nutrition throughout the developing world, the following expenditures can be noted:

- $11 billion is spent annually on ice cream in Europe.
- $17 billion is spent annually on pet food in Europe and the United States.
- $50 billion is spent on cigarettes in Europe.
- $105 billion is spent on alcoholic drinks in Europe.
- $400 billion is spent on narcotic drugs around the world.

Such statistics suggest that the ethic of individual self-aggrandizement reigns supreme in modern society, and that desires for unrestrained individualism, instant gratification, and insulated hedonism are woven into the fabric of Western culture. The popular view, generated from journalists and cultural critics, is that our increasingly individuated society expresses egoism. We are accustomed to thinking of life's possibilities and responsibilities in individualistic terms—less as interwoven with cultural relations and social problems, and more as shaped by individual decisions, capacities and incapacities, personal achievements and failures. "Narcissism" is one way to name this desocializing of people's biographies today. It is, as we subsequently argue, too sweeping to capture the daily struggles of individuals in the contemporary West, yet bears in several ways on the global transformations of our times.

When social theorists reflect on the broad contours of change influencing the private and public makeup of individualism today, they generally do so in ways that are profoundly influenced by contemporary debates on globalization. They take their cue in particular from the work of sociological authors who, struggling to grasp profound changes in social, cultural, political, and economic life, attribute major transformations to people's sense of identity, their experience of place, space, and time within the broader world, and their sense of nationhood and social belonging. Sociology has developed many conceptual angles naming different aspects of globalization. These include the "compression of time-space" through the advent of instantaneous mass communication, the intensified intermeshing of local and distant events and experiences, and the acceleration of the speed of capital and cultural flows across the globe. A list of sociological definitions of globalism would be merely scholastic, yet the transformed dimensions of individualism arising from such worldwide change might be made to come to life by reconsidering this debate from the perspective of how individuals respond—creatively, defensively, and pathologically—to globalizing social processes. This is our central concern throughout this book.

People's perceptions of a *global reality* have become increasingly important to the most emotionally felt, highly resonant, personal experience in which the textures of individualism are today fabricated. A central argument of this book is that we can understand the social impact of the development of globalization upon individualism only if we put aside traditional sociological assumptions concerning the geopolitical basis of a sense of societal belonging. For people of our times, as Ulf Hannerz perceptively notes, the notion of a "national society" is less and less vital as a source of identity and imagined community:

> There are now various kinds of people for whom the nation works less well as a source of cultural resonance. . . . it seems, rather, that in the present phase of globalization, one characteristic is the proliferation of kinds of ties that can be transnational; ties to kin, friends, colleagues, business associates, and others. In all that variety, such ties may entail a kind and a degree of tuning out, a weakened personal involvement with the nation and national culture, a shift from the disposition to take it for granted; possibly a critical distance to it. In such ways, the nation may have become more hollow than it was.

Above all, a profound change in the experience of time, work, and meaning—from a clear and fixed long-termism to a more hurried short-termism—has accompanied the rapid dynamism of technological innovation.

Sociologists like Richard Sennett have pointed to the disorienting effects of globalization on personal life—particularly how today's brave new world of impermanent contract work sets the emotional, inner life adrift. He points out that the shift to temporary, part-time, flexible employment is eroding people's capacity to create coherent narratives about their experiences of work and to create predictive narratives about the personal and social value of their lives. For one thing, the working life is shortening. In the United States, the number of men age fifty-five to sixty-four at work dropped from 80 percent in 1970 to 65 percent in 1990; these figures are much the same throughout Europe. Policy analysts predict that the working life will soon be shortened to about thirty years (from the ages of twenty-four to fifty-four). Sennett has studied, too, the damaging personal and family consequences of frequent job moves; the average American graduating from college today can expect to change jobs some eleven times, as well as change his or her skill base at least three times. The erasure of the traditional division between work time and time for family has meant not only a rise in the neglect of children but also increased levels of adult depression. Transposed to the personal realm, Sennett argues, the new flexibility demanded by unstable institutions means there is little stable ground for the individual to lodge an anchor. Keep moving and don't commit yourself is the moral to be drawn from today's hi-tech global economy.

There are some reasons to suppose that this conflict between globalization and identity has led to the kind of "hollowing out" of people's emotional intimacies as supposed by those who speak of a "culture of narcissism." But in actuality it is quite unusual to find people's biographies as emotionally stripped down as this—living without any other emotional ties, pursuing only short-term interests, completely alone and lonely. In the stories documented in *Deadly Worlds,* even the most narcissistic individuals we detail are in search of something of emotional value, something of meaning, in their relations with others, however much they find their personal difficulties intensified in a world that more and more escapes their grasp.

Individualism is and remains a master idea of modernity for a whole host of reasons, not least because ideologies pertaining to the free and autonomous individual have been essential to the patterning of relations between self and society throughout the capitalist West. Individualism promises at its core an intimate relationship with the self that explores some of the most profound issues we encounter in personal and social life. The issues of how to lead a meaningful and autonomous life, how self-development—particularly through developing abilities and skills—generates fulfillment, what intimacy and eroticism mean to the individual, and how we can open ourselves to others and explore the richness of relationships are all dimensions of our culture of individualism.

In the brave new world of globalization, new information technologies, and multinational capitalism, however, individualism has changed in three crucial ways. First, the undermining of traditions and, in particular, traditional ways of living has, as one might expect, enormously expanded the range of personal choice and opportunity for many people. As modern societies are more and more "detraditionalized" (to use a term coined by Anthony Giddens), preexisting ways of doing things become less secure, less taken for granted. It could be said that this is just a matter of the old rules and boundaries governing personal and social life dissolving, but we think not. For the import of traditions today has a reflexive aspect. Take marriage, for example. Not so long ago, marriage was widely seen as a sacred union "till death do us part." By contrast, marriage today, against a backdrop of both the sexual revolution and divorce rates soaring throughout the West, has been transformed for many into a kind of temporary arrangement, something that can be discarded. Leaving to one side the issue of whether this has been progressive or regressive, we think that what's important here is the new sense of uncertainty that such change has bred. For the likelihood of divorce must now be "factored in" by everyone contemplating getting married, a reckoning rendering marriage different from what it was in the past. At the same time, however, such changes also open our individualist culture to wider challenges and extend the terrain of emotional life beyond the inviolable character of tradition. What most complicates the thread of individualism in this connection is the *experimental feel* that much of what we do in our private and social lives takes on.

The second crucial way in which the ideology of individualism has changed in our own time is as a consequence of privatization. The neoliberal crusade to free individual initiative from the controls of the state has in recent years seen the ravages of cutbacks in welfare provisions or services, as well as the spread of a more market-led business orientation to the institutions of government, on both sides of the Atlantic. Privatism as a result becomes of central importance to large areas of contemporary urban life, especially in an age of increased mobility and digital technologies. The shrinking of communal ties and relations as a consequence of privatism is one reason that Don Watson, in *Death Sentence*, suggests economic rationalism has debased our public language. Welfare agencies try to provide better "outcomes" for "customers"; hospital managers develop "best-practice scenarios"; vice chancellors review variable university fees in order to deliver improved "educational product."

Watson's point is that a debased managerial language infects social life around the globe.

But the problem is more pervasive than any mere infection. For individualism today is intrinsically connected, we argue, with the growth of *privatized worlds*. Such worlds propel individuals into shutting others and the wider world out of their emotional lives. Under the impact of privatism, the self is denied any wider relational connection at a deeply unconscious level, and on the level of day-to-day behavior such "new individualisms" set the stage for a unique cultural constellation of anguish, anxiety, fear, disappointment, and dread. Yet to connect individualism to the new social conditions of enforced privatization is not to say that we are witnessing the end of collective ideals or, in a wider sense, the public sphere. Rather, the privatizing of identities—what we term the new individualism—becomes fundamental to the way individuals, groups, and institutions organize social things. This is the case whether people yearn for either a public, cosmopolitan lifestyle or a more traditional one.

The relation between individualism and privatization has become our central theme, and hopefully it gives the book a radical political edge for thinking about the shape of both identity and the social fabric today. The relation of individual and society has, of course, been central to the sociological tradition, of which we are, in broad terms, professional practitioners. C. Wright Mills, in his classic *The Sociological Imagination*, argued that social problems cannot have personal solutions. Notwithstanding the efforts of sociologists around the world who have taken heart from Mills's maxim in trying to foster publicly engaged social debate, the privatization of social issues has indeed become a matter of overriding political importance today. As market forces penetrate ever more deeply into the tissue of social life, what we see taking place today is a shift from a politicized culture to a privatized culture. People increasingly seek personal solutions to social problems, in the hope of shutting out the risks, terrors, and persecutions that dominate our lives in the global age.

The third important way that individualism has changed is at once more ironic and less definite than the former two. Individualism as it came to be understood after Tocqueville's observations in the 1830s was, for the most part, a value of the middle and upper classes in the European diaspora. But this does not mean that people on the social and economic margins of public life are ignorant of the lifestyles of the dominant classes. Still, the way of life enjoyed by the classically free individual, viewed as the man who removes himself from the masses, is necessarily a way of life possible only to people of means, to those able to attain and maintain a bourgeois life. The poor may aspire to the freedom, but neither the tenant farmer nor the factory worker is in a position to achieve it. Freedom, like individualism, is largely a conceit of the privileged who naively measure the differences they enjoy from the ways of the poor according to their impression that the poor simply do not know how to behave. The classical liberal principle of possessive individualism as the freedom embodied in the natural right to private property is the pure expression of the quandary of modern democratic states. They profess freedoms that can, in fact, only be attained by the landed and moneyed classes. Scratch a liberal and you'll find a Tory at worst and a democrat at best.

One of the striking facts of the current situation is the paradox that as the rich grow more distant from the poor in economic terms, the poor encroach more on the privileged cultures of the better-off. Globalization is, at least, about economics and culture. At the same time, those who think it is nothing but good tend to collapse the two, as those who think it is nothing but bad distinguish them too harshly; the reality is that the economic and cultural are both powerful forces that sometimes move in concert, sometimes in tension, but most often in complex and surprising ways. Economically the global nature of international capital has led to a net loss for the world's poorest, even as it may have pulled some into the comfortable social and economic classes. And culture in the form of mediated experiences and consumption desires has brought the rich and poor closer in the paradoxical sense that the poor cannot achieve the standards of the well-off but they can and do have a better understanding of how the other half lives.

There is ample evidence that poverty has devastating consequences for children and their families. Depression, posttraumatic stress disorder, obesity, lung and heart diseases, and starvation are rampant among the very poor, especially when they are simultaneously exposed to violence, as they are. None of these disorders of the world's social inequalities has declined, but it may be that to them is now added the affliction suffered more apparently by the middle and upper classes, that of isolation arising from being cut off from the social benefits the poor can now see plainly in the cities and towns where they beg or from which they flee. Over time, the poorer and more marginal social groups have tended to be the bearers of the traditions, religiously and ethnically most especially.

Thus, the growth of religious activism in the most impoverished regions of Africa, the Caribbean, the Middle East, and Asia is but one of the obvious instances of a cultural reaction to the inequalities of the modern world. One result has clearly been the emotional cost of the epidemic of social isolation that is always more severely visited on the poor. It makes little sense, however, to refer to the isolation of the poor as privatization if the private is taken as the interior spaces to which the individual retreats. But it does make sense if the formerly very different isolation of the poor from the means of success and self-esteem are crushed in the vacuum created by the flight of the new rich from the pains of human despair.

Throughout the book we will use the pronoun "we" and its variants as if we were speaking of all human beings on the globe. In one sense there is no universal "we" but in another there is—the we, that is, of the varieties of men and women and children who in the social inequalities are nonetheless subjected to the combined forces of globalization. Our stories are frequently, though not entirely, the stories of men and women of relative privilege. But we want to say that this is because, as is necessarily the case in the mediated world, the emotional costs of individuals of means are more visible. One is unlikely to hear about Kelly and others of whom we tell if they are not encountered in the normal course of public life. The poor are seldom on the public squares save to beg or catch a nap on the park benches, seldom portrayed on television as individuals. That their stories are less well known does not mean either that they are any less isolated or that their appeals to what traditions they may have are any less desperate than the fancier versions of the same phenomena among the world's credit card holders. If globalization has emotional costs, as surely it does, it is going to have them on the poor and wealthy alike—or, if not exactly alike, comparably. Our book is not primarily about the poor, who have always paid the greater emotional costs of life in this world. But neither is it meant to exclude them. This, simply, is an aspect of the problem about which less is known because the evidence is less available than one day it will be.

DEFINING THE NEW INDIVIDUALISM

Accounts of individualism often characterize our current cultural preoccupation with the self in terms of narcissism, emotionalism, the manipulation of individual needs or desires, and a quest for self-realization and self-fulfillment. Such accounts highlight the constraining or more negative features of our individualized culture and often present the world as shot through with traumatic consequences for people's emotional lives and relationships. As we argue in more detail in chapter 2, while these accounts contain useful insights, they fail to grasp the most central features of a new individualism sweeping the globe today. In *Deadly Worlds*, we argue that the rise of a highly individualized common language for experiencing and defining public issues is a double-edged phenomenon, one that promotes the realization of self-fulfillment as well as the cultivation of self-limitation. The culture of advanced individualism has ushered into existence a world of individual risk taking, experimentation, and self-expression—which in turn is underpinned by new forms of apprehension, anguish, and anxiety stemming from the perils of globalization.

Perhaps the most distinctive feature of the new individualism is the playing out of these positive and negative features—the cultural trends toward freedom and alienation—against a backdrop of the demise of social context. Today, people in the polished cities of the West make sense of experience on the edge of a *disappearance of context*. As science and new technologies offer alternative paradigms and possibilities for social life, we have replaced the old contexts of tradition and custom with a focus on our individual selves. This shift of focus from the old rules and boundaries to the internal world of the individual is now central to the contemporary mood. The main legacy of this cultural trend is that individuals are increasingly expected to produce context for themselves. The designing of life, of a self-project, is deeply rooted as both social norm and cultural obligation.

Everyone knows that the world is dramatically remaking itself in this period of intensive globalization. Hardly anyone doubts something like this is happening but each still asks, what changes does this carry for my personal life? How is the experience of individualism different now from days gone by? As it happens, although our experiences as individuals are very different, we tend to believe—as if instinctively—that the inner dimensions of our personal and social lives are something special, rare, precious, and thus worthy of nurturance and protection. But how to get at these "inner dimensions" of the individual experience of global transformations?

The fascination with identity in general, and individualism in particular, has encouraged us to write about the experience of globalization from the individual's perspective. There is, of course, no shortage of works purporting to account for the accelerating pace of globalization and how this impacts upon daily life. One published book has chapters on global finance and its personal impacts, globalization and mass migration, corporate power and personal development, and the democratization of globalization and its cultural consequences. Another covers topics that include contemporary states of mind, postmodern pathologies, borderline personalities, and identity crises. Our book is unlike these and contains little in the way of direct answers to the cultural problems these other books pose.

This book adopts a focused psychosocial approach to understanding the complex ways that modernity and globalization impact upon individual lives and experiences. Through this concentration on individuals and their imagined worlds, we seek to come to a better understanding of how global transformations shape, and are shaped by, human emotions. Throughout *Deadly Worlds*, we draw on interviews and informal discussions, and related material, carried out by ourselves and other researchers; some of this material dates from the late 1980s, but the bulk of it is very recent. Our aim in concentrating on the global circumstances of individualism is to unearth the jumble of emotional and social forces at work in real lives, and to that end our approach or method is plural, open-ended, reflexive. As well as making use of in-depth interviews, we have also engaged with daily experiences of people's individualism through informal discussions and ongoing encounters with our subjects. Other sources range from newspaper reports and interviews with ordinary people to more specialized material, including psychoanalytic case histories. While our discussion of the various lives documented in *Deadly Worlds* often draws from real cases or interview material, most individuals necessarily appear under pseudonyms to protect confidentiality. This, in turn, following the path-breaking lead of Susie Orbach's fictionalized case method in her provocative *Impossibility of Sex*, led us to dramatize and invent certain aspects of characters in the pages of this book. Again the impulse was to ensure anonymity, while our hope is that we have accurately captured the sense of the most deeply felt, highly resonant, emotional experience that people conveyed to us in both formal interviews and informal discussions. And finally, we make use of autobiographical reflections and of detailed biography, notably of our daughters in the opening chapter. In developing stories of what the practice of social things in global conditions is like from the individual's point of view, we try to convey something of the performative dimensions of individualism, of what is involved in *doing* identity: the emotional difficulties posed, the interpersonal and cultural issues encountered, and above all the *feel* of the new individualism.

Modernity's new individualism is not only in its accelerating globalism, massive Internet traffic and G3 technologies, proliferating fast-food outlets, increasing ease of international travel and tourism, or infernal transnational pollution problems and urban traffic jams. It is also in the expansive emotional literacy and cultural cosmopolitanism of its people who, in their diversity, have developed ways of living that are more open, experimental, and privatized than was the case in the past.

Finally, it is important to add the following qualification to the claims we develop in this book. Most of the biographical vignettes and materials presented are drawn from the Anglo-American world—specifically, from the lives of people struggling to define their individualism in contemporary Britain and the United States. The political geography that informs our thesis of an emergent new individualism should not, however, be taken to imply that such individualizing processes are dominant features of societies only in the Anglo-American world. From Singapore to Tokyo, from Seoul to Sydney, the creed of the new individualism features significantly in the private and public lives of citizens. The new individualism, we argue, is an emergent phenomenon that increasingly affects personal and social aspects of everyday life. It does not define in advance the ways people live in the world's rich states and certainly has less impact in the developing societies. But its reach, at once emotional and cultural, is increasingly global—thanks to the twin forces of globalization and the communications revolution.

CHAPTER ONE

INDIVIDUALISM FOR BEGINNERS

When Caoimhe Met Annie Somewhere in Global Space

W E WHO COME together in the writing of this book are similar only in superficial aspects. Crudely put, we are both white men of sufficient age and cultural capital to be university professors. As things go in this world, that turns out to be a not insignificant degree of similarity. Yet, otherwise, we are astonishingly different. One of us is quite a bit older, if not decrepitly so. We were born ages as well as continents apart—the one in America, the other in Australia. Even more, the American still lives in the land of his birth, while the Australian lives and works in Britain. These are real differences that in an earlier time would have made the writing of a book together improbable if not impossible. Yet, as it turns out, thanks to the efficiencies of travel and electronic communications, it is neither strange nor especially difficult to join in this work.

As it happens, the differences between us, like the similarities, are on balance relatively unimpressive when we compare ourselves to our daughters, who are both lovely and of roughly the same young age. Neither yet is in regular school. Though, by accident of their births, they live an ocean apart, these two little girls know each other, have played and had lunches together, and long after their weeklong visit they speak of each other. Yet they are different, or so we suppose, in some basic ways that people of our older generation are unlikely to have thought possible. Caoimhe is the daughter of an Australian father and an Irish mother who met in Cambridge, England. Already before she could utter words with a lovely trace of the Gaelic of her given name, Caoimhe had passed a good many months of her life in Dublin, as well as in England, and of course in Australia too. Anna Julia, the older of the two (and the one who never finished her lunch), has been away from America but once—and this on the occasion when she got to know Caoimhe; and this by virtue of a plane trip of such unbearable duration that her parents have since vowed never again to attempt such a thing until Annie is able or willing to sit still for more than a few minutes. Anna Julia thus would be a bit of a homebody by contrast to her younger friend were it not for the fact that Anna Julia has as many parents as Caoimhe has grandparents and familiar countries. Anna Julia, it happens, is beautifully brown as a result of having been born to a very white birth mom and an obviously quite black birth dad. She will never know her bio-dad, or so we assume, but she will know her bio-mom, whose photo she keeps in her room. Yet her parents—those whom she calls mom and dad—are Charles and Geri, both quite white, as well as quite taken by their daughter. As a result of the beautiful accident of *her* birth and adoption, Anna Julia may turn out to be no more a homebody than Caoimhe. Both girls will have to travel many miles over the course of their lives in order to discover and rediscover, then to decide how to feel about, their oddly disjointed places and occasions of origin. It may be that they will travel by different means—the one more by air across the global surfaces, the other on some interior plane across the emotional life. Both will take both kinds of trips, even if one logs more discount miles with the airlines.

How different, then, are Caoimhe and Anna Julia from their parents, much less from each other? In all times and places, parents have asked themselves this question. The answer, if it can be found at all, is not of course in the once exceptional, but now common, experiences of being brought up English by an Australian dad and an Irish mom, in Caoimhe's case; or of being brought up African American by two American whites, in Annie's. Though once less common than today, such international or inter-racial families, whether formed by adoption or the old-fashioned way, are not all that unusual. Certainly, they are not so beyond the pale of human understanding that their parents, or even their grandparents and other elders of the tribe, could not conceive of the circumstances of the unions and rearings-up that brought them into being. If the children just now coming into the world turn out to be different from any other previous generation of children, it will not be because of the exceptional arrangements that gave them life. Whatever else makes them different from other animals, human beings seem more able than the rest of the biological kingdom to vary, sometimes oddly, the particulars of their arrangements for birth and life, not to mention death. Exceptions always abound.

So, then, what causes two white men of professed if not proven intelligence to think that the generation of these two girls of the newest generation just might be different from children of all or most other generations of the species? The answer is that they, like a good many of *their* generation of experts on the human condition, think it is likely that, in some basic ways, the world into which today's children are born is different in kind from any other recent world of human experience. This may sound, at first, like a well-worn truism of little compelling value. Hardly anyone who thinks about it, whether parent or expert or otherwise, can fail to see that the speed of travel, the ease of communication, the multicultural politics of the world, the new transnational economic markets, and much more, have made the world either compellingly better or tragically worse (this according to differences of experience). What we, as parents of small children, trouble ourselves with is not this so much as something vastly more urgent—a something so different that, at the least, we wonder if it is possible any longer for our daughters to become individuals of the albeit different kind their fathers have become. And if not, strange as it may seem to put it this way, will our daughters still become human beings in roughly the same way that previous generations of human beings have been what they supposed they were meant to be?

The simple, if scantily remarked upon, fact is that *who* and *what* we are as individuals is always, and necessarily, a consequence of the worlds in which we grow up. To be an individual is to be the product of experience with a generous company of other individuals. Individualism, if such a basic fact of life can be an "ism," is never utterly the effect of what one does with oneself. Individualism, in other words, is not a "private matter" or a "personal dilemma," since what millions of men and women discover daily is that fashionings of the self cannot be performed outside of relations with others, who, given that they too are preoccupied with themselves, are remarkably cooperative.

If you are indeed a proper member of the European diaspora—of, that is, those social groups that are often called the "West" and those parts of the world influenced by Western culture—you might want to say, at this point, "So what's new about individualism?" Complicated perhaps, but obvious. We are both individuals and social at the same time. We live and work in the daytime with any number of rude, kind, sloppy, neat, appealing, obnoxious people; yet, at the end of the day, we fall asleep alone, even when there is someone beside us. And even during the waking hours, we spend a good bit of time in our own reveries—daydreaming on the subway, thinking of how we'd like to look while shopping, taking note of what others see when we are walking down the street alone, and more. Even then we are preoccupied with our "selves" while contending with others and what they, even strangers, may be thinking of us. We may be wrong to overestimate the extent to which anyone else, even those we live with, actually and truly care about *us*. But we are not wrong to take note that how we feel about who *we* are is very much caught up with what others just might think of us, were they paying attention. Still, turn the coin of the obvious over, and you'll see something else. If the individual is somehow a product of his relations with others, then it stands to reason that whichever others in whatever kind of social combinations makes all the difference in the world as to who we might be or become.

Why people think of themselves as possessing an enduring core of being—a Self with a capital S—is a matter of history. Ever since moderns felt that the doctrine of the Soul was a bit too religious for secular company, the idea of Self came into being. And as people once thought of themselves as having an eternal Soul, so too did modern individuals in the West come to think of themselves as having a unique Self with all the qualities that once were attributed to the Soul. But if individuals admit that their Selves are somehow a result of their social interactions, then it stands to reason that a Self can never be a once-and-for-all thing. This is because it is obvious that societies change over time (even in the time of individual lives) and that individuals move from place to place, thus exposing themselves to different social influences. Moderns travel. And travel involves new social encounters, which in turn are liable to affect us deeply. More than a few middle-aged people take a weekend in the Cotswolds or on the coast of Maine and decide to give up life as a stockbroker and become an innkeeper. More than a few students travel to Africa during college and decide to quit their economics studies and become sociologists of international development. More than a few lonely housewives fall in love with someone down the street, travel into another emotional world, and decide to give up the husband to go live with her. On it goes.

So, the question we ask is, simply: Since everyone seems to think the world as we knew it once is passing away, how does this affect who we are as individuals (or whether or not it is possible to "be" an individual at all)? We dare to write of our daughters, not because we are preoccupied with them (which we are), but because it is evident that, as the world turns in time, they were born to a day when their futures will present very different social challenges from those either of us encountered when we, at different times, were young.

ARE THE EMOTIONAL COSTS OF THE NEW INDIVIDUALISM ALREADY UPON US?

Kelly's attempt to negotiate the culture of our new individualism, sketched in the introduction, gives a very powerful indication not only of the potentially severe emotional costs of globalization but also of the future-orientated mentality demanded by this method of living. How do I look today, and how might this measure up to how I will be judged according to my looks tomorrow? Fortunately, it will be a while before our daughters begin to worry about their looks in quite this way—about, that is, how they wish they would be seen as women in the world that will have already told them how a woman ought to look. They may or may not be caught in the vicious circle that led Kelly from a doubt about her already fine feminine figure to a series of tragic remakings of her body that had the effect of an addiction that had the further and ever-more-tragic effect of cutting her off from the very world from which she drew the odd conclusion that an already beautiful woman ought to look somehow different—better according to an impossible-to-achieve bodily perfection.

Will Annie and Caoimhe become Kellys? As fathers we hope not. As fathers who think about what the worlds are becoming, we cannot be sure. At the time of our retelling of her story, Kelly was twenty-three. At the time of their first encounter in Bristol, Annie and Caoimhe were more or less twenty years younger. In the course of their growth into womanhood the global worlds will, we presume, continue to spin and turn in many of the same directions as they were shortly after the beginning of a new century. What will happen in the course of those two decades in the lives of all people, young and old, alive when the planes crashed into the towers is no more than a larger version of the question we ask of the futures of our children. Or, more directly said, the way people wonder about their futures is not so much in the abstract as in the concrete of their feelings and concerns about what the future will bring for them and those they love. Let the philosophers worry about the meaning of time and its futures. Let parents worry all the more seriously about what the world holds for those dear ones they hold when, years from now, we can no longer hold them as now we do.

It is possible to know the past, even to have a confident idea as to what is going on in the present. But the future is beyond us in more ways than one. To the extent that we think about it, we think about it with feelings. The future is a space of hopes and fears—and is thus the only human space that is filled less with facts and events than with our emotions. In a hardheaded culture where people are taught to think and speak with respect for the facts, it is sometimes difficult to accept that the emotions are every bit as real in their effects as are the facts. If anything, they are more real, not less, because facts must be argued and proven, while emotions just are what they are. To have children at any time is to be filled with emotions that sustain life—the love we feel for them (a love that dwarfs the power of the fabled romantic love that may have brought forth the children in the first place) can be ever renewing. Parents are brought to life by it even when they are weary from midnight feedings or troubled by cuts and bruises. Though it sometimes works otherwise, children are born to the parents who bear them and who in turn are reborn. Such a feeling, when it is available and embraced, is an emotional state that pays benefits again and again.

But, sadly, there are as many occasions when the emotions are costly. Sadder still is the fact that the same children who give us life compounded out of the life we give them can be the occasion for emotional debts so grave as to take it all away. We refer here not so much to the extreme cases of parents who turn abusive because they were abused, or even to others of the routine examples of depression and violence that occur all too often, as to the ways that beneficial love can be decimated by a terrible turn in the global facts of human life. Love of children (or any other beneficial emotion) must always be measured against the risks that could take away the worlds in which our emotions are structured and made possible.

Globalization is a word for the worlds whose final nature we will not know until our girls are themselves full of figure. But to the extent that we use it now, we ought use it cautiously as a way of talking about a change in the larger, perhaps the largest, social structures in which and against which all of us must live. If there is any universal *us* it is the *us* of those who, today and for the foreseeable future, must face uncertain prospects brought on by the speed and unpredictability of global transformations. What in twenty years time, any twenty years from any now, will turn out to be risks or promises of life with the mass of social others is a prospect about which we can only *feel*—feel with information, to be sure, but feel. And, in this regard, the *we* of the all that must live on the globalizing island have good reason to feel that we and our children—all those we love and all those we loathe—face as many risks as we do assurances. The very prospect of so uncertain a prospect is itself costly. The one great advantage of the modern world that stretched from about 1500 to 1991 was that, at least for those in secure positions, there was a prevailing faith in progress, hence in the likelihood that, as miserable as things may be now, there would be a better day.

When some talk about the end of modernity, they would do well to speak precisely of the loss of the promise of modern progress. We simply do not know what any future will bring, but certainly not the future in which global encounters so invade the local and personal, even intimate corners of the soul and body, that we are vulnerable in ways that twenty years and more before the new century few would have imagined possible. Yes, of course, over the centuries women bound their feet, forced their tummies into corsets, buttressed their bosoms, and much else. But only in recent years have women sought to have their bodies cut and remade in search of an ideal new individualism. And let us not forget the men who drug themselves in the search for more prominent biceps. The promptings for such decisions, we contend, go back to childhood, to the deepest hopes and dreads experienced during the very earliest years of self-definition.

Children are increasingly identified with the cultural gains of technoliteracy. This is, at any rate, what adults in the polished, expensive cities of the world—overcommitted, overstretched, and generally time-poor—tend to think about the young today. So, typically, today's generation of technokids is viewed as the product of a subsiding of industrial social structures and the increased flexibility of new information and communication technologies. The more yesterday's world of solid social structures dissolves, linked as this dissolution is to a communications revolution that bites deeply into the fabric of daily life, the more it falls to the next generation to embrace the new technologies, to figure out the latest technogadgets and their myriad uses.

In a 2005 survey collated by ChildWise, a market research agency specializing in young people, an eye-opening picture emerged of children's access to the latest technogadgets. Mobile phones, MP3 players, DVDs, Net-surfing, texting: these shape the present condition of childhood, certainly in the UK, according to ChildWise, and perhaps increasingly in the postmodern West. According to this survey of schoolchildren in England, 13 percent of five- and six-year-olds and 24 percent of seven- and eight-year-olds now possess a mobile phone. These figures rise to 58 percent among those aged ten, 89 percent of those aged twelve, 93 percent among those aged fourteen, and 95 percent of those fifteen and over. This picture of rapidly escalating mobile phone use by the very young is, in effect, repeated with other forms of technology. To list just two of the more noteworthy from ChildWise, a third of children under the age of eleven have DVD players in their bedrooms, and one in ten has an MP3 digital player. Cultural reactions to these statistics are interesting, precisely because to date there seems to be a neat divide between the positive and the negative. For the positive camp, this generation of technokids is to be welcomed in terms of useful future employment skills. Computerization and the knowledge society demand technoliteracy, and so the sooner children come to grips with the new technologies, the better. For the negative camp, such an upbeat interpretation of these figures can only be maintained if divorced from social context. That is to say, the pessimists worry that technoliteracy achieved in childhood is purchased at the cost of a loss of interpersonal maturity due to premature withdrawal from family intimacies. Technokids are, in short, antisocial, or at least asocial. Individuals ill formed and social members ill equipped.

Whether anxiety that technology is leading the young to become antisocial is misplaced is hard to say. Similarly, it is impossible to say, with any degree of certainty, whether the technoliteracy of young people today really will render them tomorrow's useful employees. But what does arise for consideration, surely, is the issue of how today's imbrication of technology, information, and communications alters or transforms not only how we experience our sense of identity and individualism but also the very process—at once social and emotional—by which young people come to think of themselves *as* individuals. In this respect it is clear that the communications revolution and new technology wear away at embedded social structures as well as traditional ways of doing things. Technology penetrates to the core of human experience, turning people's emotional exchanges into units of information, as the latest holiday snaps are compressed to jpeg files and e-mailed around the planet in seconds and the most private, intimate biographical details are routinely typed online in order to go Internet dating.

Sociologists the world over have been preoccupied in recent decades with the conditions and consequences of advanced technology as regards our social and personal lives. The advent of the term "information age" has been one outcome in the contemporary sociological imagination, as specialists in the field have sought to map the impact of global communication flows on the textures of everyday social life. French social critic Jean Baudrillard argues that our globalized era of mass communications and brilliant technology has ushered in mediated simulations of reality as never before. Perhaps more than any other theorist of the information age, Baudrillard captures how flows of communication, information, images, ideas, and ideologies pervade every aspect of daily life, from digital and satellite television to mobile phones and the Internet. Central to this analysis of the information society is a shift from modernist understandings of reality to a postmodern conceptualization of simulated reality, or of what Baudrillard calls "hyper-reality." The age of the hyperreal, he contends, "begins with a liquidation of all references." What he means to say is not simply that reality is mediated (which, to varying degrees, is true of all societies) but that our worlds today are *saturated* by media simulation. Military violence as outstripped by the globalization of terror and terrorism; sexuality as outflanked in the pornography of silicone and hard sex; fashion as raised to the second power with supermodels: media simulation for Baudrillard "implodes" the world it seeks to represent. In consequence, life in a world of 24/7 mass media is one in which people experience, struggle, and try to cope with *signs* of the real.

In a world in which fleeting signs of the real issuing from televisual media are the central building blocks of identities that are themselves fractured and split, nothing holds for long. The world "as shown on TV" is one of flickering, simulated events, disposable products, phantasmic places, sanitized information, and addictive signifiers. This is the world that the next generation accesses, and evidently with increasing ease, with the aid of the latest technologies. The extent to which individualism is grounded in new ways as a result of these technological developments is key to grasping the dilemmas of identity that the young now face the world over.

CHILDHOOD, IDENTITY, AND THE
SENSE OF EMOTIONAL FREEDOM

Shrieks of delight can be heard from the upstairs landing. Running, giggling, laughter: the unrestrained happiness of childhood. It appears from all this noise that Caoimhe and Annie have become interested in, indeed fascinated with, something. For the parents, suspicion abounds. What are they up to now? Whatever it is, we check. Our own ways of knowing pleasure link us, instinctively, to our children. And we know that such noisy pleasure probably spells trouble.

News of minor traumas travels fast on the domestic front, and this time is no exception; it filters through to us from upstairs that a lamp in Caoimhe's bedroom has been knocked over. With parents arriving on the scene, both Caoimhe and Annie stare at the lamp on the floor. What happened? Who did this? As if grasping the complex links between transgression, punishment, and guilt, both look sheepish. "Don't know," murmurs Caoimhe. Annie runs off. Caoimhe follows. Happily, the lamp isn't broken. Happily, Caoimhe and Annie don't care. Minor traumas are habitual work for parents.

Childhood is the art of making the world anew out of the world as we find it. We don't choose our parents, but we do make something with and out of them—through unconscious desire, attachment, creativity, and symbol formation. So what are we to make of Caoimhe's little white lie, of her not quite true but not alarming false account of ordinary events? One thing we might make of it is that it is perfectly normal behavior for a child. A parent or schoolteacher might rebuke a child for "lying"—for being less than fully honest. Leaving aside for the moment whether that parent or teacher could pass the same test of perfect and complete honesty in all her dealings, one might wonder whether children tell incomplete truths for a purpose. If you can imagine yourself a small child—even more, a little girl in an adult world where already you get the idea that that world treats girls differently from boys—then ask yourself what you would do to deal with such an overwhelming social world. Kids know, in some way or another, that their parents love them. But loving them can be a very abstract thing for a kid who is but a third the height and a fourth the weight of these loving monsters who ask you to sit still at tables you can hardly reach, who put twice as much food as you can eat on your plate, who watch a television screen on which the pictures are of strangers nearly your size, perhaps, but somehow adults like your parents, who are in fact much bigger. What kind of a social experience is this? And to make it worse, the loving parents seem always to know what you are doing. They make it their business. They seldom know anything about what you are thinking (mostly because you aren't really thinking anything much at all, whatever thinking might be). Still they suggest to you what they think you are thinking, and the suggestions are often quite ridiculous.

What do you do if you live in such a world, with such peculiarly attentive big people? What you do is lie. It is the only way to make some space for yourself. It is the only way to make up a world of your own. Sometimes you lie by making up playmates who don't really exist. Annie once talked to her friend "Mousie"—a little rodent that was ever present, always at the ready to take blame when things went wrong, always the one to whom she was talking when she forgot and talked out loud to herself. And so kids lie—or, that is, they make believe the world they live in is one they have a part in making (even when they know they don't—or so we parents assume).

As it happens, one of the better-established, if controversial, methods for helping human individuals understand themselves is founded on the axiom that people lie. Psychoanalytic theory—in all its many versions—provides stories about the complicated process of self-transformation, of making identities out of what we are given. And psychoanalysis begins by accepting the fact that what we do in conscious life is always similar to, if not the same as, what we do in our unconscious lives. Dreams, for example, are elaborate stories that on the surface are completely false but underneath express secrets most precious, if terrifying, to our innermost selves. Dreams may seem quite a specialized aspect of an individual's life (though a psychoanalyst would say the opposite). But they are very common if you think of the lies we tell in order to maintain a cover, in order to have a world of our own. When Caoimhe professes innocence of an audible event in her room, or Annie puts off a minor infraction of her own making on Mousie, she is speaking, in a way, in dream language. The girls are expressing what they wished were the truth—that someone else had done whatever, or that nothing had happened in the first place. And when they develop elaborate play stories, then they are dreaming while wide awake. If you suppose children are different that way, just monitor your own daily musings—catch yourself daydreaming and think about the stories you were telling yourself (or even the lie you tell your friend or mate when she asks, "What are you thinking?").

Like most stories we craft from our instinctual needs, our capacity to lie (or tell falsehoods) is rooted in fantasies—about ourselves, others, and the wider world—and the desire for passionate relationships. Freud said, time and again and in countless ways, that the unconscious is hell-bent on pleasure. You could assume from this that the inventiveness of a lie—the sheer creativity of fabricating stories about self and world—suggests the narcissistic complexity of what we do when we go about obtaining unconscious pleasure in our daily lives. In a sense, psychoanalysis has always been about, among other things, the *emotional costs of the lies we tell ourselves*. A lie, after all, gives shape to our wishes, it gives narrative direction to the self. We might think of the little white lies of childhood—of the kind we see Caoimhe and Annie experimenting with—as novel challenges to the world as it is found, to the already-made adult environment. Little white lies of childhood are thus a kind of warm-up for adult life—for the rich illusions and distortions by which selves both make sense and challenge the sense of direction of life.

There are various parallels between what we've been saying about children's capacity for the telling of lies on the one hand and the claims many people (mostly analysts or therapists) make for psychoanalysis on the other. The telling of incomplete truths can, under certain conditions, facilitate a degree of personal freedom, allowing the child to elaborate her imagination and experience shared social norms governing interconnections between the self and others. It is in and through the immediate connection and unspoken understanding of very early forms of friendship that the child gathers the necessary narcissistic support to "go beyond" the world provided by parents. The child's imagination, the child's self-transformational project, depends upon her being able to emotionally connect with others in order to explore "where she is in the world." So, too, the telling of little white lies can sometimes suspend the oppressive weight of parental expectations or cultural norms and allow one's true self to flourish. The affinities here with psychoanalysis, at least in theory, if not for all those who daily confront their inner demons with the help of an analyst, are striking. The aims of analysis, as Freud and his followers have long insisted, are for the analysand to be able to enjoy more inner freedom, achieve the relative autonomy to think alternative viewpoints, and experience emotional life in all its complexity.

When kids get together and play, in the fashion we've observed of Caoimhe and Annie, all sorts of emotional opportunities and risks gradually emerge, generating in turn both thrills and anxieties. Play, among other things, always encourages children to go public on themselves—to speak up, as it were, for their emerging identifications and visions of identity. Through interaction with (and feedback from) others, children can begin to get some kind of sense of what might be going on inside themselves, of their multiform ways of relating and responding to the world around them. Such self-investigation of character is what Erik Erikson, one of the most preeminent post-Freudian analysts, calls our need for "identity"—a relative freedom to transform cultural givens into a sense of possessing a singular self that persists over time. This need for identity often involves taking apart preconceived ideas about things or people before putting the self back together in a more complete form, thus opening a path for the toleration of anxiety, fear, and ambivalence. Although Erikson doesn't refer to friendship, children's play, or the telling of incomplete truths directly in his writings, his thinking implies that we all need a little help from our friends—from infancy through to old age. There is indeed a special role for friendship in negotiating what Erikson terms "identity crisis"—periods where people struggle to define themselves anew, taking a long, hard look at themselves. What Erikson is certain of, at any rate, is that identity is *needed* to provide "a *subjective sense* of an *invigorating sameness* and *continuity*." Caoimhe and Annie are some years away from having to deal directly with such matters. But there are preliminary strivings after identity observable from their play, in their self-absorption and immediate connection. For if growing up is a process of disillusionment, it might be said that, through their play, Caoimhe and Annie are experimenting with what one cannot provide for oneself.

Theories that stress continuity of experience and interpersonal recognition enjoy widespread popular and academic support today. Surely troubling, though, is the emphasis put on identity as smooth functioning (or what Erikson called "invigorating sameness and continuity"). This is troubling since such a viewpoint obscures something rather unsettling in the Freudian legacy: an attention to the strangeness, to the otherness, to the unpredictability of emotional life itself. Yet this may not be the worst of it. In our view, notions of "smooth-functioning identity" are completely at odds with how lives are lived today. In our age of hyperindividualism—which stresses instant transformation, flexible reinvention, and creative renewal—conventional assumptions regarding the solidity and durability of identity are increasingly disrupted.

GLOBAL DIFFERENCES AND THE
BIG LIE OF PERSONAL HONESTY

In earlier times, when the ideal of the modern individual was taking form in the new industrial cultures of America and Europe, one of the classical ideas of Western civilization remained a strong ethical principle. This idea was, of course, the notion that individuals are destined for honesty, that an individual's most fundamental civic virtue is his name, which was a way of saying that individuals were reputed to be men of integrity. In those days it was indeed an ethical expectation that applied to men who, with rare exception, were the ones among the middle and upper classes with a stake in public and commercial life. In general terms, to be a reliable individual was to be known as one whose word was good because he possessed an inner quality of honesty. To be an individual in the classes where this idea prevailed was to be honest, hence reliable.

The bourgeois idea of the honest man was, as we said, an early modern way of carrying forward the religious idea of the human soul—that core of personal being that was both the source and the standard of individual worth—and the *soul* as it came to be in Judeo-Christian cultures was itself a translation of the ancient Greek idea of the moral individual as the high-minded person. In fact, the very word for our modern term *psyche* comes from the Greek root of this ancient value of high-mindedness: *megalopsychos,* as in fact the English-language term *soul* is itself derived from the same source as *psyche.* It is evident from even a quick run through the languages that one of the deepest and most abiding expectations of the good individual is absolute honesty—from which we take the idea of integrity. To be an honest man is to have integrity, which is to say, to be one who is one, or a moral integer.

What saves this discussion of the terms from being a mere excursus is that it points to one of the fundamental dilemmas—equally psychological as sociological—in all attempts to assess the state of the modern mind. When modern social psychology began, roughly in the 1890s, writers like William James understood very well that in the new urban life of the industrial era the individual was caught in a contradiction. On the one hand, he expected of himself this classical virtue of integrity, which in James's *Principles of Psychology* was labeled *personal identity*, which itself was a turn on the words. To have an identity was to be, as James put it, the same today as one was yesterday. Or, we could say an individual's identity is the extent to which he demonstrates integrity by being the same from time to time, throughout life. At the same time, William James recognized, as did everyone else who thought about it, that in the modern world individuals were not always the same. They couldn't be. In a small town or neighborhood it was possible to achieve a degree of honesty in the sense of constancy across one's dealings with others. But this was because the others with whom one dealt were likely to be people of much the same sort. Villagers in the early modern English countryside knew themselves because they were known well by others who were lifelong neighbors and kinsmen. But put the same individuals in London in the early industrial era, not to mention today, and they will encounter strangers who do not know them. It is very hard to know who you are when others do not know you to begin with. Thus began a concept that William James, and after him many others, called the *social self.* The individual, as James put it, has as many selves as there are people who recognize him. Quite evidently this concept is a reliable way of describing the experiences one has in complex urban places where many cultures come together, making the stranger the normal individual—the one whose integrity cannot be certified by his name because his name is not known.

As a result, even early in modern life the individual faced a quandary. How do I remain an honest man of integrity while also dealing with the varieties of people I must deal with who, if they know me at all, know me only partially? A banker is known by his children in ways astonishingly different from the ways he is known by his colleagues in the bank, who must trust his integrity in a way different from how his children trust him. Arthur Miller's tragedy of the modern man, *Death of a Salesman,* turns precisely on a chance encounter in which one of the man's children encounters his father on the road as empty and fraudulent, as a man who seeks women of the streets to shield himself from the pain of personal failure children are loath to recognize in their fathers.

What this means is that moral individualism as it arose in early modern culture was always to some extent an unachievable ideal. Few individuals could honestly be one with themselves—not because they were intent upon dishonesty but because the circumstances made it nearly impossible to be the same today as one was yesterday. In fact, in the business of urban life, it is difficult to be the same right now as one was but a few minutes ago. One of the ways social theorists accounted for this dilemma was to explore, as did the American sociologist Erving Goffman, the art of impression management. In Goffman's view, impression management was mostly what the individual did to keep a face, or an honest self, in public life. Others felt he went too far, yet even Goffman's opponents could not deny that to some degree one's personality is true to its own origins as a term. Classically, a *persona* is a mask. To be a person, or to have a personality, is literally to put on a mask.

To this point, the story of the honest individual's dilemma is a difficult one, but not entirely impossible. The middle and upper classes manage still to hold firm to their professed sense of individual integrity and honesty, even as the wise among them understand that absolute moral consistency is unrealistic. But what happens when the already hard complexities of urban life are intruded upon by global differences? What makes today's London or New York or São Paulo so demanding on the individual is that, in a sense, the global city is something entirely beyond the cities of the early modern factory system. It is not just that today's London is much, much larger than the London of Charles Dickens in the mid-1800s. Today's global cities are transformed more by the varieties of people who come to them to live than by the number. Even in monolingual cultures like the United States it is hard to get by without Spanish, and it can be a risky business to hire a cab when the directions are heard by a driver from Haiti or Yemen whose grasp of English is weak and of Spanish nil. And this is only the beginning. Much is made of the fact that "everyone" is expected today to know English or American. But the fact remains that beyond the language of business are the bewildering pressures to conform or at least to understand the differences in customs businesspeople bring to the table. And this rather limited experience is itself nothing in its demands to the images from all over the world that come down into private and family life in the homes of the rich and poor alike. Bollywood films are like, but not the same as, Hollywood ones. Still, women of the aspiring classes in Bombay will try skin-lightening cream, a product that originated among American blacks who felt they needed to pass as white to survive in the urban world. After a fashion, the presence of hip-hop music and dress in China is part and parcel of the African beat in American hip-hop.

Thus—and for now we leave aside the question of whether it is a good or bad thing—women like Kelly worry fathers like us because we fear that our girls might turn out as she has. How indeed will our little girls avoid the pressures of global realities as conveyed to them by the supposed miracles of information technologies? Annie and Caoimhe were technoliterate before they could read. Caoimhe knew more about air travel before she could walk than Charles's grandmother ever knew. Annie early on somehow got the point that she was expected to get down with black culture in ways that surprised her very white parents. When a child of African American genes and phenotypically white parentage becomes a hip-hopster before she can even know about, much less sing, an American patriotic anthem, who is she? Or, better put, who is she to be? Time will tell, but it will tell one thing for certain. She will be many individuals at once because she already is, and so she will be for reasons that go far beyond her life as adopted child. After a fashion all children today are adopted. Caoimhe lives with her bio-parents but this does not make Nicola and Anthony any more "real" parents than Charles and Geri are to Annie. Nor, as we say, do Annie's early travels across the borders of her cultural mind make her all that different from Caoimhe's across the seas that separate England and Ireland and both from Australia.

It is not, we suppose, that no one ever encountered these risks and potential costs before the present day. Rather, the point is that so many do in fact and nearly all do in principle. What is the consequence, then, if it is not that what is becoming normal for the new individuals of our time, whatever their social class or cultural home, is that they can no longer aspire to the classic ideal of pure personal honesty? To live in a world where there are so *many* others, most of them virtual strangers, who recognize us—or if not this then encounter us—is to live in worlds of many colors and stripes. To get by in such a global place it is, therefore, necessary to be willing to lie. The child's play of make-believe, even children's tactical lies before damage they fear they've done, is truly child's play before the looming reality that one is expected to be like, if not exactly like, Kelly. One would hope to avoid the pain Kelly suffered. But who is to say who one is when there are so many possibilities? How do we accept our bodies, much less our "selves," for what they are when so many have their own ideas about the ideal shape of bodies or the proper way of behaving? The new individual is never really one but always several, thus constantly in search of the right way to be something more or less the same over time while also contending with the changing and challenging differences with which the others we meet may study us. No wonder, then, that Kelly retreated into the process of self-remaking, losing all the while her sense of what she wanted to be, much less who she was.

THE INDIVIDUALIST IMAGINATION

In what ways do the generational and cultural changes we've been discussing interact with transformations in personal life more generally? How do institutional changes sweeping the globe (from processes of democratization to market deregulation) connect to everyday influences upon personal conduct and our living of lives as individuals? Moreover, in our age of rampant individualism, what meaning can be given to identity? Why is it that modern men and women, in both their routine and their reflective lives, return so often to the idea of individualism? To answer these questions means interrogating key personal and political transformations associated with identity and individualism, reflecting on what individualism is and how it became something that individuals have laid claim to, as well as tracing the shifting "contents" or "objects" that make up this ambiguous phenomenon. These issues will be our central concern in this book. But to forestall possible misunderstandings, let us emphasize one central thread of our argument: *the myriad ways in which we today choose to identify ourselves as individuals—as the autonomous architects of our lifestyles—has already begun to undermine the very idea of individualism itself.* Our culture of individualism, to be sure, has become a tragically self-defeating project, one whose every act of advancement or progress turns ineluctably back upon itself to undo its own enabling conditions. Why should this be so?

On a global scale, the entrenchment of liberal ideals—from neoliberal corporatism to New Right fundamentalisms—presents itself as pivotal to the crisis of individualism. The public sphere, so various critics say, is now first and foremost the custodian of individualist cultures: consumerism, identity politics, antiglobalization warriors, New Ageists, techniques of the therapeutic, and so on and so forth. Such a critique is accurate in various senses, and we devote attention to this *individualization of the public sphere* in subsequent chapters. Yet such individualizing trends within society at large can be traced back to the origins of liberal tradition itself, for liberalism has always been, in effect, an atomized doctrine that pitted the all-privileged individual over and against the terrain of external nature, common belief, and social life. The liberal's pathologizing fear of others—and especially of dependence upon others—is

plainly evident in the doctrinal idea of the sovereign individual, introduced most notably by John Locke. Against the Hobbesian concept of
the supremacy of the modern state, Locke articulated an account of both
public and private right that emphasized that adults can reason for
themselves, and so can and should pursue their own objectives, dispose
of their own labor, and possess their own property. So far, this all seems
fairly uncontroversial (at least from the vantage point of today's world),
but it is important to emphasize the radical extent to which Locke's
atomistic doctrine abandoned each individual to her own *supposed* natural unity, dissolved all entangling cultural and civic involvements, and
projected the good society as one that recognized the mixing of
autonomous selves. The ideal of individualism, on this reckoning at least,
is thus rooted in a guaranteed, fixed essence of the self. However, in a
striking irony, this annulment of interpersonal bonds, affective ties, and
civic connections actually entails the destruction of the power of the individual to carry on in the world as a self-legislating, autonomous individual. The founding myth of a supposed unity of the self in classic
liberalism denies any relational quality to the human personality and
thus leaves the individual self bereft in a world of abstract rights and
atomized social relations.

As regards individualism in our own time, there are three major
sociostructural features throughout the Western world that have disrupted, displaced, and at times dwarfed the core liberal project of realizing a self-legislating society of autonomous individuals. These features
are commodification, the new cultural politics of the political Right,
and privatization. The intensification of processes of commodification—
uncovered in the works of Karl Marx and Georg Lukács and perhaps
best analyzed in recent times by the German critical theorist Jürgen
Habermas—depends upon the regrooving of markets through the
advent of monopolies and multinationals, as well as the promotion of
individualist values in terms of the logic of cultures of consumption.
Yet the penetration of the logic of market systems into the fabric of cultural relations and the rules governing social interaction is itself profoundly damaging. The more we come to define our lives in terms of
consumption, the more this immense market of possibilities begins to
undermine the very objective conditions by which people experience
their own needs and desires, let alone our capacities to make meaningful
emotional connections with each other. The consumer's dream of freedom can all too quickly turn into its opposite, as narcissistic satisfaction

("I am what I buy") turns into a cry of bitter despair ("All this is so vacuous and meaningless").

The remaking of ourselves and the larger society in the image of cultures of consumption, however, is not the only reason for the disintegration of individualism. It is also a consequence of a seemingly unstoppable political shift toward a new conservatism and reactionary intellectual consciousness. Radical Right politics in the West, inaugurated in the United States by President Ronald Reagan and in Britain by Prime Minister Margaret Thatcher, was responsible for destroying human communities and solidarity on a scale not previously witnessed, and for providing the powerful ideological substitute of market deregulation that shaped (and has continued to influence) the attitudes, expectations, outlooks, and sensibilities of each of us. In the monetarist era after Reagan and Thatcher, transnational capitalism promoted such individualist forms as central to lifestyle and the maximizing of individual potential, and as a result private and public values were rapidly remolded. This ideological remolding produced in turn various concrete, specific political forms: the market came to be cast as the absolute measure of all worth, freedom was refigured as the unencumbered right to buy and sell, and money was designated as the final arbiter of life and thus of the future. The creative destruction of the market has, of course, always been at the core of capitalism, the only supposed way to guarantee an opening of economic opportunities and personal possibilities for everyone. But the rush to neoliberal privatization contains the promise of more than merely increased economic freedom to act. Privatization, it is said, will produce a worldwide transformation of barriers, of public and private spaces. The intimate connection, forged over many years in the collective psyche, between the domain of government and the public good is today rendered a fantasy of a bygone era, as the world is remade according to capital mobility and the selling off of governmental assets to the private sector. In the end, the separation between the public and the private looks decidedly shaky, as previously protected public spaces—from education to health care—are sold to the highest bidders.

If capitalism in its advanced stage of multinational globalism has bred a plethora of corporate vices, ranging from arrogance and greed to tunnel vision and institutionalized deceit, so too other kinds of pathological consequences have been discernible in personal and cultural life. Some of these pathological consequences are easy to see: witness the devastating implications of the Enron scandal for thousands of U.S. employees, who find themselves without that much-needed privatized retirement portfolio, and thus devalued and demoralized in a world where money is the measure of all things. Other distortions are harder to spot, but they are at work, reshaping the needs and desires of individuals who are increasingly encouraged to think of their lives in terms of market options, risk calculations, and lifestyle segmentations. "In Bush's 'Ownership Society,' Citizens Would Take More Risk" runs the February 28, 2005, headline of the *Wall Street Journal*, which announces that under George W. Bush's rewriting of the government's social contract, "the emphasis would be on the individual" in controlling retirement savings, as well as planning for education, job training, and health insurance. Similar rejoinders to the individualizing challenges of our era have been developed in Tony Blair's Britain and John Howard's Australia and by other governments throughout the postmodern West.

Much has recently been made of the ways in which mass privatization and deregulation breed social exclusion. Critic Naomi Klein, in *Fences and Windows,* contends that the privatization of public assets has produced large segments of people who are locked out from various fundamental social provisions—shut out of hospitals, schools, workplaces, their own homes and communities. Leaving aside the issue of the complex relations between corporate power, global production networks, and mass deregulation, one might responsibly wonder whether those individuals socially excluded from such service provisions are merely locked out or whether the fences—both real and virtual—erected through privatization haven't created more permanent, structural barriers. For example, the overall effect of denying countries loans from the International Monetary Fund for failure to curb government spending, as occurred in the case of Argentina in recent times, institutionalizes privatization as a kind of command and coercion of transnational state action.

But things run still deeper, and this takes us to the third and most important feature of institutional change affecting the texture of individualism throughout the world, which is that of privatization. Privatization—best critiqued in the writings of the sociologist Zygmunt Bauman—concerns the spread of neoliberal economic doctrines into the tissue of our social practice itself. This process expands market deregulation into personal and intimate life, producing in turn isolating, deadening, calculating forms of life. As we understand it, this process concerns above all the emotional isolation generated as a consequence of privatized spaces and privatized worlds. In a society awash with flashy commodities, and against the backdrop of the commodification of water, electricity, music, sex, and ideas (just to name a few things that the market ruthlessly colonizes), our language for representing and elaborating our image of self-identity is more and more fixed into a syntax of possession, ownership, control, and market value. What we are suggesting is that people today increasingly suffer from an emotionally pathologizing version of neoliberalism. More and more, individuals translate—in the sense of projecting desires, reimagining Self with a capital S—experience in society, in business, and also in private life as reducible to self-regulation, self-management, and self-sufficiency. Understood this way, the individual self—in extending its imperial sway over the social environment—liquidates the solidity and substance of the world into a privatized terrain of needs and desires. Such flights of fancy (fantasies which, to repeat, are essential to our culture of hyperindividualism) involve, fundamentally, a denial of dependency. "Privatized" could here be roughly translated as the imperative: "Don't rely on anyone for long, and avoid support or help from others, as survival depends on going it alone, constantly changing partners and networks, and always looking out for Number One." Fear of dependence, in turn, places a further strain on the intrinsically lonely parameters of privatized life, as individuals head off manically in search of all sorts of illusory substitutes to fill in for what is missing in their private and public lives.

New information and communication technologies play a fundamental role in this translation of public, private issues into privatized experience. More and more, and for increasing numbers of us, the mass media are where we get our language, where we learn to construct narrative continuity of self and world. So it is worth asking, and this we pursue in following chapters, how much of the heavy-handed selling of risk-avoidance strategies and commodities comes to be translated in such a way as to make sense only at an individual level, for the self alone. From the marketing of exercise machines (to keep the body fit and stave off illness) to home alarm systems (to keep others out of one's privatized space), the translation of broader collective problems (health care, crime) into privatized dangers and risks is at once spellbinding and amnesiac, such that we come to feel trapped inside our privatized worlds like a goldfish in its bowl. This brings us back to the emotional costs of globalization, the considerable costs that men and women condemned to live a privatized existence will do so much to avoid or deny, partly, as it happens, by deploying risk-avoidance merchandise to soothe their anxieties. As a form of emotional defense, therefore, risk-avoidance merchandise feeds into that part of the mind that reassures us and becomes very parenting.

It is this social condition of privatization—of social things continually eroded into individualized dilemmas—into which Caoimhe and Annie have been born, and from which the lasting social differences that will mark their lives have already impacted their emergent identities, ways of relating, and ways of responding. Such a deregulated, liquidized, and privatized world may offer considerable illusion or magic: the posttraditional social environment into which Caoimhe and Annie have been cast offers new levels of freedom to do whatever one may choose, on the terms one may choose, without too much regard for social convention or cultural prejudice. Yet while a world privatized, a world in which everything goes, can be exhilarating, those negotiating that world are not immune to anxiety. For even the freedom to pursue anything can become crippling, as the anxiety of choice floats unhinged from both practical and ethical considerations as to what is worth pursuing.

Too much choice.

CHAPTER

TWO

~

WAS THE FREE INDIVIDUAL JUST A DREAM?

Snapshots of Individualism and the Illusion of the Good Society

WHATEVER ONE thinks about the world today—whether even it is possible to speak of a *world*, as opposed to *worlds*—one unavoidable fact of life, so early in the twenty-first century, is that it has been shaped decisively by the dream of human freedom, which itself has largely been a dream of "the free individual."

In 1782, when the culture of modern world, or modernity, was taking on its definitive shape, one of Europe's most influential, and controversial, writers began a most unusual book with the following astonishing proclamation:

I have begun on a work which is without precedent, whose accomplishment will have no imitator. I propose to set before my fellow-mortals a man in all the truth of nature; and this man shall be myself.

I have studied mankind and know my heart; I am not made like any one I have been acquainted with, perhaps like no one in existence;

39

if not better, I at least claim originality, and whether Nature has
acted rightly or wrongly in destroying the mold in which she cast
me, can only be decided after I have been read.

These are the words with which Jean-Jacques Rousseau began his *Confessions*,
a personal narrative of his life through which, as the words reveal, he
claimed nothing less than to set forth the claim the he was an utterly
unique human individual. Centuries later, such a claim would not seem
so outrageous. Even in 1782, not all of Rousseau's readers would be surprised by his audacity.

This was a time when the modern dream of the free and absolute
individual was still being forged out of bits and pieces of social thought
that had been coming together for the good while of the preceding two
centuries. It was the eve of the French Revolution and just at the end of
the American War of Independence from the British. The year 1782 was,
in short, precisely the moment when moderns began to imagine their
new world, a world that would still be a long time coming—and, important to add, a dreamed world that might have been doomed to remain a
dream unconsummated by any enduring reality.

Rousseau was far from the first individual to contemplate his
uniqueness, nor was he the first to write a confession of the details of his
personal life. Still, Rousseau the man and the book he wrote were different in their way. While nearly fourteen centuries before, in 397 C.E.,
Augustine of Hippo wrote his own famous *Confessions*, Augustine's memoir was really a spiritual document, an account of his personal struggle
with his own very powerful human appetites and of how he overcame
them, an overcoming that led to the sanctification of his career as one of
the Western world's exemplary religious writers and leaders. Augustine's
purpose was to spread the faith and build up the Christian church.
Likewise, well more than a century before Rousseau, in 1637, René
Descartes famously proclaimed his *Cogito ergo sum* doctrine—the principle that consciousness of one's own ability to know was proof positive of
the existence of autonomous human self: *I think—that is, I know—therefore
I am.* But Descartes' purpose was philosophical: to establish the self-
conscious individual as the beginning point for modern knowledge.

Rousseau's purpose, like his claim, was different from any that came
before. His confession was not so much an apology for his life as an asser-
tion of *his* unique value as a model for the new and free individual. What
lent weight to Rousseau's audacity was that he had, through his previous

writings, already done much to establish the political actor as the ground-work of the French and other revolutions that would make the modern world what it would become. That Rousseau had reason to trust that his uniqueness might serve as an example to others is shown by two facts of his extraordinary life.

First, he *was* an individual in that he lived the life of a vagabond. Cast off by fate from his native town, Geneva, he found his way as a child to a foster mother, who became his lover. Thereafter, as he grew to adult-hood, he moved from place to place seeking the comforts of patrons, who like his adoptive mother tended to offer him more than warm meals and a roof over his head (like Augustine, Rousseau had a voracious appetite for pleasure). His vagabondage was often required by the need to find personal or political asylum from his opponents. Rousseau lived, in other words, as the modern exile—the one constantly in search of the better home as a way to the good life.

Second, Rousseau was the social theorist par excellence of modern social and political life. His famous doctrine of the social contract as the essential structural feature of modern society was a decisive break with the more abstract doctrines of the individual found in the writings of English and Scottish philosophers of the early modern world. John Locke, for example, had earlier taken Descartes' principle of the con-scious self an important step forward by asserting that the one definite basis of human knowledge was the self-evident sense of the individual experience. Locke's political ideas were, in their way, nearly as important as Rousseau's on American revolutionaries like Thomas Jefferson and Ben Franklin.

Still, Rousseau stood on different ground from other early philoso-phers of the individual. His purpose was to define the primacy of the social in the new world order. Yet, ironically, his method was to proclaim that the collective life, while the first fact of society, was itself derived from the general will of the individuals gathered into the social contract. Rousseau's astonishing claim to put himself forward as the one "if not better, at least original" served, in effect, to solidify centuries of uncer-tain development in social thought about the Individual—the effect of which was to prepare the way for the dream of free individualism that would define and frustrate the struggles over the two centuries follow-ing his confession and the French Revolution it helped spark.

In 1791, in the Paris Rousseau had fled on more than one occasion, and just a decade after Rousseau completed his *Confessions*, *The Autobiography of Benjamin Franklin* was published. Franklin had written his own memoir (decidedly not a confession of any kind) over the last years of his life, which ended in Philadelphia just the year before. (Rousseau himself had died three years before that, in 1778.) Though today neither Rousseau nor Franklin is widely read save by those with a special interest in philosophy and history, in the crucial years of the revolutionary eighteenth century their stories and ideas were among the most famous of any living individuals'. And, of the two, Franklin was the more famous, as he was very possibly the most conspicuous celebrity of his day.

Benjamin Franklin was, more or less justifiably, known for the "discovery" of electricity in his bold and legendary experiment with kites and lightning. In fact, his mind was constantly at work with one or another scientific experiment. Even as a very old man, sailing home to Philadelphia for the last time, he invented a method for measuring the temperature of the ocean depths as a way of mapping currents.

Still, as honored as Franklin was for his science, he was, if anything, better known for his careers as a diplomat and a philosopher. As diplomat he negotiated the treaty with France that sent military and financial support to the Americans in revolt against the British. And when the American colonies had won their independence, he negotiated the peace treaty with the British on terms favorable to the Americans. And Franklin's philosophy was unlike any other philosophy then going under the name. Not even Rousseau's very public philosophy was quite as public as Franklin's.

From the days of his youth, well before he had entered political life, Franklin had been a printer, which gave him the means to become a public writer by printing and publishing occasional pieces of his opinions (often under the guise of fiction). Soon enough he formed familiar, often business, relations with newspaper publishers (and eventually became one himself). These relations ensured him regular access to the reading public for his clever musings on the events and struggles of the restive British colonies. Then, in time, he settled on the unusual practice of publishing personal advice, most famously in his regularly appearing *Poor Richard's Almanac*. Franklin's social philosophy, though it often addressed political issues, was based first and foremost on offering his personal wisdom as to how others ought to live. In this, Franklin took Rousseau's audacity one step further. While Rousseau had dared to "set before my fellow-mortals a man [himself] in all the truth of nature," Franklin's practical aphorisms were not so much a model of the ideal individual life as direct instruction as to how individuals might live their individual lives.

It surely would not have been possible for Ben Franklin to give advice that stood any chance of being taken were it not for the fact that in many ways he was the modern world's first international celebrity. Today, we would describe him as a global personage much on the order of figures like Muhammad Ali, David Beckham, Aung San Suu Kyi, and others whose human appeal somehow transcends their personal accomplishments. Franklin was truly an accomplished man, a writer, scientist, revolutionary, diplomat, and philosopher. But of all these, it is surely his brilliance as a diplomat of the pre- and post-Revolutionary American colonies that made him famous.

Well before 1776, Franklin was a delegate of the colonies to London, where his assignment was to mollify the Crown in the face of growing rebellion in Britain's North American colonial interests. His position was strengthened by the fact that at the time he considered himself loyal to the Crown, while opposing the arrogant and increasingly ruthless behavior of the king's colonial administrators. Franklin sought reform in the system, not revolution. Yet, though he would gradually come over to the side of the revolutionaries back home, his genius as a diplomat had less to do with the convenience of his convictions than with his marvelously patient and canny method in relations with others. Franklin was a splendid storyteller, a raconteur who entertained many a social gathering with tales and yarns told always for a purpose. He used the fiction and the legend of his own personage as an indirect method for making a point (in this he was surely a pioneer in the narrative method of diplomatic signaling). The ploy worked so well because Franklin was a person of extraordinary charm, one who was slow to attack his enemies and quick to forgive them when possible, as he was steadfastly patient in the building of relations with others (perhaps most notably with young women who found him irresistible in more ways than the merely platonic). It did not hurt, of course, that he was, in the UK and Europe generally, thought to be the most famous American of his day. The word of his writings on so many subjects had spread rapidly beyond the circles of those with a direct interest in North America. He was, thus, a global man before the word—a personality whose appeal touched corners of the European world, and even a few nooks and crannies beyond it.

Once the Revolution broke into open warfare after 1776, Franklin was sent to Paris to negotiate the interests of the rebellious colonies. The

Americans needed loans from those nations that opposed the British (of which none were so interested in curbing British power as France). They needed, and got, munitions and military support. But in the early days they needed most of all the assurance that the French would do nothing to advance the British cause, which in effect was the same as providing the aid they required. As apparent as it might have seemed that the French would oppose the British, the fact is that in that day nationhood was not so well defined as later it would be. Before the collapse of the old regimes of inherited royal authority, the several royal houses in Europe were of course bound to each other by marriages of diplomatic convenience. Thus, for one instance, the French were not entirely free to offer unilateral support to the Americans without the consent of the Spanish, with whom they enjoyed diplomatic family ties, not to mention their own colonies and ventures in the New World. This was the challenge Franklin faced, when he arrived in Paris accompanied by his illegitimate son and personal secretary and a very few others. He faced long odds with a small staff.

What was Franklin's method? It was, very simply, the deployment of charm. He installed himself in a home in Passy made available by the generosity of a Parisian notable. Soon Franklin's afternoon levee blossomed into one of the hottest social events in town. His evenings were spent in social dining and other less discreet adventures with the influential and wealthy of Paris. Though his command of the French language was uncertain, he soon became one of France's most visible characters. His method, again, was the employment of his grace as an exceptional individual. To be sure, he obeyed the social conventions that governed courtly social life. But Ben Franklin's obedience to the norms was always marked by striking symbols of individuality. Both in London and Paris, he very often declined to wear the wig customary for gentlemen and dressed himself in the plain clothes others would associate with the rough-hewn people of the New World. (Franklin himself was anything but rough-hewn, though he could put the image into play.) In Paris, his most exceptional display of individual image making was the habit of wearing about town, often on his social calls, a fur cap, which itself quickly became the fashion rage of the day in Paris, a most fashion-conscious town.

Franklin was, in short, the studied performer of the conceits of *the* individual of the New World. Over the years, Franklin's embodiment of the ethical principles of the pure individual—thus of individualism itself—

was recognized after a lapse of geography and time. More than a century later, in Germany, the great turn-of-the-twentieth-century sociologist Max Weber made Benjamin Franklin the key to the evolution of modern economic and social life. By 1905, Weber, just then recovering from a devastating period of incapacity due to depression, had finished the essays that would come to be his most famous book, *The Protestant Ethic and the Spirit of Capitalism*. Just the year before, 1904, Weber had paid a long visit to the United States, where he was particularly impressed by the diffusion of the ethic he meant to define by the phrase "spirit of capitalism."

In brief, Weber's idea was that, though it was perfectly evident by the beginning of the twentieth century that capitalism (the economic system) had become the "tremendous cosmos" of the modern world, there remained an important question about the enormity of it all. Where did the capitalists come from? The question turned on the evident point that capitalism required a specific type of individual—one who was willing to work hard, with self-sacrificing discipline, carefully marshaling his resources, then investing time and cash money in enterprises that promised a profitable payoff. But, of course, the promise was hardly ensured. The essential virtue of the capitalist entrepreneur was that of an individual willing to take risks for gain but ready to calculate the odds that the risks might pay off. The capitalist of Weber's sociological imagination was, in short, the rugged individualist—a figure already well in evidence in his day even in Europe but especially in the burgeoning industry of the American North.

To be sure, Weber's book is read mostly by college students and academic specialists, who to this day debate his claim that the source of the new spirit of the entrepreneurial individualism was in the doctrines of sixteenth-century Calvinism. Yet, among those who have never bothered to read Weber (and would likely be put off by the complexity of his academic language) there would hardly be many who have not heard the expression "the work ethic," which is a shorthand version of Weber's so-called Protestant ethic. The capitalist work ethic was and is the attitude of calculated discipline that may have started in the obscure details of Puritan religious thinking but which came into full bloom over the years of the eighteenth and nineteenth centuries in the widespread ethic of the new entrepreneurial individual of rising industrialism that would become the tremendous cosmos of capitalism.

And how did Weber make his point in this otherwise difficult book? As it happens, and it did not happen by accident, he defined and described the emerging entrepreneurial spirit by using none other than Benjamin Franklin as the evidence. Though Weber doctored up the method (that of the "ideal type") whereby this one remarkable individual could be made to represent the new individualism of the modern world, the choice could well have been made quite independently of his methodological plan. What better proof could there be of the spread of a new entrepreneurial ethic than the fact that it may have existed well before industrial capitalism (which emerged strongly late in the nineteenth century) and well after the religious philosophies from which the ethic may have sprung, which were native to the sixteenth and seventeenth centuries? And what better certification of the spread of this new ethic of the forward-looking, calculating individual could there be than the existence of a man like Franklin, and of the near universal popularity of his writings? Not only was Franklin the celebrity of his time, and a global man at that, but he was also the very nearly pure and exceptional source of the teachings that appear to be necessary for the rise of a class of entrepreneurs.

Who has not heard some version of Franklin's preachments on the new individualism of the eighteenth century?

> Remember, time is money. He that can earn ten shillings a day by his labour, and goes abroad, or sits idle, one half of that day, though he spends but sixpence during his diversion or idleness, ought not to reckon that the only expense; he has really spent, or rather thrown away, five shillings besides.

This is from one of Franklin's earliest bits of public advice and wisdom (in this case *Advice to a Young Tradesman* from 1748). It contains all the ingredients of Franklin's ethical rules: *Time is money and both must be invested with discipline. Idleness is a waste. Industry is the key to individual success.* To which is added Weber's shrewd insight that the very popularity of the rules handed down by the famous eighteenth-century man is proof positive of the origins and nature of the modern individual of the new industrial world.

It hardly need be said that *individualism* implies (as Rousseau's first line allows) an infinite variety of *individuals* each with his own peculiar tastes and philosophies. Yet, there would hardly be a modern world—the one shaped by the revolutions to which Rousseau and Franklin contributed and, just as important, Weber's new world of industrial capitalism that came to be—were there not some common element that bound however loosely the infinity of individuals into an accord of some sort as to the importance of *individualism*.

This precisely is the key to the distinctiveness of the modern world as it was for a good two centuries or more. But this individualism is precisely also the subject of a very considerable debate early in the twenty-first century—a debate that suggests there now may be a series of very different ways of looking at individualism, or perhaps we should say ways that define another *new individualism* by the terms of its contradictions.

The debate as it has come to pass early in a new millennium earns a good bit of its urgency from the acute and global sense that all previous ideals of the new individual may have failed at the near impossible task they were meant to achieve. Near impossible, we say, precisely because the goal of the early modern ethic of individualism was no less than the establishment of a final, and evident, Good Society. Though in the course of the years since Rousseau and Franklin there have been good moments for the dream of the Good Society, there have also been as many, or more, bad moments—periods in which, by the cumulative weight of social violence and human misery, the dream of the potent moral individual as the cohesive force of the morally good commonwealth has turned from sour to bitter. So bitter has been the failure of the social whole to provide stable and reliable goods for its individuals that the dream withers against the growing terror of social failure into, for many, an illusion.

In a sense, the failure of the dream should surprise no one, and would not, had not so much social hope been vested in it. The prospect that the autonomous and robust individual, trusting her own inner strengths, would be sufficient to bind a social whole of any serious complexity is, on the face of it, implausible. It would be laughable were it not for the early witness of men like Rousseau and Franklin and so many of their contemporaries among the French philosophes and the American revolutionaries—men who were anything but fools, men who emboldened subsequent generations to trust that if only they could do as these men had done, they would bring to consummation the revolutionary social order of which the modern West had dreamt so fervently. That it has not come to pass—or, more modestly put, that it has not become a self-evident prospect—is perhaps nothing more than the fine underbelly under the thin skin of modernity's self-confidence. And from this angle, it may well be that the reason there is such a controversy today over the still newer new individualism is that moderns—or even their postmodern kin—are so reluctant to give up the only dream they ever knew.

INDIVIDUALISM, INDIVIDUALISMS

The term *individualism* today conjures up an unusual, though sociologically revealing, diversity of associations. Ours is the era of identities individualized, and our current fascination for the making, reinvention, and transformation of selves is, in some sense or another, integral to contemporary living. Living in an age of individualism requires individuals capable of designing and directing their own biographies, of defining identities in terms of self-actualization and of deploying social goods and cultural symbols to represent individual expression and personality. Yet in current social circumstances—in which our lives are reshaped by technology-induced globalization and the transformation of capitalism— it is not the particular individuality of an individual that is most important. What is increasingly significant is how individuals create identities, the cultural forms through which people symbolize individual expression and desire, and perhaps above all the speed with which identities can be reinvented and instantly transformed.

This paradoxical situation is perhaps especially evident in contemporary representations of individualism in popular culture and the media, particularly the selling of "lifestyles" and of do-it-yourself (DIY) identities to mass audiences. Apple Computer's 1998 Think Different campaign illustrates this well:

> Here's to the crazy ones. The misfits. The rebels. The troublemakers. The round pegs in the square holes. The ones who see things differently. They're not fond of rules. And they have no respect for the status quo. You can praise them, quote them, disbelieve them, glorify them or vilify them. But the only thing you can't do is ignore them. Because they change things. They invent. They imagine. They heal. They explore. They create. They inspire. They push the human race forward. Maybe they have to be crazy. . . . we make tools for these kinds of people. Because while some see them as the crazy ones, we see genius.

Whatever else individualism may offer—and in the "Think Different" campaign the promises are undeniably large and varied, from imagination to rebellion to craziness—identity embodies a palpable cultural contradiction. Apple draws a direct connection between its high-tech aesthetics and individual expression, between the technological revolution and personal genius. And yet the campaign, paradoxically, sells individuality to a mass audience.

How did such a cultural contradiction come about? How can it be that individualism—which, one might think, is by definition opposed to cultural regulation or social consensus—has ended up, in some social contexts, opposed to autonomy? More generally, how might the meanings we attach to individuality influence our lives and our worlds? And what models of individualism best capture the conflicting trends of globalization and identity?

We do not attempt in this chapter to provide anything like a comprehensive account of the development of notions of individualism. Given that the concept of individualism is one of the most widely used in the social sciences and humanities, any summary treatment of scholarly research would be only superficial. Rather, we situate our discussion of individualism throughout this chapter in the context of changing relations between identity and globalization. The snapshots of individualism presented here are crucial for grasping social changes currently sweeping the globe, as well as the basis upon which we develop hypotheses regarding the emergence of a new individualism throughout this book. There are three contemporary compelling, and widely discussed, theories of individualism with respect to issues of the globalization of life, meaning, self-actualization, and identity. We describe these as *manipulated individualism, isolated privatism,* and *reflexive individualization.*

Manipulated Individualism

In the absence of possessive individualism speaking to our contemporary cultural condition, how should individualism now be characterized? Individualism in the present age has been cast by some within a broader field of historical and economic determinations, and, with some degree of oversimplification, two variant perspectives may be recognized here. A first group consists of those who argue that public life is contaminated by the manipulation of human capacities by transnational corporations and global elites. A second group argues that social control or political domination within our individualist culture is more complex and paradoxical than some Orwellian dystopia of the unconstrained powers of

Big Brother; instead, political domination arises from an acute contradiction within the very global, technological frameworks that shape individualism's ideological needs. Such critics thus seek to juxtapose the intensification of globalization processes and the impersonality of large-scale institutions with the corrosion of intimacies of personal life. Needless to say, each of these conceptual orientations has influenced the other, although the political differences between them remain reasonably clear.

We can find an interesting starting point for such orientations in the classical sociology of George Simmel. In his *Fundamental Problems of Sociology*, Simmel speaks of a "new individualism" stemming from the modern metropolis and the money economy. Liberated from the grip of tradition (or what Simmel calls "the rusty chains of guild, birth right and church"), the meanings that motivate modern people are no longer fixed through external categories but arise rather through an intensification of processes of strong self-definition. "The individual," writes Simmel, "seeks his *self* as if he did not yet have it, and yet, at the same time, is certain that his only fixed point is this self." Simmel's self-actualizing individual is all about the work of self-assembly, self-construction, liveliness, and playfulness; in short, life lived as artfulness. And yet, while enlightening and exciting, this modernist approach to individualism also implies its opposite, a negation of meaning and total loss of personality. There is a sense in which modern culture is at once enabling and constraining, which is the story Simmel seeks to plot through the extremities of our individualist age. In a metropolitan, urban world— under the pressures of the city crowd and alienating structures of economic exchange—individual identities are necessarily egoistic, calculating, and blasé. In such a way, people seek reassurance of their independence and power in an overwhelmingly indifferent and impersonal world. The overemphasis placed on individualism is thus, on Simmel's reckoning at least, a "retracted acuity," the expression of unfreedom rather than liberation.

In contrast to the liberal concept of moral individualism, with its ideal of a flowering, all-round development of individual human powers, what arises from this critical orientation is a relentless focus on exploitative social relations. The study of the material and emotional devastation that capitalism has unleashed is especially interesting in this context. Arguably, the single most important body of ideas that addresses social division and alienation comes from the German tradition of critical theory, sometimes referred to as the "Frankfurt School." While the Frankfurt School was broadly Marxist in orientation, its strong interest in identity (and especially new forms of individualism) necessitated a shift away from class struggle and materialism narrowly conceived. The key perspectives advanced in German critical theory—particularly evident in the writings of Max Horkheimer, Theodor Adorno, and Herbert Marcuse—were shaped largely by the twentieth-century experience of fascism, particularly the Nazi reign of terror in Western Europe. For the Frankfurt School social analysts, or for those whose approach has been influenced in some significant way by this school of thought, the individual is viewed as an instrument of domination and alienation. A variety of terms were introduced to capture this crippling constitution of individualism under conditions of advanced capitalism, from Adorno's critique of "the authoritarian personality" to Marcuse's portrait of "one-dimensional man."

In Frankfurt School sociology, if there is one area that stands out in terms of dramatizing the transformed social conditions in which individualism operates in our own time, it is that of mass culture. The critical theorists were especially interested in how individuals are shaped as consumers through the mass media, a process that in their analyses demands both the manipulation and domination of mass consciousness. Tracing the dynamics of irrational authoritarianism in communications media, the critical theorists suggested that popular culture is manufactured under conditions that reflect the interest of media conglomerates. "The culture industry," writes Adorno, "intentionally integrates its consumers from above." Technology itself, even the use of household technologies such as radio and television, determines the responses and reactions of individuals. This rigid control of mass media, for the early critical theorists, is itself the result of a broadcast language of command—in which the reflectiveness of the individual is instantly nullified. As Adorno puts this, "The repetitiveness, the selfsameness, and the ubiquity of modern mass culture tend to make for automatized reactions and to weaken the forces of individual resistance." In some ways, Adorno's comments offer a suggestive critique of the broadcast activities of such diverse media companies as MTV, CNN, and Time Warner. Yet there are many obvious respects in which the relation between markets and consumers is not as neatly unified as some formulations of the critical theorists suggest. Still, there is little doubt that Frankfurt School theory has provided an inspired approach to various aspects of the relationship between individualist identities and media entertainment, particularly as regards film, TV, even jazz and other forms of popular music.

The ideas of the Frankfurt School have been taken up in a number of ways to make sense of our age of rampant individualism. For the most part, many writers influenced by the assumptions of critical theory have tended to view individualism and a preoccupation with identity as an outgrowth of monopoly capitalism and processes of commercialization. It was to fall to what has been called the second generation of critical theorists to develop a more sociologically sophisticated critique of the cultural consequences of the spread of globalizing social forces into the private sphere as a whole. Today the most prominent critical theorist is Jürgen Habermas, who has put forward a sweeping and challenging social theory of how the accelerating pace of modernization reshapes the boundaries between public and private life. Though Habermas's analysis of the changing boundaries between public and private life is sociologically dense and historically complex, the broad thrust of the argument, succinctly put, is this: In the societies of early, or market, capitalism, individuals performed a vital role in mediating between the differentiated spheres of the state and civil society through interpersonal interaction, business dealings, and civic association. The model of the so-called public sphere that Habermas defends is, essentially, one that can be traced to the life of the polis in classical Greece. In ancient Greece, the public sphere was constituted as a profoundly dialogical arena, a place where individuals came to engage in a public discourse of critical reason and to debate issues of common interest.

Habermas's account of democratic and public participatory processes takes its cue from reasoned debate, logical thinking, and consensus; indeed, his critique of the rise of the bourgeois public sphere draws parallels between the polis of classical Greek city-states and the literary salons and coffeehouses of early eighteenth-century Europe, where different groups met to exchange opinions on a dizzying array of ideas and ideologies. As the state came to penetrate more and more into the economy and civil society, however, the public sphere—so valued by Habermas—entered into a period of unprecedented decline. The global expansion of capitalism, and the associated intensification of commodification, spelled the disintegration of the public sphere. The public sphere shrank, according to Habermas, as the corrosive bureaucratizing logic of capitalist society came to eat away at the practical and civic agencies of everyday life as well as eroding the influence of broader cultural traditions.

For Habermas, this is how it is in our own time—but perhaps even more so. New communication technologies, like television, cable, and satellite, are viewed as weakening both the private sphere and civic association; the public sphere itself becomes desiccated. Though he does not address these concerns in any great detail in his more recent writings, Habermas does explicitly recognize the potential gains to democracy generated by the advent of electronic media. He acknowledges that the dramatic proliferation of communication technologies and media services might contribute to the democratizing potentials of cosmopolitanism, and he also recognizes that some commentators view the Internet and digital interactive technology as heralding a second spectacular age for a revitalized and democratic public sphere. Yet Habermas, for the most part, remains unconvinced. The use of the Internet and related interactive technology may create new forms of publicness, but this is a degradation of genuine civic engagement and public political debate. It is degradation as individuals today mostly engage with mass communications and mass culture in privatized terms, as isolated selves obsessed with mediated spectacles. "In comparison with printed communications," writes Habermas, "the programmes sent by the new media curtail the reactions of their recipients in a peculiar way. They draw the eyes and ears of the public under their spell but at the same time, by taking away its distance, place it under 'tutelage', which is to say they deprive it of the opportunity to say something and to disagree. . . . The sounding board of an educated stratum tutored in the public use of reason has been shattered: the public is split apart into minorities of specialists who put their reason to use nonpublicly and a great mass of consumers whose receptiveness is public but uncritical." Our age of mediated conversation (TV chat shows, radio talkback) is that of politics trivialized. As Habermas writes, "today the conversation itself is administered"; the privatized appropriation of such mediated conversation is such that it may be pointless to speak of a robust public sphere at all. Indeed, in his mature writings, Habermas writes of a "colonization" of the private sphere by the rationalizing, bureaucratizing forces of large-scale institutions.

There are quite a number of criticisms of the thesis of manipulated individualism, both of Frankfurt School thinking and of authors working within a broadly critical theory tradition. Some critics argue that, while advocates of such a line of thinking are mostly accurate in their description of the socioeconomic shifts of the present day, they nevertheless fail to put those shifts into context at the level of the individual.

Few would deny, for instance, that the rise of mass culture and consumerism has, in some sense or another, contributed to a pervasive instrumentalism within private affairs and social relations. And yet it's surely too simplistic to suggest, as some authors indebted to contemporary critical theory have, that what people make out of popular culture and communication media is entirely controlled by corporate power or manipulated through ideology. Equally contentious is the assumption that individuals are increasingly powerless in the face of global forces, with all this implies for a downgrading of human agency, resistance, and social knowledgeability. As Cambridge sociologist John B. Thompson queries, "Why do members of the life-world *not* perceive that what they are threatened by is the uncontrolled growth of system complexities, rooted ultimately in the dynamics of capital accumulation and valorization? Why do they not resist this growth directly and demand, in an open and widespread way, the transformation of the economic system which underlies it?" Thompson's remarks are directed at Habermas, but equally apply to variants of the thesis of manipulated individualism.

Isolated Privatism

Individualism as isolated privatism is, as we define it here at any rate, more culturalist than sociological. Its major protagonists describe modern culture as heralding the death of personal autonomy, involving the replacement of authentic, reflective subjectivity with a narcissistic, hedonistic attitude toward other people and the wider world. Whereas theories of manipulated individualism tend to concentrate on the overshadowing of selfhood by large-scale institutional forces, adherents of the thesis of isolated privatism derive their notions from transformations in ideology, culture, art, and literature as well as in economic life. While the previous group of social critics recasts the material foundations of life in terms of the restructuring of capitalism and globalism, the latter theorizes today's world more in terms of cross-cultural fertilizations and psychological upheavals.

Many of the leading figures of the thesis of isolated privatism (though they would no doubt reject such a label) are to be found not in Europe but in the United States. In a widely influential treatment of how contemporary cultural life has become progressively uncoupled from politics and the economy, Daniel Bell shows how a modernist ideological context of secular Puritanism transmuted into consumerist imperatives of purchasing and pleasure seeking. In stimulating consumer desires, multinationals and business conglomerates today encourage people to think only of their own private satisfactions, which in turn weakens the spirit of active citizenship. Yet despite the cultural supremacism of consumer freedom, Bell contends that today's hyperindividualist idiom enters into an embarrassing contradiction with the moral fabric of society. A similar capacious moralizing characterizes the work of Allan Bloom, who lambastes what he calls—in defensive, mildly anxious tones—our "culture of moral relativism." Like Bell, Bloom says the contemporary epoch inaugurates an isolated privatism at the level of the individual; but Bloom in particular harbors a neoconservative suspicion of social changes such as the rise of feminism and sexual permissiveness, which he sees as culturally regressive. People today, writes Bloom, are "spiritually unclad, unconnected, isolated, with no inherited or unconditional connection with anything or anyone."

If individuals today are unable to muster the commitment necessary to sustain interpersonal relationships and civic participation, this is because an unchecked narcissism empties out both the emotional depths of the self and the affective texture of interpersonal communication. Thus Richard Sennett, in *The Fall of Public Man* (1978), explains the demise of public life as a consequence of pathological narcissism and character disorders. The deadening of public political space, says Sennett, arises not simply from impinging forces of commodification or bureaucratization but from the dominance of notions of self-fulfillment, sensual gratification, and self-absorption at the expense of social bonds. An equally influential version of the thesis of societal narcissism has been put forward by the late American historian Christopher Lasch, who speaks of a "minimal self" in an age of survivalism. Lasch's self is one focused on the experience of living "one day at a time," of everyday life as a "succession of minor emergencies."

Robert Bellah and a group of California academics, standing somewhere in the middle of the left-liberal wing of individualism theory, believe that much of the language of contemporary individualism profoundly constrains the ways in which people think about their identities, relationships with others, and also involvements with the wider world. In *Habits of the Heart*, a book that explores the relationship between culture and character in contemporary America, Bellah and his associates argue that the balance between public commitments and private attachments has tipped overwhelmingly in favor of the latter at the expense of the former. Through in-depth interviews with Americans from various walks of life, Bellah and his associates hold that the fierce individualism pervading American culture today is in danger of producing selves either obsessed with material gain and private success on the one hand, or with forms of pseudocommitment to, and concern for, fellow citizens on the other. Here we have what we might call a popular conception of individualism, or at least a popular-academic take on the political costs of an individualist culture. It is therefore all the more perplexing that hardly any of this critique captures the changing, conflicting trends of globalization and identity.

Interestingly Bellah and his associates, who contextualize practices of individualism in terms of cultural tradition, political ideology, and social history, see the problems facing our society less in terms of invasive economic forces eating away at the fabric of social practices and cultural traditions than as a lifting of individualist ideologies to the second power. They speak of many of their interviewees as trapped in a language of isolating individualism, a language that ultimately distorts human capacities for genuine personal growth, ongoing commitments to others, and involvement in public affairs. "We are concerned," they write, "that individualism may have grow cancerous . . . that it may be threatening the survival of freedom itself."

Yet Bellah and his associates are constrained by their liberal definition of individualism to dismiss as distorting or pathological any kind of social practices that do not fit with their rather traditionalist understanding of the civic-regarding character of the public sphere. Hence, their laments about consumption-oriented lifestyles, TV culture, and the packaged good life. But this, notwithstanding its liberal sneering and lofty academic remoteness, falsely assumes that the language of "public" and "private," or "the cultural" and "the personal," is adequate for comprehending the global webs in which forms of identity and individualism are today constituted. Part of the problem, in our view, stems from the overvaluation Bellah and his associates place on religious and republican traditions as unquestionable sources of spontaneous and enriching forms of self-definition. Conversely, they can find precious little of this in what they term "utilitarian individualism" and "expressive individualism." They are thus left celebrating an image of individualism from a bygone age, one that idealizes individual rationality and logical reasoning and likewise denigrates spontaneous subjectivity and emotional literacy. This ultimately maneuvers them into the absurd position of saying that the writings of, say, Tocqueville or the actions of cultural heroes like cowboys speak to authentic individuation; whereas they argue that our culture of therapy and appetite for consumerism are only pseudo-individualistic in form.

In Robert D. Putnam's *Bowling Alone: The Collapse and Revival of American Community*, the same sweeping generalizations take on a decidedly populist flavor. According to Putnam, the crisis of the American community is that of broken bonds and deteriorating democracy. He uses the metaphor of bowling to capture recent social changes through which individuals are more and more disconnected from family life, friends, colleagues, neighbors, and the social system itself. Here's Putnam's argument in a nutshell: where people once bowled in league teams during their leisure time after work, now they bowl alone, as solitary entertainment. Putnam makes claims similar to those made by Lasch and Bellah about the need to avoid cultural nostalgia, but it is interesting that his analysis proceeds from juxtaposing the communal character of yesteryear with the impersonality of today's world. Civic engagement as opposed to disconnected individualism, cooperative community as opposed to commercialized competition, genuine relationships as opposed to episodic encounters: these are the oppositions through which Putnam summarizes the decline of social life.

American feminist and sociologist Arlie Hochschild's book *The Commercialization of Intimate Life* similarly warns of the emotional dangers of global consumer capitalism for our experiences of identity, gender, sexuality, and family life. Much like Lasch and Sennett before her, she believes that globalization is eating away at the fabric of private life, degrading individualism into self-obsession and unchecked narcissism. For Hochschild, the new global galaxy of digital communications, market institutions, and transnational corporations gives rise to what she calls "a spirit of instrumental detachment." Isolated, adrift, anxious, and empty: these are defining emotional contours of the individual self in a globalizing world. Especially evident today is what Hochschild calls a "cultural cooling" affecting people's attitudes toward sex, relationships, and love. She contrasts the patriarchal world of yesteryear, where rigid, predefined gender relationships ruled, with the new postmodern world of more open communication and fluid boundaries between the sexes. Paradoxically, the vanished world of "till death do us part" seems to have provided for greater emotional warmth than the cooler emotional strategies demanded today. Examining in detail women's best-selling advice books for clues as to this cultural cooling of intimate life, Hochschild speaks of an "abduction of feminism." With the spirit of feminism now displaced onto private life, Hochschild's "perfectly packaged woman" takes her cue from the postmodern sexual revolution, as represented in *Sex and the City*. Diet, dress sexily, dye your hair, and get a face-lift: such is the relentless media advice, says Hochschild, on how women should negotiate today's high-risk relationships market.

Whichever variant you choose in the debate over isolated privatism, one thing is clear: contemporary culture remakes the individual ego-centric, and so also in the shadow of a narcissistic society. Self-enclosed, self-obsessed, market-style identities are cultivated by late modern or postmodern culture: a surface concern with self, others, and the wider world, much like surfing the Net, is the only game in town. Yet while we do not deny that privatism—the privatization of human experience—is an undoubted characteristic of contemporary culture, we fundamentally disagree with the elitist and anachronistic assumptions that individualism today is rendered merely surface oriented, media driven, and focused on personal or apolitical issues. For one thing, ours is a time of collapsing distinctions between public and private life, of the erasure of traditional distinctions between private issues and political matters, but it also brings with it new experiences of where culture and politics actually reside. The cultural characterization of pathological narcissism, from Lasch to Hochschild, is ill suited to analyzing current patterns of individualism, primarily since global transformations render self-identity itself a profoundly political arena. Many such transformations date from the late 1960s and early 1970s, when a number of genuinely transnational social movements—feminism, gay and lesbian rights, indigenous movements, and environmentalism—ushered in a widespread acceptance of the politicization of issues previously portrayed as private. Today popular culture, however distasteful or degraded to some cultural critics, is where millions of people negotiate some of the central political issues of the day, those to do with contested notions of gender, sexuality, race, ethnicity, and on and on.

Criticizing individuals for ongoing interest in, and engagement with, communications media and popular culture on the grounds that this represents a retreat from the public sphere and genuine citizenship is also too simplistic. In conditions of globalization, in which media networks and new communication technologies powerfully influence many aspects of our lives, popular culture and the mass media are where many encounter political issues and negotiate identities. It's certainly true, as Lasch and others contend, that the mass media are entertainment orientated, celebrity driven, and sometimes focused on reducing complex political issues to private concerns. Yet popular media move in many directions simultaneously, and there is considerable research to indicate that interaction between audiences and media messages has become increasingly complex, contradictory, and discontinuous in the digital age. It's estimated, for example, that a newspaper today contains as many bits of information as people living in premodern societies might have encountered during the course of their lives. There's little doubt that the information revolution has reshaped individualism as we know it, yet the failure to consider with full seriousness the consequences of this communications transformation renders accounts of isolated privatism backward looking and blinkered.

Reflexive Individualization

We live in a world that places a premium on instant gratification. Thanks to technology-induced globalization, the desire for immediate results—for gratification now—has never been so pervasive or acute. We are accustomed to sending e-mail across the planet in seconds. To shopping in stores stocked with goods from all over the world. And to drifting through relations with other people (both intimate and at work) without long-term commitments. The vanished world of self-restraint has truly been replaced by a culture of immediacy.

If globalization raises our lust for instant gratification to the second power, it also powerfully reshapes—as theories of manipulated individualism and isolated privatism make clear—the way we conceive of our individualism and ourselves. Awareness of a new individualism unleashed by the forces of globalization is also a key concern that unites a variety of intellectuals trying to grasp the novel ways societies "institutionalize" these transformed relations of private and public, self and society, individual and history. This brings us to the theory of individualization. The ideas of authors and activists associated with notions of individualization are perhaps best described as center-left politically and strongly sociological, since social forces play such a large role in them. For proponents of the theory of individualization, the social vision of intrusive, large-scale governmental forces and capitalistic conglomerates into the tissue of daily life and the personal sphere is not sufficient for grasping the core opportunities and risks of contemporary culture. Rather than "big institutions" ruling the lives of "small individuals"—a social vision especially to the fore in variants of the thesis of manipulated individualism—the theory of individualization holds that people today are only partly integrated into the social network. The leading thinker associated with this approach, German sociologist Ulrich Beck, argues that people today must constantly undertake the work of inventive and resourceful self-building and self-design in order to avoid their identities breaking into pieces. Explicitly rejecting the notion of individualism, Beck's ideas emphasize the global transformations of everyday life and of the relationship of the individual self to society.

In his ground-breaking study *The Reinvention of Politics*, a riposte to the theories of both manipulated individualism and isolated privatism, Beck contends that the making of identities today is an innovative, institutionalized process, not an outgrowth of inner desires or forces of socialization. Beck sketches something he calls "institutional individualization," in which people's ability to create a biographical narrative—and continuously revise their self-definition—becomes fundamental to our age of pervasive globalization. In a world of interconnected information technologies and diversified communication networks, he argues, people are always revising, reworking, and reinventing their personal habits and identities in the light of knowledge about the state and direction of the world.

At the center of Beck's work is the claim that the shift from tradition to modernity has unleashed a profoundly novel process of self-formation—one that, notwithstanding regional differences and cultural variations, is everywhere similar. According to Beck, traditional societies gave people little room for individual autonomy, as categories of meaning were pregiven. Religion is perhaps the obvious example here. In modern, secular society, by contrast, the construction of identity and individualism becomes detached from history, particularly in the West. It becomes increasingly difficult to rely on traditional frameworks of understanding in the orientation of one's life and activities, principally owing to the vast explosion in social possibilities and cultural horizons generated by modernity. Individualization, or the reflexive organization of the self, demands that people explain themselves, become open to discourse or reflective deliberation, both internally and externally. Against this backdrop, Beck tracks the spiraling of insecurities experienced by people the world over in their attempts at self-definition and particularly their ways of coping with globalization. Reflecting on the complex negotiations people make in juggling the conflicting demands of career, family, friends, work, and love, Beck opens up new ways of understanding self-experience and individualism. Perceptively, he speaks of an emergent "self-driven culture," of self-designed biographies, and of do-it-yourself identities. The French philosopher Jean-Paul Sartre once quipped that it is not enough to be born a bourgeois, rather one must live one's life as a bourgeois. Beck takes this idea and pushes it further. Pressure to become what one is—and especially to demonstrate to family, friends, and colleagues that one has truly "made it"—is perhaps a central defining feature of contemporary Western living. The evidence is all around: in the seemingly unstoppable desire to shop and consume luxury goods; in new conditions of work, where networking, short-term teamwork, and instant self-reinvention are all the rage; and also in the craving for instant celebrity and the packaged good life that goes with it.

It's a provocative thesis, and one that chimes nicely with the vast expansion of media culture, interconnected virtuality, and the information technology revolution—all of which have served to provide many with a glimpse of alternative horizons and symbolic possibilities on a scale that did not exist previously. Beck sketches what these big social changes mean for people in the following way:

> "Individualisation" means, *first*, the disembedding of industrial-society ways of life and, *second*, the re-embedding of new ones, in which the individuals must produce, stage and cobble together their biographies. . . . [P]ut in plain terms, "individualisation" means the disintegration of the certainties of industrial society as well as the compulsion to find and invent new certainties for oneself and others without them.

This search for "new certainties" in a world of heightened ambivalence is shaped by the interwoven trends of individualization and globalization. But Beck argues that globalization is not a single process; rather, globalization is a complex mix of forces—usually messy, often contradictory—that produce novelties, complexities, and disjunctures in patterns of individualism and forms of identity.

The self today thus becomes a kind of DIY survival specialist, imbuing with expansive and polyarchic meanings a world stripped of pregiven significances and traditionalist structures, rules, and processes. The individual self in an age of individualization can find only a privatized, contingent kind of foundation for the activities one sustains in the world, which in turn both defies presumptions about traditional ways of doing things and spurs further the self-design and self-construction of all phases of life. This kind of individualism is for Beck the sole source of meaning and value, though that is not to say that the subject's ceaseless biographical productivity springs from inner depth, emotional resilience, or personality. What constitutes the individuality of the individual self in Beck's sociological doctrine is the ongoing negotiation and strenuous modification of complex identity processes: interlocking networks, civic initiatives, social movements, ethnic and racial clusters, business pyramids, and on and on.

This kind of individualization is not confined only to the private sphere (though this is surely often a common fantasy); individualization is *socially produced*. All processes of individualization thus become political, even though the political consequences of today's DIY biographies are often better grasped in hindsight. As Beck characterizes the endless push and pull, conflicts and compromises, of individualization, "Decisions, possibly undecidable decisions, [are] certainly not free, but forced by others and wrested out of oneself, under conditions that lead into dilemmas."

GLOBALIZATION AND THE INTERIORS OF THE NEW INDIVIDUALISM

It is time for us to take stock. From the early critical theorists to Habermas, the corrosive intrusion of large-scale, impersonal systems (social and technological) into core areas of personal life is seen to drain civil society and the public sphere of any vitality they once possessed. Yet none of the parties to this debate stops to question whether it is sociologically meaningful, in an age of pervasive globalization, to set a conception of modern institutions as remote, distant, and cut off from the terrain of lived experience and everyday life. From Bell to Putnam, a rampant individualism is said to threaten the moral fabric of society; in particular, consumerist imperatives of pleasure, play, and privatization put at risk established social rules governing manners and morals. But again, critics don't stop to consider that the thesis of a decline of public life and the death of genuine individuality might be grounded in elitist or anachronistic assumptions about the private realm, public debate, and political life. Few critics question the equation of selfhood with critical reason, continuity of cognition, and logic, as well as a related downgrading of the emotional realm of the passions and the political power of subconscious forces and unconscious desires. Few critics stop to consider that individualism, and particularly the politicization of identities, today cuts forcefully against the grain of traditional conceptions of public debate (as rehearsed in universities) or institutional politics (as played out in parliaments).

Is there a way of approaching identity and individualism that avoids the limitations of the approaches we have considered so far? Is it possible to question the currently fashionable distaste for the very idea of the free individual and autonomous individualism, but without sliding into a political fatalism that views modernity and globalization as producing a wholesale emptying out of selfhood and interpersonal relationships? In this final section of the chapter we shall outline, in a necessarily provisional manner, what we term a social theory of the "interiors of the new individualism." Like Giddens and Beck, we are interested in the development of reflexivity as pertaining to the domains of self-constitution and self-reproduction. But unlike them, we seek to focus the reflexivity of contemporary practices of individualism on affective notions of the interior life. It is the necessary relation between globalizing social processes and the affective contours of reflexivity that, we agree, holds the key to new forms of identity and individualism.

In characterizing individualism in this way, we return to Marshall Berman's classic, *All That Is Solid Melts into Air*. For Berman, "to be modern is to find ourselves in an environment that promises us adventure, power, joy, growth, transformation of ourselves and the world—and, at the same time, that threatens to destroy everything we have, everything we know, everything we are." Berman's portrait of modernity is both exhilarating and disturbing. As Perry Anderson has summarized the contradictions inherent in this account of self and society:

> On the one hand, capitalism—in Marx's unforgettable phrase of the *Communist Manifesto*, which forms the leitmotif of Berman's book—tears down every ancestral confinement and feudal restriction, social immobility and claustral tradition, in an immense clearing operation of cultural and customary debris across the globe. To that process corresponds a tremendous emancipation of the possibility and sensibility of the individual self, now increasingly released

from the fixed social status and rigid role-hierarchy of the pre-capitalist past, with its narrow morality and cramped imaginative range. On the other hand, as Marx emphasized, the very same onrush of capitalist economic development also generates a brutally alienated and atomized society, riven by callous economic exploitation and cold social indifference, destructive of every cultural and political value whose potential it has itself brought into being. Likewise, on the psychological plane, self-development in these conditions could only mean a profound disorientation and insecurity, frustration and despair, concomitant with—indeed inseparable from—the sense of enlargement and exhilaration, the new capacities and feelings, liberated at the same time.

Anderson eloquently makes the point that use of a binary opposition between modernity and individualism, or globalization and identity for that matter, is only of very limited explanatory value for grasping the complexity of personal and political life today.

The essence of our approach can be stated thus: the new individualism that shapes, and is shaped by, our times involves *ongoing emotional struggles* to relate internal and external experience in which both processes and structures of self-definition are explicitly examined, revised, and transformed. How does such a formulation differ from the notion of individualization? And, for that matter, from personal reflexivity? Our approach emphasizes what societal processes of individualism are like from the inside out, from the viewpoint of the individual self. The focus is on individual experiences of, and reactions to, individualization. In the account that we develop here, processes of individualism and identity construction involve the emotional experiences of individuals who are situated within an *imaginary domain*, a domain that has a fundamental impact on self/society relations.

We use the notion of an imaginary domain, which we contend lies at the heart of global transformations shaping the new individualism, in a very specific sense: it bears the weight of a tradition of interpretation that, since the uncovering of the repressed unconscious by Freud, has been concerned with problems of interior life, of desire, as well as the thread connecting internal and external aspects of human experience. Psychoanalysis, which we have drawn upon for the interpretation of individual narratives as well as for the reinterpretation of theoretical issues of a more specific methodological kind, reminds us forcefully that our principal object of study—individuals seeking to remake themselves from the inside, in order to adjust to new global conditions—is a rich imaginary domain of representations, including stocks of precognitive knowledge, affects, drives, and related defenses. It is this focus on human imagination that leads us to be skeptical of social theories that are complacently antipsychological.

Yet if psychoanalysis can be used to develop a better understanding of human emotions and their impact upon the new individualism, this does not mean that it is necessary to choose between "subjective" and "objective" conceptions of identity or lived experience. Rather, our contention is that social theory needs to recognize the political urgency of connecting a revised account of individualization (as elaborated by Beck and his followers) with psychoanalytic theory in order to develop a critical perspective on the new individualism. What social theory today must grasp is how social processes of individualization are fundamentally interwoven with imaginings of the psyche and the self. In breaking from the foregoing accounts that keep apart the social and the psyche, we have to grasp how social and cultural processes affecting individualizing trends are given shape internally. We need to see that unconscious imaginings of the self are always at work within the individualizing acts and speech-acts of individuals. Individualism is never predetermined or prepackaged; rather, the individual construction and reconstruction of the new individualism is built upon operations of fantasy and its unconscious contortions—anxieties about difference, about otherness and strangeness, about intimacy and proximity—in the wider frame of cultural life and social institutions. In saying this, we do not claim that new individualisms only involve the realm of fantasy and that the only features that ought to be taken into account are those of imagination and repressed desire. This clearly is not the case, and as the social theories examined in this chapter suggest, there are many institutional forces at work influencing the individualizing of social life today, including multinational capitalism and restructurings of the political field, as well as processes of advanced modernization and modernity. To this list of institutional forces shaping constructions of individualism in the contemporary age we need to add the impacts of globalization, which will be examined in detail in the following chapter. But our central point is that even forms of individualism heavily constructed around institutional webs of, say, business interests or new social movements also involve the imaginary domain; all forms of individualism involve individuals battling internally with the conflicting desires and dreads that lie at the core of the preoccupations of the contemporary age. The new individualism of our time involves emotional and social struggles with issues of dependency and independence, with the demands of change and of keeping pace with sweeping global change, with reflexive awareness of living experimentally and with people breaking new ground for themselves.

The rich multiplicity of the new individualism is becoming increasingly apparent, but at a theoretical level it has only been as a consequence of the slow melding of sociology and psychoanalysis that we have been in a stronger position to understand the processes of modernity and globalization in relation to the individual subject. In seeking to unfold the potential of psychoanalysis without succumbing to its limitations (for too often followers of this tradition have simply by-passed issues of social conflict and political domination), the critique of the new individualism we present in this book is one that finds a wealth of contemporary identity strategies. Some are conforming, some privatized; others are individualizing and genuinely autonomous. These latter forms of individualism emerge from unique personal histories, as identities reinvented with imagination and ethical courage—of which more shortly.

A further word on psychoanalysis, however, as much has been said about this tradition of thought in the preceding pages. Some readers may find it odd that we have devoted attention to psychoanalysis in a chapter concerning the social theory of individualism; others may find it equally surprising that, in our subsequent analysis of life histories and personal stories throughout the book, we refer only rarely to specific psychoanalytic ideas or concepts. Our reasons for this are straightforward: in our professional careers as sociologists, both of us have been affected by various psychoanalytic theories and writers. We have each, in quite different ways, written on the relationship between social theory and psychoanalysis. Furthermore, we both acknowledge the significance of contemporary psychoanalysis to our sociological outlooks: Lacan, Laplanche, Kristeva, and Castoriadis; the work of American analysts such as Ogden, Spezzano, and Prager, and especially Meadow and her associates at the Boston Institute of Psychoanalysis; and the theoretical departures of Winnicott, Bion, and Bollas. That said, psychoanalysis is rarely foregrounded in our analysis of vignettes for demonstrating the social significance of the new individualism. Because of our focus on the *experience* of the new individualism, we have decided not to distract the reader with extensive references to current theory.

In emphasizing the importance of fantasy and the imaginary domain, however, we do focus centrally on the subjective experience of individuals to processes of identity construction, individualism, and individualization. In the vignettes we present throughout this book—of Kelly, Larry, Xavier and Joe, Simon and Ruth, Norman, Phyllis, and Annie and Caoimhe—our aim is to show how both emotional and social constructions of individualism work on many different levels. Following the psychoanalytic departures of Freud and his followers, this involves crucial attention to the feelings and affects—positive, negative, and ambivalent emotion—stirred up in individuals through responding to the individualizing challenges brought about through conditions of globalization. This approach also involves attention to the individual's *personal associations* to the individualizing and privatizing of social processes.

While our understanding of the complex, contradictory ways in which societal processes and cultural forms are internally anchored in the psychic lives of individuals has been extended by many theorists, including Herbert Marcuse, Erich Fromm, Jacques Lacan, Franz Fanon, Julia Kristeva, Slavoj Zizek, and Judith Butler, we still need to know more about how the global (and processes of globalization) comes to be lived internally. Much contemporary psychoanalysis has been preoccupied with theorizing the structure of multiple identifications in the constitution of personal identity and a sense of individualism, but at the same time the larger question of social forces and institutional transformations has been sidelined from critical scrutiny. Our argument is that social theory must try to develop an account of the new individualism increasingly prevalent throughout the West today that, while attending to the specificity of psychic processes of multiple identifications and of the centrality of the passions, brings out the broader social and global significance of this phenomenon. Individualism can never be free of the emotional constructs and multiple identifications of the individual involved in producing and performing identities; what aspects of cultural life and of globalization individuals choose to emphasize and concentrate upon, and equally what they choose to ignore or set aside, is fundamental to any sober assessment of subjective reactions to processes of individualization.

The new individualism is both personal autonomy and longing for utopia, the possibility of postmodernism and the reality of living in a radically pluralistic world in which "anything goes," the fact of confessional culture and the value of self-questioning and personal transformation.

Contrary to theories of manipulated individualism and isolated privatism, the new forms of individualism assembled today are not imposed by society, nor are they a defensive response from within the self; sources of self-development emerge from an uncanny mix of globalizing processes (spread unequally in their effects across the globe) and subjective definitions of individualizing trends within society at large.

When some complain about the decline of moral values, they tend to mean the liberal values of the free individual. They forget that this is but one of the ethical traditions to be drawn upon. It is true that ethical rules that rely on time-honored philosophical truths or religion-based precepts are called into question more robustly today, as for a good century or more they have been. But it hardly need be said that values, and most especially religious values, have not disappeared—anything but. In the United States, the 2004 national election was, it seems, decided largely by the influence of mostly conservative religious beliefs. Around the world, similarly, new religious movements of various sources (most strikingly, though, of Islamic origins) are a major factor in world culture and politics. There are two common themes in these movements worldwide. One is that they are most popular among the poorer classes and social groups, especially in the Middle East. The second is that, though they are called "fundamentalist," they are better described as retreats to traditional ways where the ethical rules were clearly described and more easily discerned.

Yet, these traditionalist religious and moral movements could just as well be described as part of the global mix. One of the reasons they have become so dominant in, say, the last twenty years or so is that this is the period when the effects of globalization have grown more prominent and thus forced individuals everywhere to make fundamental choices about who they are. If you think about it, whenever individuals are forced to confront a world changed dramatically from the one they were taught in childhood to trust, they have only three fundamental choices. One is to retreat into the traditions, to reaffirm them (often in overly simplified terms), even to use them to attack what they consider to be the cause of the change. A second is to deny the change and to pretend that life goes on as usual, that this too will pass if one only keeps cool. This may be more the way taken by those in the privileged classes around the world, those able to insulate themselves from the pain and suffering that go with change. The third, however, is the one we are calling attention to: the new individualisms are ways of attempting to come to terms with change by remaking oneself from the inside to adjust to a new outside. This way may be most prominent among the middle classes, but as we say, it is just as likely to be a force in the lives of those on the margins who are less able to insulate themselves from change. This way is not necessarily pretty, but it is to be admired. And, we would emphasize, it is *not* immoral or amoral—hardly that. In fact, history has taught us that in times of change, moral values are more, not less, important, if only because the conventional routines of daily life that people take as the way to live are collapsing, so those unwilling to retreat or unable to stand above the fray are forced to look at themselves and what they believe.

When some, usually on the right, complain about the loss of traditions, the decline in family values, the moral corruption of the world, what they are complaining about is the loss of the values *they* know and believe in. And, though they can be irritating in their self-righteousness, they deserve a good measure of human sympathy. To have lost the social supports that sustain what you believe in, and be unwilling or unable to find new ones, is to put yourself in the terrible position of trying to keep back the floods by sticking your thumb in the moral dike. It hurts. Still, retreatist attitudes should not be a justification for thinking there is no longer any interest in moral living or ethical reasoning.

If anything, the people whose stories we tell in this book are intent on inventing new ethical rules. In some ways, it would not be too far off to say that the new individualism is about new moralities as much as it is about anything else. After all, how does anyone reinvent herself without reinventing the standards and values by which she assesses and practices her life as a new individual?

~

CHAPTER THREE

LIVING IN A
PRIVATIZED WORLD
Coping with Globalization

E WAS ALWAYS punctual and approached psychotherapy as though it were simply one of the many business
transactions he conducted daily. A good-looking man,
a forty-eight-year-old high-tech computer whiz, Larry had accumulated
buckets of money during the dot.com revolution and was now a mil-
lionaire several times over. He was, by his own reckoning, "self-made,"
and remarked that he really only felt secure when he was "in control" of
a situation—which, for him, meant defining how things should be.
Psychotherapy was no exception.

The idea that other people could engender different emotional states
or frames of mind in him was foreign. It simply never arose for his consideration. People, much like things, were there for his pleasure, his
manipulation. Not that he approached the world in a cynical way, he
stressed. It was just the way the world worked. Period.

"People see me as something of a control freak I know, and they may
be right," he said. "But that desire for control goes all the way down, and
it is, ultimately, a result of the way my mother related to me. She always
said it was important to fit in, to belong. But that was just a cover, a way

of getting me to do what she wanted, to dance to her tune. And so, this is where projection comes in. I've taken what happened from my childhood, what was done to me, and I'm now putting it on others, making them dance to my tune."

Larry's reference to "projection" gives some indication of the way he approached psychotherapy, the latest of his attempts to purchase care of the self. Before beginning therapy, he had got hold of all the books his psychoanalyst—a prominent and respected professional—had written. He read them intensely, as if studying for exams. He'd also immersed himself in the self-help literature. It was as if he believed the only way he could reflect on the psychological meanings of his life was to affect a kind of "therapy-speak," as if copying a discourse promoted by experts.

The language of therapy is, in fact, a form of talk that by and large ignores the socially and historically fragile, but fundamental, division between public and private life, and perhaps nowhere is this more true than in the therapeutic injunction to free associate. The notion of free association appealed to Larry's finely tuned commercial instincts: Freud's precept that the patient should be released to a kind of unconscious dreaming had become, in Larry's hands, a new way into thinking about the behavioral imperatives of the global marketplace for flexibility, fluidity, and continual self-reinvention. If he could successfully organize his daily working life and manage to negotiate all sorts of significant changes within the company that he owned, then surely self-change wasn't going to be that difficult. Flexibility creates dynamism in the marketplace and so may actually induce big emotional changes in personal life also. But how to be flexible? Really flexible. Emotionally flexible.

Larry's desire for flexibility was somewhat constrained by his inflexible attitude that all things had to be done quickly. Speed was a supreme value in his life—the accelerating pace of technology, after all, had made him a rich man. But not so therapy, which—as Larry discovered—works with an altogether different understanding of time. Therapy isn't exactly famous for getting fast results. A colleague had told him to read a well-known book on self-therapy, a kind of guide to becoming one's own therapist.

> Possibly you're feeling restless. Or you may feel overwhelmed by the demands of wife, husband, children, or job. You may feel unappreciated by those people closest to you. Perhaps you feel angry that life is passing you by and you haven't accomplished all those great

things you had hoped to do. Something feels missing from your life. You were attracted by the title of this book and wish that you really were in charge. What to do?

Though he was skeptical of the California cult of therapy, this book— *Self-Therapy* by Janette Rainwater—struck a chord with Larry. Something certainly was missing from his life, and he was quite prepared to try self-therapy. This was all to the good, he thought, since it cut out the awkwardness of having to discuss embarrassing personal problems with another person. Larry would be his own therapist. And he could work at his own pace: fast.

And so he did. Larry's dedication to "taking charge of one's life," as therapy-speak has it, was single-minded. He followed, almost to the letter, all of Rainwater's recommendations. He kept a journal. He sought to break with habit, with his routine ways of doing things. He thought long and hard about traumatic phases of his childhood (what Rainwater calls "autobiographical thinking"—as if there might be another kind?), especially the loss of his mother's affections during his earliest years. He thought about the future. Imagining what Rainwater terms a "dialogue with time," he tried to envisage what his life might be like without work, without that familiar structure that he used to screen out questions about what he actually wanted to do, what he felt like doing. And he tried to think about death Rainwater-style: not as time running out but as an active engagement with the present and his own desires.

Still, all the time he was getting anxious and more depressed. His addiction to feverish work was threatening his own health, and he could not seem to hold things together at work in the manner he once could. He went to see his doctor, who recommended yet another therapy, psychoanalysis, which is how his story has come to be told here.

Coming to psychoanalysis had been perhaps even more difficult for Larry than it might have been, partly because he concluded that this meant his self-therapy was a failure. Rather than viewing his experiment with self-therapy as having opened emotional questions that led to psychoanalysis, Larry preferred to carve up his world into neat starts and endings, successes and failures, the good and the bad.

Larry liked being analytical in analysis. He would routinely stand back from his described feeling states—as if still the self-therapist—and pronounce on his psychological condition. He spoke of resistances in himself, of projection and transference, and of repression. He had almost convinced himself that he did in fact understand what was going on in his emotional life when he did not. This posed obvious problems. Such was his desire to be always in control, to assume total knowledge, that it was anything but simple for Larry to tolerate uncertainty or ambivalence. From pop-psychology handbooks to his psychoanalyst's latest technical papers, Larry used whatever he read to protect against a fear of not knowing.

Before Larry could pursue this fear and attempt to come to terms with its emotional significance, he needed to acknowledge his inability to feel at a loss about what he wanted and needed. This came slowly, through long and often painful therapeutic work. More often than not, any step forward would generate a few steps backward. His unconscious anger poured out. A workaholic, Larry knew one guaranteed way out of the emotional messiness the analysis was reflecting: work. Feverish work.

Yet even work wasn't what it used to be for Larry. It was increasingly unable to protect him from the seemingly chaotic feelings of which he was more and more aware. In fact, it was work—or, rather, a failure to work—that brought Larry into psychoanalysis in the first place. There were two especially telling incidents. The first arose when Larry was seeking to clinch a business deal, ironically enough while using a mobile phone. The anxiety was extreme. Suddenly, it was as if there was too much confusion; Larry had to get one of his associates to take over the negotiations. The second incident occurred several months later, again when Larry was with business associates. Executives from a company based in London were in Los Angeles, seeking to finalize an agreement with Larry's company. After the first round of meetings, Larry invited the associates to dinner at an exclusive restaurant. While Larry was waiting to be seated at the restaurant, anxiety flooded in again. Intolerable anxiety. Larry felt "temporarily deranged." He was confused and couldn't think; he fled the restaurant.

PRIVATE STRUGGLES, GLOBAL TROUBLES

What does Larry's story say about our changing social condition? What does the constrained, and constraining, nature of his choices say about the world's shape? How does Larry's struggle to come to terms with his inner, emotional life reflect broader social transformations across the globe?

We've already noted that Larry works in the field of computer technology and is at home in the world of big business. Like almost every company executive, Larry has for many years lived in a homogeneous culture of airport lounges and Hilton hotel rooms, eating McDonald's, using Microsoft, and watching CNN wherever he happens to be. Video conferencing, mobile phones, and the Internet are his preferred methods for tracking the positions of others and for maintaining his own visibility within the company. Larry says he feels "wired" into international communication networks, even though he cautiously acknowledges the alienation he has come to sometimes feel as a consequence of living this way.

For many, there is a widely shared sense that such developments in communications, culture, and identity are evidence of the twenty-first-century world remaking itself, and rapidly. Hardly anyone doubts this is happening. Hardly any two agree as to why it might be happening, though there is a broad consensus that what this something is, is best called "globalization."

The adventures of the concept of globalization have fast become the central metanarrative in a world that supposedly has dispensed with overarching story lines. Whatever may be the political differences between advocates and critics of globalization, one of the most astonishing things about this debate has been how quickly it has colonized public attention; in a relatively short period of time, discussion of globalization has gone from being marginal or nowhere in public life and the academy to being everywhere. Just fifteen or so years ago, many, if not all, social scientists tended to use quite specific terms for analyzing social change—from intersocietal to international idioms—and, with rare exception, talk of global transformations didn't figure. Today however, and in that relatively short period of time, the term *globalization* has pretty much gone global. The concept is now everywhere—in the newspapers and business magazines, on radio and television, in universities and what remains of the public spheres in the various regions of the states of the European diaspora. Indeed, talk of globalization has fast emerged as the international theoretical currency for thinking about rapid social change in the twenty-first century.

The notion of globalization, many agree, captures something about the ways the world in which we live is now continuously changing. Hence, the preoccupation in globalization theory with, among others, forces of multilayered political governance, shifting patterns of postindustrial production, global financial flows, and exchange rates. Each of these clusters is a subject of intense debate in academic circles, and it is telling that such debates are played out globally or at least throughout the contemporary West, in universities and government think tanks from San Francisco to Sydney. Yet globalization as a concept involves considerably more than academic debate alone. We refer not only to the globalized protest strategies of antiglobalizers in Seattle, Genoa, Porto Alegre, and elsewhere but also to the myriad ways in which the forces of globalism impact on both the personal and the social aspects of everyday life. Today, there is good reason to think that the world really has changed, and profoundly. For anyone wanting to understand these changes, it is necessary to come to grips with what globalization is, with what it is doing to our societies, and with the profound consequences it carries for personal and emotional life.

When social analysts first started to speak of the globalizing implications of modernity—what, for want of a better term, we call the Globalization I debate—many reacted in a skeptical manner. The thesis that the historical and economic processes of the modern age mark an overall movement toward "one world," even though the proponents of globalization never quite expressed it thus, was considered fatally flawed—not only by academics but also by policy analysts and politicians. The skeptics were, in short, unconvinced and cited trade and investment figures from the late nineteenth century to question the idea that national economic interdependence had entered a historically unprecedented stage in the late twentieth century. Critics of the "myth of globalization" pointed out that, in contrast to the colonizing spirit of the age of world empires, the majority of economic activity across the international economy occurred primarily in the OECD (Organisation for Economic Cooperation and Development) countries. Regionalization rather than globalization, it was said, defined the shape of the worldwide economy. Some went so far as to claim that, because of the heavy regionalization of such trading blocs as the European Union and North America, the world economy was becoming less, not more, global. Most agreed, at any rate, that nation-states were not becoming progressively less sovereign; on the contrary, internationalization was regarded as fundamentally dependent on the regulatory control of national governments.

Alongside the skeptics of globalization were to be found the antiglobalizers. The antiglobalization brigade, in all its manifestations from anticapitalist protesters to policy think tanks, put forward a list of powerful charges cataloging the sins of globalization. Globalism was allegedly empowering multinational corporations and speculative finance, compounding inequality and eroding democracy, promoting Western imperialism and the Americanization of the world, and destroying environmental standards, as well as brutalizing the public sphere and the state governmental structures through which it operates. The emergence of a planetary-scale global market with ever-decreasing tariffs, ever greater international production, and more-integrated financial markets with higher trade flows had unleashed a turbocharged capitalism of unprecedented forms of economic exploitation and political oppression. Or so argued the antiglobalizers.

The antiglobalizers' link between global Westernization or Americanization on the one hand and turbocapitalist exploitation on the other is an interesting one. Somewhere behind it lurks the Marxist conviction that capitalism exhibits a pathological expansionist logic, one that now expands the geographical reach of Western corporations and markets to the nth degree. The imperial West, it is argued, has carved up and redivided the world into exclusive trade, investment, and financial sectors and flows, with new institutions—such as the G8 and the World Bank—exercising global surveillance and domination. Yet, significantly, there is no recognition here of the monolithic, unitary, and ultimately all-controlling logic attributed to globalization processes; rather, the antiglobalizers tended toward the flat-footed platitude that globalism was a total system with only negative impacts—from which viewpoint the discrepancy between the economic processes of globalization and the daily experience of globalism could only appear as unbridgeable. Certainly it is hard to see how the antiglobalizers can justify the grounds of their own social critique on the basis of the fatalistic theory they espouse. In any event, the assumption that the globe is always geared to perfectly integrated markets is certainly deficient. That is, such critics have reductively equated globalism with an economistic version of globalization. Yet, as we will see, concentrating solely on processes of economic integration, and thus neglecting current social, cultural, and political transformations, leads to an impoverished understanding of how globalization is constituted, contested, and shaped.

One of the most sophisticated analysts of globalization is David Held, who has tackled head-on the critics, both skeptics and antiglobalizers. Held, a professor at the London School of Economics, has quickly emerged as a leading expert on globalization. He powerfully argues that the critics are wrong on almost all the major points. Globalization as the driver of Americanization? Yes, the United States is the major player in shaping economic markets, but globalization, says Held, is not just an American phenomenon. As he points out, American companies account for around only one-fifth of world total imports and approximately one-quarter of total exports. The compounding of inequalities? Individual income differences in the wealthiest and poorest countries are greater than ever, but perhaps the most significant development is that the number of those living in the very poorest conditions appears to the on the decline worldwide. Global markets triumphant over national governments? In the West, government expenditure and taxation levels have generally risen. Globalization, says Held, "has not simply eroded or undermined the power of states; rather it has reshaped and reconfigured it." The globalizing of communications threatening national cultures? The diffusion of instant communication across large parts of the world cannot be doubted, but Held argues that available evidence indicates that local and national cultures remain robust.

Over the last ten to fifteen years, while the Globalization I debate raged, few could have anticipated just how quickly the spread of a "borderless" world was to occur. Some consider that the acceleration and deepening of worldwide interconnectedness sprang directly from the collapse of Soviet communism and the end of the Cold War. Some see the rise of universal consumerism as responsible. Others identify new information technologies as crucial. Whatever the exact play of forces, it is increasingly evident that globalism is nowadays not merely catching up with the discourse of globalization but is, in various senses, outstripping it. That is, cultural transformations associated with globalism have called into question many of the economistic assumptions informing mainstream accounts of globalization. There is certainly something drearily homogeneous about economistic conceptions of globalization, or so argue some of today's leading advocates of globalism. One such figure is sociologist Roland Robertson, who captures well the key limitations of the Globalization I debate:

> The tendency to regard globalization in more or less exclusively economic terms is a particularly disturbing form of reductionism, indeed of fundamentalism. Nowadays invocation of the word "globalization" almost automatically seems to raise issues concerning so-called economic neoliberalism, deregulation, privatization, marketization and the crystallization of what many call a global economy (or global capitalism).

Robertson suggestively seeks to open the globalization debate to factors previously screened from consideration. The global, he insists, involves more than institutional transformations affecting how people live. Rather, the condition of globalism actually changes how people think— about themselves, about others and the wider world. From this angle, the global involves "the compression of the world and the intensification of consciousness of the world as a whole."

There can be little doubt that the debate over globalization in recent years—what we term Globalization II—has advanced a much richer, multidimensional framework for analyzing the shape of world affairs today. In the age of the satellite and instantaneous digital communications, fewer and fewer social analysts approach globalization in only economic terms. We need to still be cautious in saying this, however, and it is necessary to enter some judicious qualifications. Much newspaper commentary the world over, for instance, tends to still assume that globalization refers only to marketization and integrated financial markets. Yet, to repeat, it is increasingly evident that—in both the academy and public political debate—the impacts of globalization are no longer viewed as limited to economic actions and decisions alone and that various cultural, social, and political aspects of daily life are seen as inextricably caught up with the forces of globalism.

The globalization of communication media is especially consequential in this regard. For if globalization is about, among other things, the emergence of one-worldism, then perhaps nowhere is this better dramatized than in popular understandings of the social impact of communication technologies and the growth of the media industries. A key reference point here is the early 1970s, when the first telecommunications satellites were positioned in geosynchronous orbits, thus allowing for the emergence of virtually instantaneous electronic communication between individuals, institutions, societies, and cultures. From the perspective of daily life in the West, the integration of satellites into telecommunications networks is a taken-for-granted phenomenon, an operational backdrop that allows individuals to use mobile phones, faxes, e-mail, and related Internet services the world over. Yet the expansion of global markets is fundamentally interwoven with the spread of such technologies, whose scope is truly staggering. The activities of twenty-four-hour money markets, for example, are constituted and reproduced through global networks of communications, producing a daily turnover in 2003 that exceeded $1.2 trillion.

That said, the globalization of communication does not spell the globalization of culture. Money flows and electronic communications might be as central to the global economy as forests and rivers are to the ecosystem, but the central point is that different individuals and societies produce very different conceptions of globalism through their daily social practices and, equally significantly, take up globally produced services and goods in particularly local ways. The more global space becomes commodified and standardized, the more some critics have assumed a one-size-fits-all model of both individualism and cultural reception. The available scholarly evidence, however, contradicts such unsubtle readings of globalization. While the rise of satellite and digital technologies has made instant communication possible across large parts of the globe, it does not follow that people are exposed to globalism in a unified fashion. Although research remains fragmentary, many studies indicate the extraordinary diversity of orientations and worldviews through which people interpret global communications and thus make sense of their lives and the societies in which they live. This is especially the case as regards cultural countertrends to global consumerist culture. "The large Western city of today," as Saskia Sassen comments, "concentrates diversity. Its spaces are inscribed with the dominant corporate culture, but also with a multiplicity of other cultures and identities. The slippage is evident: the dominant culture can encompass only part of the city. And while corporate power inscribes these cultures and identifies them with 'otherness' thereby devaluing them, they are present everywhere." A relentless globalizing of the economy and communications thus finds its counterpart in a multiplicity of cultural orientations and social differences, all the way from national differences between participants in the global affairs of foreign exchange markets to the localization of fashion trends and the endless market proliferation of designer jeans.

Yet while globalization may not betoken an incipient cultural unity, social theory must come to terms with those aspects of globalism associated with increasing awareness or reflexivity of the sheer pace and scale of change in our lives today. The conditions of globalization on the one hand and reflexivity of globalism on the other are intimately linked, as many recent thought-provoking sociological diagnoses make evident. Zygmunt Bauman speaks of "the globals," those extraterritorial, rootless jet-setters for whom postmodern life involves constantly shifting experiences and events. Jeremy Rifkin writes of the emergence of "global consciousness." Roland Robertson theorizes an "intensification of con-

sciousness of the world as a whole." And Ulrich Beck traces individualized ways of living to assumptions that treat the whole earth as "one
place." Central to such globalist viewpoints is a conception of globalization involving a significant transformation in the ways people imagine
themselves, experience others, and engage in forms of global interconnectedness in everyday life. At the core of this globalist orientation lies
a concern with transformations of the self: its mentalities, interactions,
ideologies, dispositions, and affects. In this respect, the social, cultural,
and political processes of globalism extend into the core of the self, initiating a reordering of relations between forms of individualism and
global trends.

Transformations in individualism and globalization do not, however,
lead to the production of "globalized identities." We do not mean to deny
the existence of many kinds of global consciousness—evident at times of,
say, megaevents such as the Olympics or worldwide political crises such
as the terrorist attacks of 9/11. But such emergent forms of global consciousness do not result in a common way of global thinking, if only
because there is no global pool of memories to draw from. Contemporary
forms of global interconnectedness do not, of themselves, predetermine
a particular set of cultural experiences, social values, or ideological reactions. And yet globalization, involving very different patterns of transnational interactions, flows, and networks, remains above all about *people*.
Global transformations are deeply inscribed in people's sense of their own
individualism, at once demanding significant levels of psychic commitment and reorganization. It follows that a social theory responsive to
such changes must seek to grasp the complex, contradictory ways in
which individuals constitute, reproduce, and transform their sense of
self-identity and individualism in relation to processes of globalization.

LIVING WITH GLOBALISM

For those who fear globalization and its impacts, Larry's story might seem
an instructive warning: a man who has "made it," primarily through traversing the global, and one whose personal sense of satisfaction gained
from capitalist society (material affluence, power, symbolic prestige)
enters into sharp contradiction with the ideologies of that world (security, freedom, and happiness). Larry is, by his own account, self-made,
autonomous, his own boss, blissfully self-determining. And yet, paradoxically, all of Larry's reflections on his life in therapy attest to a sense

of displacement, decentering, and division. His own biography, he implies, is continually written over by outside forces; but also, and more interestingly, such dislocating forces penetrate to the core of his identity. Caught within the denied difference between the rhetoric and the reality of global postmodernist culture, Larry is at once self-identical and decentered, manically narcissistic and defensively depressed.

Larry's reflections on the determining power of "outside forces" provide a salutary example of the risks issuing from globalization, especially of its perceived threats and terrors. Interestingly, Larry has his own perspective on the global. During therapy, he expressed deep reservations about the intricate links between corporate power and the new global economy—reservations that reflect anxieties about the myriad ways his own life has been transformed as a consequence of globalization. The trouble with globalization, he reasoned, is that it is ultimately menacing, soul-destroying, and all-controlling. The relentless commercial pressure to compete, to continually cut costs, and to find more flexible and cheaper methods of service delivery cuts directly across any sense of loyalty and commitment to his staff as well as the building of a larger organizational identity. He felt saddened that money, materialism, and managerialism so obviously held the upper hand over loyalty, commitment, and community. From this angle, the economic and cultural consequences of globalization can only be thought of in terms of deadlock, the former displacing and disfiguring the latter. The media, he reckons, mythologize the virtues of global forces like digital communications, especially the capacity to broaden the mind, to allow one to learn from, and experiment with, other forms of life, other cultures. But for Larry this isn't what happens at all. The something happening in our brave new world, unleashed by the unknown and unseen forces of globalization, is that which takes control of one's life, both professionally and personally, rendering one defensive and depressed.

For all the wealth the new global capitalism has brought him, Larry is clearly prone to speaking a language of victimhood. The hard-nosed entrepreneur in him welcomes the greater competitiveness and intense individualism that globalization has spawned. And yet his own experience, as one whose lifestyle of globalism leaves him feeling far removed from his own emotional world as well as emotional contact with others, leads him time and again to blame external forces. And nothing, it seems, is quite such a menacing external force as globalism. Although Larry only used the term globalization on rare occasions, many of the issues he was preoccupied with in therapy go to the very core of this phenomenon. In particular, corporate downsizing and constant technological change had made him permanently uneasy, self-doubting, anxiously preoccupied with matters of professional standing and social hierarchy. Torn between liberal rhetoric about the economic benefits of globalization and the realities of corporate reengineering and general short-termism, it was as if Larry couldn't decide whether, as boss of the company, he's a winner or a loser. Again, however, what comes through most clearly in therapy is his sense of a lack of emotional freedom. For Larry has come to blame the counterfeit flexibility promoted by globalizing economic forces for this sense of emotional deficit pervading his life.

As Larry speaks of it, this brave new world of corporate reengineering and technological networking is primarily about economic globalization. Yet there is a sense also in which the global economy spills over into the cultural sphere and at the same time transforms and reconfigures it. For example, Larry often referred to his business as a "control machine." When this was explored in therapy, it became clear that he imagined not only that this "machine" controlled the activities, thoughts, and dispositions of both employees and senior management but also that this omnipotent force extended to the commercial operations of the organization itself—thereby filling in a range of societal connections with other communication networks, corporations, and, ultimately, the global marketplace. Tellingly, it had never occurred to Larry that these fantasies about corporate surveillance or social control might be worth exploring further for himself, for what they might suggest about both his ties with other people and the changed relations between institutional and personal life. Larry's analyst suggested that it might be fruitful to think about this some more, and in time it emerged that there was a link in Larry's mind between the corporate, technical, and organized world of global systems on the one hand and the draining or emptying out of passion, spontaneity, and interpersonal engagement in personal life on the other. The more Larry immersed himself in the world of business and the dynamics of the global economy, the less sure he felt of his inner self and of his emotional connection with others. This was the theme—organized globalization contrasted with dislocations of the intimacies of personal life—that dominated many analytic sessions.

What, exactly, is the personal dislocation of which Larry speaks? What is being explored here is the fear (and, no doubt, the wish) of relinquishing personal agency. In a globalizing world, in which past ways of doing things are continually revised and overturned, personal reflexivity becomes paramount. There are of course various ways in which individuals can avoid or displace these pressures of globalism, and strategies of passivity, resigned acceptance, or denial are all ways of limiting the difficult emotional task of relating inner and outer, self and world, identity and difference. And yet such strategies, notwithstanding their own emotional brittleness, run directly into conflict with the deadly worlds of globalization. Such is the heavy emphasis on individualism today that people are compelled, and daily, to be pro-active or self-legislating in all aspects of life. Only those practiced in the arts of escape, from daydreaming to artistic and literary expression, manage to hold to a sense of what is tantalizing in the very thought of subjective escape. For what we need to escape from—others, work, the system—says a great deal about both ourselves and our contemporary cultural malaise.

Here is where sociology enters in an interesting way, as there has been no shortage of intellectual assessments of the conditions of political domination structuring the desire for social escape. Inspired by various kinds of literary and sociological works—from Weber's envisioned "iron cage of bureaucracy" to Orwell's *1984*—many have portrayed the development of the modern age in terms of escalating and unstoppable levels of social control, with an accompanying radical deterioration of individual initiative and sense of personal freedom. Thus the sociological melodrama of "Big Brother society," in which the world of organized capitalism and bureaucratic rationality produce ever-intensifying levels of private fear, foreboding, and fragmentation.

Many contemporary accounts of globalization do, in fact, present an explanation of the ills of society in terms of the determining power of structures in people's lives; it is then but a short step to fill in the missing pieces of the jigsaw by uncovering how individuals, identities, desires, dispositions, environments, and cultures are reshaped, usually in a brutally linear fashion, by the omnipotent forces of globalism. The central conceptual and political limitation of conceptualizing globalization purely as an external force, however, is that it prevents us from seeing with sufficient clarity the myriad ways in which individuals engage, respond, escape, reproduce, or transform the whole gamut of globalizing forces that they necessarily encounter in their everyday lives. What is ironic is that such top-heavy accounts of globalism—even if they were proved an accurate account of current social realities—cannot provide an adequate means of grasping how individuals respond to both the expansive and the debilitating impacts of such worldwide transformations. People who retreat inward, like Larry, are merely cast as the dupes of a particular Western set of ideological values or consumption patterns; what is passed over in silence is the multiplicity of emotions that shape the distinctive and idiosyncratic ways in which individuals cope with the multiple cruising speeds of globalization.

The opposite of social control, one might say, is choice. Precisely how we come to think about the scope of available choices in our lives, at any particular moment, has consequences for how we imagine the ways the world affects us. In the language of some analysts of worldwide social transformations, globalization is viewed as both condition and consequence of people exercising choice in their daily lives. A triumph, one might think, of neoliberal ideology? A reinstatement of the modernist dream of the free individual at precisely the historical moment when global conglomerates reign supreme? Or, perhaps, simply a consumerist discourse raised to the second power? Not necessarily, as choice in this context cannot be explained exhaustively in terms of the marketplace and the new capitalism. Those who think it feasible to speak of a more nuanced idea of how personal choice intersects with globalization have in mind, perhaps above all, the crisis (or, better, ever-erupting crises) of the late modern age, and in particular they focus on the complex ways in which ordinary people reframe global troubles in terms of individual responsibilities, emotional conundrums, and ethical dilemmas. Here is how Anthony Giddens, renowned sociologist and a leading figure in British Third Way politics, describes how choice is shaped by, and reshapes, globalizing processes:

> The more tradition looses its hold, and the more daily life is reconstituted in terms of the dialectical interplay of the local and the global, the more individuals are forced to negotiate lifestyle choices among a diversity of options. Of course, there are standardising influences too—most notably, in the form of commodification, since capitalistic production and distribution forms core components of modernity's institutions. Yet because of the "openness" of social life today, the pluralisation of contexts of action and the diversity of "authorities," lifestyle choice is increasingly important in the constitution of self-identity and daily activity.

Not so much a phenomenon "out there," globalization is, rather, internal to the way we go about making choices and performing activities in daily life. Globalization is not merely a constraint, a kind of brake, on personal autonomy, though undoubtedly it sometimes feels like this. For Giddens, the global—which penetrates to the core of lifestyle options—is inextricably bound up with the local, the way we live now.

The Global Unleashing of Privatized Lives

The problem of individualism today, it might be argued, is that it seems increasingly disconnected from "life" as globalized capitalist society is coming to define it. Certainly, it is far from obvious what the political and ideological reach of individualism—as both concept and lived experience—is in a world of transnational conglomerates and mass-produced products such as designer clothes and mobile phones. The dilemma is that the modernist creed of individualist self-making appears to have been brought low by a postmodernist cult of discontinuity, displacement, and disengagement. Real-life accounts of personal life today, as we are beginning to see, are those of people struggling, among other things, with the difficulties of mass consumer culture and its prepackaged scripts for living. In an age that privileges rapid disposal over durability, as well as instant replacement over continuing relationships, the language of individualism looks increasingly fictional, even though it may still represent for many a kind of utopian aspiration.

There is, however, a powerful postmodern solution to the current societal dilemma of individualism, and it is one that seeks to make a virtue of the alleged deficiencies of current global transformations. In this kind of orientation to life, there is not much room for long-term projects, grand designs, ongoing commitments, or moral and societal ideals. This isn't necessarily bad news for individualism (or at least, and more accurately, for a privatized form of individualized experience). For if globalization has sliced life into a series of episodes and momentary experiences, then the same may equally be true of the individualist identities that are increasingly fast consumed and disposed of by people in the contemporary West. These are identities with a wondrous capacity for continual change and instant transformation. To be more precise, these are identities that have taken the modern individualist impulse for self-constitution and self-improvement and raised it to the second power, thus giving a radical postmodern slant on choosing, changing, and transforming as ends in themselves.

Such is the world inhabited by Joe and Xavier. Lovers for only a few months, they are both effortlessly elegant, dressed in black designer wear—with Joe calm and in control in a stereotypical masculine way, and Xavier more obviously quiet and introverted. They sit in a luxuriously appointed boutique hotel in Paris, just off boulevard St. Germain, sipping bottles of cold Japanese lager. A striking couple, they attract looks from most passing through the hotel lobby, which in itself seems to bring pleasure—especially to Joe.

Xavier and Joe begin to talk about their plans for the night: dinner at La Coupole, drinks at Aux Deux Magots, then clubbing. It is clear that it's of the utmost importance to be seen at the right places. And as for most couples dedicated to following "what is in," the Internet remains a privileged site for tracking news on the latest trends. Joe walks over to the hotel's flat-screen terminal and asks Xavier which city he wants to visit next. A week away from his native New York, Joe is already feeling restless. He suggests Berlin, a city he instinctively feels is "right" for their designer-led relationship, and Xavier agrees—provided they can get a suite with a Jacuzzi and an extra-large flat-screen TV. Joe impatiently scrolls through Google. After several false leads, Xavier takes over the search for their hotel paradise in Berlin. Joe heads back to the bar for another beer.

A reasonably confident though emotionally immature man, and a shy, anxious man: common enough versions of masculinity certainly, but what does the story of Joe and Xavier suggest about contemporary social conditions? It would be easy to argue that consumerism is at the core of things here. And yet these social changes Joe and Xavier confront and are confronted by reach well beyond transformations in the marketplace and consumer culture. Both Joe and Xavier love their lifestyles and to different degrees have found aspects of their relationship rewarding, but neither of them wants to relinquish his personal freedom for the security of coupledom. Both are preoccupied, again in quite different ways, with the fear that something—their relationship, work, life itself?—may overtake them. Deeply aware that they live in a time when there is no choice but to make continual choices (from lifestyles and careers to travel and relationships), and yet also sensing that the pace of global change today devalues everything that one may choose as desirable, Joe and Xavier battle internally with the dominant orientation currently available for the design of life strategies. These orientations include desires for independence; impulses to avoid becoming too tightly connected to any given person, situation, network, or job for very long; a general sense of dissatisfaction and impatience with the structure of all social things; and, perhaps above all, a preoccupation with keeping on the move and moving on.

Orientations such as these are threaded through their ways of relating to others and the wider world, and indeed cut to the core of their relationship. For not only do Joe and Xavier struggle with matters of independence, expressing a continual need to avoid any sense of dependence on others, but also the ground rule of their being together is one that—in advance—stresses the centrality of multiple sexual partners and the pleasures of ever-new experiences and enjoying the moment, as well as the need for fast exits. That they both have secured in recent years good incomes—although Joe has experienced periods of unemployment—allows them escape from predictable routines and fixed ways of doing things. And that they are in flight from their pasts—Joe in particular seeking to escape his unhappy upbringing—also gives shape to their embrace of the high-tech culture of globalization.

There is a psychological disposition toward dismantling and deconstruction built into the newly individualized forms of individualism as expressed by Joe and Xavier. A fear of the long-term, of time itself, is what theorists of individualization like Ulrich Beck have picked up on. The cult of the ever-new and of short-termism has produced a code of self-searching and self-discovery riddled with contradictions. As Beck expresses this:

> People end up more and more in a labyrinth of self-doubt and uncertainty. The infinite regress involved in this self-questioning—'Am I really happy?', 'Am I really fulfilled?', 'Who exactly is the I saying and asking this?'—leads to ever new kinds of response, which then often provide a market niche for experts, industries and religious movements. In their quest for self-fulfilment people scour the travel brochures and go to the four corners of the earth; they throw away the best marriages and rapidly enter new ties; they undergo retraining, diet and job; they shift from one therapy group to another and swear by quite different therapies and therapists. They pull themselves up by the roots, to see whether the roots are really healthy.

Whether self-questioning individuals like Joe and Xavier are in a position to take stock of the state of the roots they have pulled up, in any kind of reflective manner, is an open question. Certainly, their lives are dedicated to the pulling up of roots—to transforming, changing, choosing—and yet much of this seems conditioned by global promptings rather than arising from their own making.

Joe in particular says he feels passive in the face of global forces. Focusing on his work as a cameraman—currently filming pop music videos—he remarks, "You know, the work comes and goes, and when it comes I follow, one month Los Angeles, Sydney the next, London the next and on and on. Sure, the money is good, but I'm just a pawn of the media agencies, who in turn are run by music conglomerates like Sony and EMI." Yet Joe's pessimism isn't conditioned only by distant economic forces (media agencies, music conglomerates); rather, it's the structure of the work itself that fuels his pent-up anxiety. The average length of his employment in any job project, which may encompass several video promotions, is about three weeks. The opportunity to get to know colleagues under such conditions is obviously extremely limited. "This business today," comments Joe, "is about networking and getting the best agency connections. When we're filming, people basically keep their distance." In any event, Joe can never be sure how long he'll be working with people, whether he'll cross paths with them again, or for that matter when and where the next project will arise.

It's the last of these factors that plays most uneasily on his mind. The short-term project time of video production certainly seems to preclude the building of lasting work relationships and a sense of solidarity with colleagues. Yet the worst of it for Joe is the absence of firm prospects and guaranteed commitments. He knows only too well that his media skills are expendable, disposable, and he knows that his projected future in work depends primarily upon current job successes. His past experience of working in television for some eight years certainly seems to count for little, as it did when he was laid off by NBC in the mid-1990s. This immobilizing period of unemployment held Joe in the grip of depression for eighteen months until he recovered and returned to the present-day dispersed, deregulated processes of the media industries. Most people he now encounters seem to accept the episodic nature of their work, taking into account that the likelihood of future successes depends on current risk taking. And while there seems to be no shortage of short-term or rolling contracts at present, Joe still worries that he'll be unable to keep pace with changes in the industry and, perhaps above all, that any current failure will be too difficult to combat within the unforgiving world of transnational media.

It is worth asking why what makes sense for the long-term working mentality no longer makes so much sense in our own time of short-termism. What exactly has changed? It is not, of course, that global capitalism has managed to tame unemployment. On the contrary, mass unemployment has become more pervasive, although poverty under conditions of globalization becomes considerably more individuated, at least in the West. What has changed is the distribution of poverty and unemployment, away from a traditional reserve army of labor groups and toward segments of the individual working life in which poverty is for some a temporary condition. This is what sociologists today call "dynamic poverty," the dispersal or scattering of unemployment across individual biographies. From this angle, Joe might be said to be suffering from a kind of anxiety arising from our "75-15-10 society," with 75 percent never having known unemployment, some 15 percent having been out of work temporarily, and the remaining 10 percent more permanently excluded from the job market. As Beck summarizes this trend, today "poverty and unemployment first enter people's lives not as permanent facts but as a less forbidding temporary condition, coming and going and only at certain times becoming more settled." In such conditions, people find themselves—even those arrogantly convinced of their "membership" in the 75 percent grouping—less and less protected against exposure to periods of unemployment. And this may be why Joe, having been already excluded by the forces of capital once, is prone to jadedness.

Like a good many other hyperglobalists living, working, and traveling the polished cities of the West, Joe deploys various strategies for avoiding awareness of this global economic situation. He believes that his seemingly random work life, with its unpredictable shifts and drifts across the earth's surface, represents the aesthetic of postmodernism exquisitely, a new mode of living and labor informed by the principle of "anything goes." But for the most part he is not interested in connecting the living of his life to current social trends; he says he hates people who think there's some intrinsic logic to our fate as individuals. Such hostility to any kind of historical or sociological thinking may help to explain his enthusiasm for quickly consumed and disposed-of consumerist experiences, which he interestingly enough interprets as a form of repetition of early family dramas. Raised principally by his emotionally volatile mother, Joe was brought up in the Bronx, where his father worked as a department store manager. Adrift and amnesic, Joe's father was a "ladies' man," attracted to the "finer things in life"—primarily money and material possessions. The father appears as a man who "didn't give a damn": Joe's disappointment that his father didn't care enough for him (he deserted the family when Joe was only four) is the emotional backdrop to his own exaggerated self-reliance and fear of dependency. In a curious paradox, Joe thinks he's copied his father's own emotional style.

There may well be something to this, but, significantly, one unintended consequence of Joe's familial narrative is that it displaces attention from the social conditions that make globalization disorientating at an emotional level. A key assumption of his familial narrative is that Joe feels an acute sense of disappointment that his father had not loved him and that his style of coping with this loss was, in effect, to become a version of his father himself. If this is correct, it is perhaps not surprising that he chooses to live as a hyperglobalist. But this still removes him from the troubled waters of thinking about how the brave new world of globalization creates ever-new forms of exclusion and disappointment. In *Wasted Lives*, a brilliant analysis of human waste as an unavoidable side-effect of globalization, Zygmunt Bauman writes:

> What we all seem to fear . . . is abandonment, exclusion, being rejected, blackballed, disowned, dropped, stripped of what we are, being refused what we wish to be. We fear being left alone, helpless and hapless. Barred company, loving hearts and helping hands. We fear to be dumped—our term for the scrapyard. What we miss most badly is the certainty that all that won't happen—not to us.

An ambient fear—of being dumped, of becoming waste, of exclusion—has become the emotional backdrop to the theater of globalization.

When people feel horror of exclusion, they can become more decidedly dependent upon external social or cultural guidelines in a bid for immunity against feared rejections. Indeed, it could be said that this kind of free-floating, ambient anxiety trickles directly on to a market level of ready-made answers proffered by experts, culture industries, and therapeutic movements. Take Larry's deep ambivalence about his own wishes and needs, how these self-concerns should be related to his current working regime, and even the dire potential consequences he imagines might flow if he deviated too far from a preplanned, regulated working life. It is not that Larry is uninterested in interior life, but it does appear that he is uncomfortable with (and perhaps ashamed of) his inner drives and desires. If he was interested in therapy and psychoanalysis, it was partly because

Freudian ideas seemed to offer expert guidance on how to better tie together his internal and external worlds. Despite his disbelief at what he saw as the "failure" of an expert system, Larry's world came to life as he discovered in therapy the lack of fit between his inner and outer worlds.

This raises the vexed question of whether it might be possible to speak of a psychology of globalism—or, perhaps more appropriately, of the *emotional climates of globalization*. This chapter has presented a classification of this kind, based on the profiles of two quite different men (should we say globalizers?) going about their daily business of coping with, responding to, and creatively engaging with the global forces currently transforming society at different levels. It is necessary, finally, to proceed upward to the cultural dynamic of the global itself, which in any event partly determines the individual experience, and ask, how have Larry and Joe—in their particular worlds and personal styles—developed individualist responses to the shape of contemporary globalization? How might these individual experiences of individualization, that is, be mapped in relation to the flows, networks, and interactions that constitute the deadly worlds of globalization? Here the typology of possible shapes that globalization might take as developed by Held and his associates, which involves particular stress on the dimensions of extensity, intensity, velocity, and impact, guides our conclusions. (For further discussion of Held's model, which we seek to transpose in a strictly limited fashion from institutional political concerns to individuals and individualizing concerns, see "Notes and Sources").

Much has been made of the fact that Larry is a man living an extraterritorial and globe-trotting lifestyle. Of course, in the eyes of many ordinary people, it would surely be obvious that Larry's habitat is itself global. From his very high degree of international mobility to his use of the latest technologies, globalization is integral to the constantly shifting opportunities and challenges that define Larry's life. But, at the same time, we have seen that Larry withdraws from, and indeed feels high levels of anxiety in the face of, the complexity and sharp contradictions of a globalizing world. Sociality is difficult, people remote. There is little doubt that his jet-setting lifestyle has promoted his work interests, and yet his life in the global fast lane is one largely devoid of inner texture and reflective experience. His dealings with others, as indeed with himself, remain singularly instrumental.

It is against this personal and professional background that we contend that Larry inhabits a world of *diffused globalization*. What is this diffusion of the global? We use this term to refer to high levels of extensity and intensity of global social forces in which the impact of such forces is highly regulated. This characterization of globalism is particularly relevant to Larry's experience of work, in which his exposure to the worldwide stretching of economic flows and technological interactions was high. If we bear in mind these features of globalization, we can see why Larry has come to take work very seriously, so seriously that the attitude often spills over into a defensive repudiation of other aspects of life. Development of his company within a web of global networks was undertaken to, among other things, prove himself clever and commanding; work pursuits offered a largely impersonal context in which he could mold a vision of himself as successful. And yet, as we have seen, the more control Larry exerted over the field of work, the more restrictive and oppressive became his sense of self-identity.

Through therapy, the emergence of an increased capacity for introspection highlighted for Larry that a sense of meaninglessness underlay the strictly controlled and repetitive quality of his working life. It was from this insight that Larry came to recognize that his heart was no longer in work the way it had been previously. What is equally noteworthy, however, is the choice of therapy itself, from which Larry embarked on such self-exploration. The rise of therapy as a phenomenon of globalization has received much attention in recent public debate and scholarly literature, and we consider this development in some detail in chapter 4. Therapy undoubtedly created new opportunities for Larry to reflect on the direction of his life. But there was also a very palpable sense in which Larry turned to therapy as a means to limit the emotional impacts of globalization. From the very start of his interest in therapy, Larry's use of self-help manuals and psychological experts involved a kind of defensiveness that endowed the therapist or expert with an omnipotent knowledge of the necessary guidelines for free and successful living. Therapy in this sense became a trap in much the same way that work had been a trap. To the extent, of course, that therapy is viewed as a cultivated diversion of the privileged (and there are many critics who take such a view), Larry's use of therapy might be said to have promoted only narcissistic withdrawal. We do not believe that this was in fact the case, if only because therapy in seemingly failing Larry actually provided him with a fresh means of moving beyond his routinized work identity. The point that needs to be stressed in conclusion, however, is that there can be no denying that Larry initially used therapy as an "expert system" to beat back the challenges and threats of a globalizing world.

By contrast, Joe's world is *thickly globalized*, structured to its core by high exposure to the intensity of global networks. As in any life set within the parameters of thick globalization, Joe lives several concurrent stories. There is his narrative of unpredictable work moves and shifts, set within the broader confines of his previous experience of temporary unemployment and fear of exclusion. There is his experience of global consumerist landscapes, of designer clothes and boutique hotels, invested emotionally with considerable affect as a kind of scramble away from the disorientating consequences of economic globalization. The mirrorlike sensuousness of consumer culture thus provides a kind of emotional break from the impersonality of corporate capitalism. And there is, finally, the narrative of his relationship with Xavier, imagined in terms of erotic intensities and unexplored gratifying passions, all set within cultural scripts of "easy exits" and "anything goes."

CHAPTER

FOUR

~

ON THE INDIVIDUALIST
ARTS OF SEX
Intimacy, Eroticism, and
the Newly Lost Individual

S OMETIMES INTIMACY seems like a promised land where
couples are bound together in mutual understanding, solidarity, and friendship. Yet a need to escape the myth of
mutuality is more and more typical of the interwoven desires and anxieties of contemporary women and men. Simon is recently divorced, a college teacher, just turned forty, yet still in the grip of ambivalence and
frustration about the direction of his life:

> It's an enormous relief, you know, getting divorced, admitting my
> mistakes with Lisa and acknowledging how long I've lived with a
> certain amount of guilt and regret. It's tremendously freeing, and
> exciting. That's what it feels like. But if I'm honest I also feel a lit-
> tle fearful. Though I was sexually bored with Lisa, she was a good
> friend, and she did make me feel secure. Now, there's no safety net.

Things may have been bad before for Simon, life may have been difficult,
his relationship with Lisa may have been unsatisfying, but there was

always the possibility of improvement. A fantasy of future perfection. Yet now, single and footloose, Simon can't help finding the future intimidating.

What has gone wrong? Apart from the obvious sense of loss resulting from the fact that he has ended the relationship with his wife of some eleven years, there is also an apparently subtler reason for Simon's personal discontent. Simon's uncomfortable feelings about himself center on sex, principally what he considers the terrible tensions involved in being a man in a changing and uncertain world. Simon describes in fairly precise terms how his home life has always felt like a refuge from a heartless world, how all this centered on Lisa, and the importance of his friendship with her, given an inability to make friends. Home was where he went to escape the pressures of the world. "I used to come home from teaching, relax, and usually spend the night with Lisa—watching TV or listening to music. Nothing too exciting, we didn't have that many friends—but I quite liked it that way. I had my own access to a different social scene at any rate."

What Simon refers to here is his erotic interest in women and casual sex and the thrill he gets from sexual experimentation. For sex is with Simon a compulsion; he feels that he's rarely at a "safe distance" from desire and is always on the lookout for new sexual encounters. "It's not like I want to get to know these women or anything, or that I get intensely involved with them. It's rather the buzz, the excitement, that comes from meeting all these women clandestinely, and of course the sexual high that comes from screwing someone you don't know." In true New Lad fashion, though he's far from being a lad any longer, Simon likes his sexual encounters impersonal, discreet, and—truth be told—a little brutal. Episodic sex is hot, sexual commitment is cool. And Simon can't help finding that the best sex is free of complications.

There's much more at stake here than the traditional male "double standard," although that does, of course, enter into it. For along with the mixture of excitement and guilt that Simon derives from regular sexual encounters with strangers, he is also held in thrall to the process of his "sex addiction." New information technologies, mass communications, and culture are all involved. Withdrawn and cut off from colleagues at work, Simon relies on sexual contact magazines and singles bars as the principal means for his calculated pursuit of sex. He's also drawn to the "wonders" of mobile phones for developing "sex contacts." Texting erotic messages, sending and receiving digital photos prior to meeting, and pursuing various desired objects at a distance—all this seems to Simon much less strained than clubbing or other more traditional means of scoring a one-night stand. At any rate, his new G3 phone allows him to experiment, to try on different ways of being, to enact different forms of sexual fantasy. This might suggest, at least as an initial approximation, that there is here an emotional openness or willingness to embrace others, and yet Simon is in many ways a vivid illustration of how the use of new technologies can be debilitating with respect to fostering interpersonal relationships. For while Simon might feel he's missing out on nothing, is never unaware of the power of sex, his compulsive sexual encounters involve a kind of psychic withdrawal. Episodic sex for Simon had become a form of emotional deadness acted out in the presence of others:

> I'm trying to think how to capture this in words. It's a bit like that feeling when, as a kid, you found something really good that didn't belong to you—and you got to keep it. Having sex with these women is just wild, it releases me from all these personal and work pressures. It's like the one time I know I can be happy, not in the sense of contentment but in terms of doing what I like doing and doing it when I want. It's my own freedom really—a place I can be myself, truly, you know just switch off from the pressures of everyone and everything—and then afterwards, refreshed, I feel I can confront the world again.

Narcissism and a sense of otherness, identity and difference, have hooked Simon on the fleetingness of sexual encounters.

In this interplay of home and away, internal security and external arousal, there is a deeper sexual history. Simon was born and grew up in London, the second of two sons of an American father and an English mother. His father, a company executive, was regularly overseas on business, which left his mother to "keep the family afloat." Simon especially identified with his older brother and relished the opportunity to hang out with him as they were growing up in the metropolitan buzz of London. The "big brother" was streetwise and smart; he always "did well with the girls." Not so Simon, who not only experienced uncomfortable feelings of rivalry and competitiveness with his brother but also seemed to lose out when his father returned from overseas trips. For his father, it seems, got best with the older brother—though it was "only Mum he was ever really interested in."

In the bare bones of this family structure there was not much for Simon to build upon, in the sense of nourishing family ties from which a degree of continuity of identity is sustained. Rather, Simon kept an image of his family as soap opera—all bit parts, isolated scenes, and low-level drama. "My parents," he says, "only had time for each other. What my brother and I wanted or needed was only ever an afterthought. It wasn't that they didn't care for us—they did. But it was so hard to make contact with them, impossible to know what they were thinking." This mystery as to what the parents were really thinking made it especially difficult for Simon to trust himself to the friendship of others. If engaging with friends involves a kind of "reading" of both need and desire, Simon was, in a sense, semi-illiterate.

This failure in emotional literacy is important. Still fascinated by the "mysterious" relationship of his parents, though uncomfortable with the display of emotion in his private relationships, Simon has worked out a form of reconciliation with his troubled past. He tells of a recent experience of phoning in to a radio talk show and of feeling unusually at ease with himself when discussing concerns and secrets of his private life. The radio host became, in effect, Simon's therapist:

> He was very courteous, very professional, and didn't use any "psychobabble." Talking about some of the sordid secrets of my sex life wasn't exactly easy, but I'd heard the show before and it's all very accepting and nonjudgmental. He just let me talk, really, and waited for me to bring up the more intensely private stuff. He said that I was brave and honest in confronting my private problems.

While averse to the public display of emotion, Simon found the touchy-feely therapy of the radio program strangely soothing. On this calmer, reflective ground, he feels positive about life's possibilities.

Compare Simon's story with that of Ruth, a married woman in her late fifties. Unlike Simon, who has experienced inner turmoil, Ruth describes herself as contented, for the most part, with her life. Marriage, companionship, sex, children—she has them all. Her love for her children has been the core of her marriage: "Max and I have four wonderful sons, and I've little doubt that the early years of being at home and looking after them were the best of my life. It was certainly the time when I felt most needed—that what I was doing was really valuable and made a difference."

So far so good. But Ruth has discovered that marriage can't be fully anchored in children alone, a fact brought out especially as her children have now grown up and moved out of the family home. She describes herself as having felt "gutted" when her youngest left home to go to university in London some three years ago. She misses him—she misses all of her sons—a lot. Since that time, she has been going through "a period of self-realization." All her married life Ruth had displayed an attitude of benign neglect toward her husband, Max. Their marriage seemed to work well enough "as he got on with his work and career— he's a real workaholic—and I focused on the children." But now that has all radically changed. Ruth misses the intimacy she shared with her sons, and life with Max alone seems a bit lonely.

Ruth has developed an increasingly reflexive self-consciousness about her identity, brought about partly by the departure of her sons from the family home and partly by the impact of new technologies on her emotional life—of which more shortly. The oldest child of a prosperous German family in which the parents enforced quite strict codes of moral behavior, Ruth had been a very quiet, shy young woman who worked as a nurse until she met and fell in love with Max, an investment banker. She saw marriage as a means of escaping the stifling atmosphere of her own family life and quickly abandoned her career in nursing to support the aspirations of her husband and concentrate on raising children. Looking back, she says she now sees the extent to which her sense of self-worth became dependent upon her husband and life with the children. Yet it emerges that the dependency was more complex than this characterization might suggest, since Ruth relied on different aspects of family life in order to both emotionally contain and stimulate herself. In many ways, she depended upon her husband to hold herself together, to give some shape to the future. But it was always the children in whom she found stimulation; they were not just soothing but genuinely exciting.

In recent years, Ruth has been trying to patch things up with her husband, an effort she describes in terms of "making a success" of the marriage. But she has also been trying to recapture something of the lost excitement she found in the relationship with her children. And she says she has found it in cyberspace, through surfing the Net. Here she is on the thrill of chat rooms and how the Internet has "allowed me to put myself back together":

Not that I was ever particularly interested in computers, and I couldn't care less about electronic mail and such things. But the anonymity of chat rooms was such an eye-opener, just marvelous. I've got to find out all sorts of things—about people and exciting ideas, but above all about myself. My online experience, particularly when the discussions concern more explicitly sexual things, has taken me far beyond what I knew about my identity.

The utopianism in this is almost attractive. Though she doesn't use the term herself, Netsex has given Ruth a place to belong and a new sense of identity. Enacting alternative selves, performing different sexual scripts, she finds herself looking out in a new way and reflecting differently on her internal world. So much so that she confides in many of her new interlocutors on the Net, confessing her personal failures, sexual inadequacies, and feelings of vulnerability. Ruth feels this has been very positive. It is as if the Internet has given her a greater emotional range.

RELATIONSHIPS WITHOUT SEX, SEX WITHOUT RELATIONSHIPS: THE NEWLY LOST INDIVIDUAL

Sex thrives on ideas about sex. This ongoing self-evaluation and self-exploration of sexual desire is highly evident in the lives of both Simon and Ruth. Through it all, life is lived reflecting on life. Sexual satisfaction means exploration of the erotic. For Simon, being adventurous and sexy and alive are the same thing. For Ruth, too, to be networked is to be at the center of things.

Eroticism in the language of psychoanalysis is an imaginary force, a construct of fantasy, from which desire flows incessantly. In psychoanalysis we find a radical defense of sexual diversity, a plea for understanding of erotic variety, from which we might reflect on the real-life sexualities of Simon and Ruth. Freud thought that sex communicates the core of the self, and in a certain sense both Simon and Ruth might tend to agree. And yet Freud's psychological and political reflections run much deeper than this, underscoring as his writings do the dramatic extent to which the expression of sexuality is always interwoven with the receptions and reactions of others, as well as the traumatic and impenetrable pleasure we derive from our attempts to fathom the fantasy-ridden worlds of our deepest presocial desires. After all, that's the end point of Freudianism: the *polymorphous plasticity of sex*, by which Freud sought to underscore the massive fluidity of sexual desires. But if this is true, then the new world of sex inaugurated by globalization gives even greater impetus to an eroticism that ceaselessly turns back upon itself, calling up a staging of sexuality that is exploratory and reflective in equal measure. Specifically there are a number of recent social developments that bear upon this increased personal and cultural awareness of the fluidity of sexual desires; many of these developments are touched on throughout this chapter: the impact of new technologies from the Internet to mobile phones; the rapid explosion of interest in sex through magazines, lifestyle television programs, and self-help manuals; the commodification of sex and the partial globalization of the "porn industry"; and the establishment of sexualities as a field of academic study and specialization.

Over the past few decades, there has been a marked series of changes affecting sex, intimacy, and eroticism within the advanced societies of the West. These changes are a product of both consumer capitalism and globalization, though it is not always easy to determine which is more significant. Two factors, however, are especially relevant here. The first is a rapid rise in what we call *discursive sexuality*. That is, sexuality increasingly becomes a terrain on which the impact of global capital, ideas, and ideologies is brought to bear. This is particularly clear in terms of the ways in which sexuality is framed and regulated today through advertising, mass media, and information culture. Second, sexuality becomes a key focus of personal identity, a reflexive condition of meaning in social relationships, intimacy, and eroticism. Let us briefly consider these two intersecting developments.

There has been considerable recent public debate concerning the extent to which moral values and sexual orthodoxies have been vigorously challenged and undermined by contemporary cultural influences and new technologies. Some see in the rise of both consumer culture and sexual progressivism an overturning of the mores and traditions that had been consolidated throughout the nineteenth century in private life, law, medical practice, and social regulations. Yet rather than pose the modern (or indeed, postmodern) against the traditional, it is necessary to see more recent and sometimes dramatic global change both as interwoven with a long historical process and as highly uneven in its impact. Those who counterpose "contemporary values" with "traditional values" often display an ahistorical attitude toward sexual mores and sometimes altogether bypass the complex ways in which current transformations in sexuality intersect with the residues of deeply sedimented traditions.

One area in which we can clearly see the more visible signs of profound change in personal dispositions as well as in social attitudes to traditional values is the dramatic rise in literature about sex. From the late
1960s on, largely under the impact of the feminist sexual revolution, our
cultural fascination with sexual literature expanded dramatically. This
expansion ranged from self-help literature and soft-core porn to highly
academic analyses of desire, sex and sexualities, eroticism and gender. This
post-1960s politicization of sex was memorably captured by Betty
Friedan's judgment that, in modern social conditions, the question of
gender identity has become—for everyone—"the problem that has no
name." Added to this there should be mentioned various developments
in the social sciences and humanities, such as the critiques of sexuality
launched by psychoanalytic feminists, deconstructionists, poststruc-
turalists, and postmodernists. These developments in turn widened the
debate over sex and sexualities to a broader concern with, among others,
issues of the body and its pleasures, repressed desire, multiple identities,
new cultural techniques of sexual surveillance, and cybersex.

Yet contemporary interest in sex and sexuality stems also from certain emphases on beauty, youth, desire, pleasure, and playfulness that
are the hallmarks of consumer capitalism. While it is arguable that much
of the interest in sex in the social sciences and humanities may have
evolved as a kind of cultural extension of 1960s radical politics, in our
own time capitalism has ruthlessly colonized sex to sell everything from
movies to mobile phones. In one sense, the market has of course always
worked on the premise that sex sells; it's just that now it appears that
there's nothing sexier than sex. A number of highly influential theorists
have expressed such views about the regulation of contemporary sexuality. For the late cultural historian Christopher Lasch, the Western infat-
uation with all things sexual is itself symptomatic of an escalating
culture of narcissism. For those more influenced by the philosophical
doctrines of poststructuralism and postmodernism, the cultural fascination with sex has, in fact, been an imposition—a complex effect of the
forces of power and domination.

Given the widespread availability of both information about sexuality and entertainment enacting the spectacle of sex, alongside the spread
of new technologies from the Internet to artificial insemination, it is
hardly surprising that we have become fascinated in new ways by intimacy,
love, and eroticism. The British sociologist Anthony Giddens has
described these current changes affecting men and women in terms of a

"reflexive monitoring" of the personal sphere, in which information produced by our high-tech media culture is continually woven into the fabric of daily life. As Giddens explains: "Increased geographical mobility, the mass media and a host of other factors have undercut elements of tradition in social life which long resisted—or became adapted to—modernity. The continual reflexive incorporation of knowledge not only steps into the breach; it provides precisely a basic impetus to the changes which sweep through personal, as well as global, contexts of action." From the latest statistics on divorce as covered by the national press to the emergence of questions of gender and sexuality in current political debates about human rights, the horizons of understanding of individuals are rapidly expanded through exposure to global communication networks. Reflexivity on the level of ordinary, everyday practices is for Giddens a kind of "knowledge multiplier" from which women and men renew efforts to take control of their lives, relationships, and commitments.

Giddens argues that we are in the midst of a global transformation of intimacy, a transformation initially ignited by the sexual revolution of the 1960s but significantly enriched and accentuated in our own time as a consequence of globalization. In conditions of advanced globalization, he argues, not only are our preexisting traditions increasingly undermined but also the massive expansion of new information technologies opens up new possibilities and new risks for everyone on a scale that previously did not exist. The democratization of the personal sphere, the freedom to choose lifestyles, the emotional satisfactions and dilemmas of intimate relationships—individuals are increasingly called upon to negotiate the meaning of sexuality on their own terms, and they consequently find it more and more difficult to rely on traditional frameworks of understanding, which are now everywhere in question.

The idea of "reflexivity" may seem fairly abstract, the province of specialized sociological debate. But it becomes interesting when you see it opening a window onto psychological and political life, deeply private and significantly public at the same time. Simon, having been emotionally dependent and also having cheated on his former wife, isn't exactly an ideal candidate for the "reflexive" label. In many ways, his is a story about male disquiet and male sexual compulsiveness in a brave new world of open relationships and negotiated intimacy. When Simon says his former wife, Lisa, offered a "safety net," he doesn't refer to emotional satisfaction but rather to an avoidance of the demands and anxieties of the present age; what he had with Lisa seemed the only safe place from which to launch his wider sexual experimentation with others. Yet, in a more restrictive sense, a reflexive orientation to others and the wider world did influence Simon's attempts to escape the oppressive nature of his marriage. From this angle, his use of singles bars, sexual contact magazines, and telecommunications was an aid for the difficult psychological challenge of questioning the more oppressive conditions of his marriage as well as his home life.

Reflexivity may be considered a metaphor for one of the greatest private conundrums of the present age—namely, how to cope with the information blizzard that defines our global media age and relate such mediated experience to the personal and social contexts of our day-to-day lives. The concept of reflexivity has been sharply criticized by some authors for exaggerating the degree to which people actually take control of their lives; proponents of the thesis of reflexivity, it is argued, tend to pass over the insidious ways in which globalization eats away at the moral fabric of both identity and social relations. A full discussion of these arguments goes beyond the scope of this book, but we find that the very propagation of the concept of reflexivity testifies to the continuation of at least some of the values attached to modernist notions of agency that many fear the contemporary age has eroded. This is not to say that reflexivity, at least in the hands of some of its theoreticians, hasn't been cast in an "inhuman" mode—obsessive, extremist, fetishizing process, and drained of emotion. Yet, for Giddens at least, there can be no durable reflexivity that is not firmly anchored in dialogue with some of the more constraining or repressive aspects of both self-organization and social relations.

Giddens tells us that reflexivity, powered by processes of globalization, stands closest to autonomy. In a world in which tradition has more thoroughly been swept away than ever before, contingency appears unavoidable. And with contingency comes the potential to remake the world and negotiate lifestyle options about who to be, how to act, whom to love, and how to live together. The promised autonomy of reflexivity is, however, also a problem, since choice necessarily brings with it ambivalence, doubt, and uncertainty. There is no way out of this paradox, though of the various, necessarily unsuccessful, attempts people make to avoid the dilemmas of reflexivity Giddens identifies "addiction" as of key importance to the present age. As he writes:

> Once institutional reflexivity reaches into virtually all parts of everyday social life, almost any pattern or habit can become an addic-

tion. The idea of addiction makes little sense in a traditional culture, where it is normal to do today what one did yesterday. . . . Addictions, then, are a negative index of the degree to which the reflexive project of the self moves to centre-stage in late modernity.

Reflexivity's promise of freedom carries with it the burden of continual choice and deals with all the complexities of emotional life. "Every addiction," writes Giddens, "is a defensive reaction, and an escape, a recognition of lack of autonomy that casts a shadow over the competence of the self."

Simon, in the grip of a sexual compulsion he feels powerless to control, underlines the point that a certain self-consciousness about sexuality can constrict and counterfeit intimacy. In his calculated pursuit of sexual conquests, the bolstering of a very fragile sense of self-identity was maintained only as long as he derived a certain kind of "psychological high" from these clandestine activities. Part of the special high he obtained from these episodic encounters came from a feeling of sexual triumph, but part of the addiction also came from the secret nature of these activities. Yet it is the instrumental rationalism implicit in Simon's self-justification for cheating on Lisa that perhaps most deserves attention. There is a kind of automated quality to the way in which he describes his need for extramarital sexual relations; certainly there is little feeling of spontaneity here, however much he believes himself to be acting "naturally" or "like a man." Indeed, it is as if eroticism in Simon's case is a monstrous by-product of calculated planning, desire only emerging as an outgrowth of exercising strict control over the segmentation of his life. In Simon everything is rational and calculated, but in spite of that, the addictive nature of his behavior reveals the anguish of his life.

So too it is tempting to cast Ruth's love affair with seductive technology as a form of addictive psychological escape. For one thing, her need for constant self-approval derived through virtual sex might cause her to be seen as a woman seeking a form of reassurance online that she hadn't managed to obtain in everyday life. Ruth had long felt insecure about her physical appearance, and indeed this was doubly so as she felt herself growing older. Yet the virtual context of Netsex changed all that, and at the press of a button. She experienced a wonderful sense of loss of her built-up identity in performing various virtual personae, a moment of release through these online interactions in which she imagined herself young, slender, tall, and devastatingly good-looking. This intoxicating loss of self was addictive precisely because the emotional fix derived online jostled uneasily with feelings of emptiness and despair afterward, thus opening a disabling gap between Ruth's virtual self and her actual self. Yet also addictive was the more active and sometimes aggressive form of sexuality that Ruth adopted online, a form of sexuality she was now trying to integrate into other aspects of her life, principally her relationship with her husband.

Before deciding whether Ruth's behavior might be considered some form of sex addiction in the interweaving of her online and daily experiences, however, we have to look more closely at her wish to be neither compliant nor complacent but rather the active agent she has always believed she really is. "I was always envious," she reflects, "of the power and freedom enjoyed by both my father and my husband and felt unfairly shut out from this aspect of life. My own boys allowed me to experiment with a kind of freedom, I suppose, and to some extent I've pushed this further with the characters I've created online." Ruth is clearly engaged in some sort of search for self-identity through the use of Netsex, however frustrated that search may be. What, after all, makes the hours that her husband spends engaged in investment banking necessarily more creative or freeing than the hours Ruth spends spinning off online personae? Might the addictive nature of Ruth's online activities seem less problematic if she were receiving an income from them?

A reliance on symbolic resources accessed through both traditional and mediated forms of communication to expand the horizons of self-identity has been well documented in a variety of recent studies. The literary scholar Janice Radway has forcefully argued that when women read romance novels, they are not necessarily withdrawing from the world but potentially developing practical knowledge for dealing with the complexities of intimate relationships. Reading romance fiction can provide a practical lesson in emotional literacy for people whose possibilities for happiness in their existing relationships are seriously constrained. Such a perspective, sensitive to the creative ways that individuals construct accounts of who they are and of what the future may hold, is widely shared in contemporary media studies. John B. Thompson, for example, speaks of the ever-increasing "relevance structure" of mediated experience that arises as a consequence of the rapid expansion of global communication networks today. According to Thompson, while some people still orient their lives primarily around local paths of daily life, it is increasingly common for individuals to draw upon the many global forms of mediated experience in the construction of self-identity.

Mediated experience, Thompson contends, is a regular and integral feature of the shaping of individualism today. "Taken to an extreme," he writes, "mediated experience may even supplant or become confused with lived experience in such a way that individuals may find it difficult to distinguish between them."

The same emphasis on creative self-making appears in the writings of a number of analysts of new information technologies, particularly as regards the effects of computers on our psychological lives. Richard A. Lanham's book *The Electronic Word* celebrates the creative activity of open-ended screen text, with its endless possibilities for cutting, pasting, and rearranging text and meaning. In a similar spirit, Sherry Turkle's *Life on the Screen* argues that the uncertain relationship between mind and body—as well as that of self and others—is now pushed to its limits in the new electronic age. The Internet, says Turkle, is where people navigate simulated worlds and create virtual realities in the hope of transforming their inherited ways of thinking about identity, sexuality, relationships, even politics and society. Her analysis of Netsex is especially relevant in this connection. Focusing in particular upon Internet relay chat rooms and text-based virtual reality sites, Turkle looks at the complex ways people reinvent themselves as they go along, exploring, constructing, and reconstructing their identities. The beauty of Netsex, according to Turkle, is that anything goes. People can change their genders, sexual orientations, or personalities, devising a Net self that continually outstrips the real-life self. Cyberspace sex for Turkle is intrinsically fragmentary and episodic. At the push of a button, one can shift from flirtation to cross-dressing, from sadomasochism to fetishism.

Such an emphasis on fluidity and multiplicity brings us directly into contact with some influential contemporary currents, sometimes labeled "postmodern," on the nature of self-experience. By postmodern, we refer, in the most general terms, to contemporary philosophical standpoints that reject epic narratives, solid metaphysical foundations to knowledge and everyday life, universal values, self-identical identities, and so on. While the ideas of postmodernists are notoriously difficult to define succinctly, there are various ways in which postmodernism might be highly attuned to contemporary circumstances. This is perhaps nowhere more obvious than at the level of self-identity, where a "decentered subject"—nonlinear, fluid, and fractured—is widely seen as having replaced the modernist dream of self-certitude, of stable, linear, logical, and, above all, autonomous identities. Here the writings of French social analysts—particularly Jacques

Derrida and Jacques Lacan—are especially pertinent, particularly the conviction that language, or "discourse" or "text," is fundamental to any conception of subjectivity.

If to dwell within the postmodern condition is to live a discontinuous, fractured, episodic, consequences-avoiding life, then it might seem reasonably evident that postmodernism mirrors the experience of identity for citizens of the polished, expensive, high-tech cities of the West in these early days of the twenty-first century. This is certainly the view of Turkle, who contends that "the Internet brings postmodernism down to earth." In this age of media saturation, she argues, people increasingly experience their lives as a collection of fragments and episodes, and it is precisely this sense of discontinuity that the Internet allows people to explore. The same emphasis on discontinuity as a consequence of media simulation appears in the writings of the French media theorist Jean Baudrillard. Perhaps the most controversial cultural analyst writing in Europe today, Baudrillard is best known for questioning whether the first Gulf war ever took place. Many, inside and outside academia, were offended by the claim. But forgotten in all the intellectual frenzy was Baudrillard's underscoring of our high-tech media world, of televisual wars, of what he terms "hyper-reality." Baudrillard's notion of the hyper-real underwrites the endless play of signs dramatized through the mass media today, in which individuals become more and more caught up in a multiplication of representations. Media simulations such as MTV, the Disney Channel, and CNN become more vivid, more seductive, and more intense than that which we typically think of as "reality," so that the individual self enters into a new terrain of perception in which hallucination, schizophrenia, and virtualization rule.

How accurate is such an account of the experience of individualism in the contemporary media age? Certainly it could be said that the social impact of today's media may seem to beget a personality structure constantly "in catch-up," as people attempt, with varying levels of interest, determination, and success, to come to terms with an overload of information. Baudrillard takes this to a kind of perverse extreme in suggesting that the hyperreality of information blizzards produces individuals who are bored, lifeless, drained, and atomized. The self has, in this view, been liquidized into the media simulations that define contemporary culture, with the result that the most one can reasonably hope to do is channel hop or surf the Net. Some people, to be sure, might live aspects of their lives absorbing the trivial details of trash TV and tabloid culture; it might also be said that what especially worries some cultural critics about all this is the missing dimension of an internal conversation investing the culture with significance. Yet what may seem apolitical, trivial, or boring to some is heady stuff for others. It could be said that what we read, see, and hear in media culture, whether humorous or heavy, goes to the core of how we see ourselves in relation with others and the wider community and in that sense is part of the oxygen of contemporary politics.

In terms of transformations of intimacy, we can see that aspects of the contemporary media age can protect people from the anxiety of feeling overwhelmingly alone. This has been true of Simon and Ruth, both of whom in quite different ways have drawn upon new information technologies to explore possibilities, invent fantasies, and experiment with alternative definitions of the self. Simon's use of mobile G3 technology and Ruth's exploration of the Internet have opened their lives to others beyond the local determinations of everyday life. Both of them have been able to explore and experiment with others in ways that they obviously felt previously unable to do through traditional face-to-face interaction. In these modes of mediated interaction, Simon and Ruth have generated and invented, in daydreaming, reveries, and fantasy, new ways of connecting their imagination and wishes to everyday life.

And yet mediated experience seems to be a problem of some kind for both Simon and Ruth. It isn't as if either of them just uses communications media as an enriching resource for self-development; the Internet for Ruth and mobile G3 technology for Simon are not merely a resource for the self but its central fixation. That both of them equate eroticism with "life on the screen" is an indication of this addiction, absorption, and helplessness.

Some of the negative consequences of Ruth's addictive preoccupation with Internet chat rooms are revealed in the way she now relates to—or, as she puts it, "handles"—her husband. Getting over the emotional loss of her children's leaving home has meant being less troubled, less needy. For Ruth this means typing real-time erotica with others in cyberspace. Yet she can't be sure if this is taking her closer to, or away from, intimate eroticism, for her husband's principal objection to her online sexual intimacies centers precisely on "the kind of talk" that he thought was an exclusive feature of their marriage. Whether he could manage or accept Ruth's having an actual affair he is uncertain; and yet the "just chatting" that makes up Ruth's experience of Netsex seems equally difficult to tolerate or understand. As Ruth says, without the slightest trace of irony, "my husband still holds to the old-fashioned notion that talking lies at the core of sex."

In many ways, for all her fascination with the Internet as an arena for self-experimentation, Ruth thrives on her personal isolation. It is as if she became aware, when her sons moved away from home, that we all inhabit many disparate worlds at once. Her answer to this realization was to compartmentalize imagination on the one side and the solid everyday world on the other, to divide the softness of her Netsex dreams from the hard reality of her marriage and family. This, too, is why Netsex and intimacy are for her opposed to one another, rather than related.

COMMUNICATING CONFESSION: THE SHIFTING BOUNDARIES OF PRIVATE AND PUBLIC LIFE

Ruth's closest friends in recent years have all been met through the Internet, and her main desire in life has been to discuss the nature of her sexual desire online. She's very dependent on her "online friends"—as provisional and fleeting as they are—to bolster her newly (re)invented sense of self-identity, while insisting that her cyberlife in no way detracts from her marriage, family, or other social commitments. How many people around the world are connected to the Internet and pursue, like Ruth, the thrills of sex talk via chat rooms is unknown, but it has been estimated that since 1985 the Internet has grown at a rate of 200 percent annually. What is increasingly agreed is that transformations in media technology are at the very heart of change in personal and emotional life, and this is perhaps nowhere more obvious than in the ways sexual confessional discourse has infiltrated the remaking and reconstruction of identities through various forms of communications media.

Giddens argues that, in a world of stunning technological change, people continuously revise the settled patterns of their relationships and question the established certainties of their private and public lives because no one can any longer be sure what the future holds. Uncertainty about the future, to some degree, affects all societies. Yet thanks to developments in globalization and media technologies, problems arising from the circularity of social knowledge have become particularly acute. The future is open-ended, and so in a sense is the self. Against this backdrop, choice increasingly becomes the key—decisions about our relationships, about our sense of sexuality, about the meanings we attach to our self-experience.

Ruth says that, thanks to the virtual support she obtains online, she is ten times more confident than she used to be. A good part of this newly discovered online assurance derives, it seems, from confessing to others her private insecurities and sexual anxieties, excavating her own past life within an alternative Internet subculture of self-affirmation. The rediscovery of sex has been central in the struggle for a reinvented sense of self and identity. For Simon, too, though he is less assured than Ruth that sexuality is a prime site for self-discovery, life has become an arena for experimentation, for trying things out and on. Many of the joys of sex detailed by Simon to his talk-radio therapist are, for some at least, common practice—picking up women through contact magazines, episodic sex, mutual masturbation. What is perhaps most interesting here is not Simon's apparent comfort with exploring the erotic (which in his case has a distinctly compulsive quality about it) but rather his emotional investment in the therapeutic value of public confession. Both Simon and Ruth have found certain degrees of pleasure in enacting sexual desires and fears in public, in media-driven interaction, where a fundamental aspect for remaking of the self has involved speaking about emotions through a language of confession.

The central tenets of confessional therapeutic culture can be found in various sectors of contemporary institutional life, from religious confession to the therapist's couch, from TV talk shows such as *Oprah*, *Ricki Lake*, and *Geraldo* to confessional autobiographies like Elizabeth Wurtzel's *Prozac Nation*. Indeed, from the late 1970s on, the literature about therapy culture has become huge, ranging from self-help to highbrow academic studies of public confessional discourse. Notwithstanding differences of opinion as to the cultural reach and impact of therapy culture, most analysts of these trends agree that contemporary media culture has shifted the language of confession away from its religious anchorings and toward a new kind of private psychological therapy. This is a form of therapy played out in living rooms across the globe, as a mass-mediated spectacle of private anxieties is dramatized for public consumption. Radio talkback, TV talk shows, and cybertherapy are all at the core of this restructuring of the "talking cure" through the twin forces of multimedia and popular culture.

Against the backdrop of these cultural developments, we want to consider further the ways in which a confessional therapeutics infiltrates the construction of individualism in modern societies, in a process that powerfully reconstitutes the boundaries between private and public life.

How can we best understand the impact of confessional therapeutics upon the process of self-formation today? And how should we understand the role of new communication media in restructuring the relation between individualism and confessional culture?

It is only in relatively recent times, historically speaking, that our society's lust for therapeutic culture has become deeply interwoven with modernist ideologies of individualism, individual choice, self-awareness, and psychological well-being. The key pioneering social analysts of this historical trend include, among others, Phillip Rieff and Christopher Lasch, both of whom added a psychoanalytic dimension to sociological accounts of how large-scale changes at the level of modernity and modernism ushered into existence profound restructurings of individual desire and the psyche. Rieff's provocative book of the late 1950s, *The Triumph of the Therapeutic*, brilliantly captured the early stage of development of consumer culture's colonization, marketing, and rebranding of psychological illness and of the cultural trend toward therapeutic scrutiny of personal unhappiness and the quest for emotional health. The sociological corollary of this triumph of the therapeutic, for Rieff, was a crisis in political authority and the death of culture. Lasch introduced a related question of whether the increasing dominance of therapeutics isn't, in some deep emotional way, at the heart of a broader restructuring of the political sphere away from collective problems and toward personal issues that in the end are always presented as amenable to therapeutic intervention. For Lasch, the growth of narcissistic politics opens the way for a therapeutic imperative in which crisis becomes both permanent and personalized.

Another, highly illuminating, account of such cultural processes can be found in the writings of the influential French historian and social theorist Michel Foucault, especially his late work *The History of Sexuality*. In this ground-breaking book, Foucault developed an argument about the centrality of confession to the process of self-formation and the changing relations between sexuality, identity, and power. The core of his argument, succinctly put, concerns the complex ways in which confession manufactures a truth in the ongoing production of narratives of the self. This is a "truth" that goes to the core of a person's identity—something about her innermost feelings, her deepest desires or fears, her most personal thoughts. And yet this is also a "truth," argues Foucault, that the individual constructs through the very act of confession—it does not exist prior to the confessional act. As Foucault writes of the spread and acceleration of a discourse that has gradually given rise to a kind of "confessional society":

> The confession has spread its effects far and wide. It plays a part in justice, medicine, education, family relationships, and love relations, in the most ordinary affairs of everyday life, and in the most solemn rites; one confesses one's crimes, one's sins, one's thoughts and desires, one's illnesses and troubles; one goes about telling, with the greatest precision, whatever is most difficult to tell.

According to Foucault, individuals are increasingly caught up in a new system of power in which confession functions as a means of control. Such control is not necessarily exercised by authority figures (say, police officers or priests) acting coercively over and above the individual— though the history of the Catholic Church certainly suggests that confession has functioned as a ritual in which individuals believe in the power of the priest to absolve them of sin. In developing this argument Foucault traces a move during the late nineteenth century in the language of confession away from the church and onto the psychoanalyst's couch, where the worried well could manufacture new identity truths through the "talking cure."

Foucault developed his account of the relations between self and sexuality as disclosed through confessional practices during the late 1970s and early 1980s. Holding the post of visiting professor in French at the University of California at Berkeley, Foucault was personally much taken by the West Coast, where he developed ideas concerning a confessional trend within American culture as represented in, say, psychotherapy or psychoanalysis. "In the Californian cult of the self," Foucault remarked during an interview, "one is supposed to discover one's true self, to separate it from what might obscure or alienate it, to decipher its truth thanks to psychological or psychoanalytic science." In developing the argument that confession is a way of producing a truth about the self, Foucault undoubtedly called attention to a major set of issues about the cultural organization of power and identity. We will not examine Foucault's analysis of confessional practices of the self in further detail here, though subsequently we will argue that Foucault's suggestion that therapy has become an extension of religious confession is less than convincing. What we draw attention to is the changing ways in which contemporary confessions take place in public. Had Foucault been able to consider the role of new communication technologies upon the formation and reformation of the self, he might have seen just how powerfully confessional culture constructs new privatized relations—in which, contrary to his sometimes fatalistic account of how power mysteriously operates behind the backs of individuals, there is considerable dynamism between individualism, institutions, and social relations.

Many of the trends identified by therapy-as-depoliticization theorists—the growth of emotional fatalism, the decline of tradition, the rise of narcissism—have been taken up and given a new twist in our own time. Globalization, many argue, has dramatically fostered a process whereby cultural processes of self-definition become increasingly self-referential, so that therapy and the "psy" professions supposedly offer an ideologically neutral means of cultivating the self. In particular, the speeding up and deepening impact of electronic communications, digital flows, and patterns of media interaction fuel new manifestations of the therapeutic ethos, as confessional culture moves beyond the consulting room and into every facet of popular culture and society at large. Of key importance in this respect is the dissemination of technologies that restructure confessional practices of contemporary individualism. Today's new individualism promotes the deployment of confessional discourse not only through radio talkback and TV talk shows but also through mobile phones, computers, and the Internet. From one angle, this astonishing reorganization of individualism is primarily sociological. Individualism today is plugged into vast systems of electronic and digital communications, interfaced with others negotiating the demands of confessional culture through complex information systems. Both Simon and Ruth, in this reading, can be viewed as points in circuits of global communication networks: Simon's dramatization of his sexual practices on radio talkback casts him as a "voice agent" of confessional culture, while Ruth presents as a "textualized agent" of Internet interfaced exchange. From another angle, however, there is also something more psychologically fluid, creative, productive, and entertaining about this individualist turn of confessional culture. Both Simon and Ruth feel that the dramatic revelation of their personal lives and sexual fantasies should have been an anxious, guilt-ridden, and destabilizing experience. But it wasn't. On the contrary, the experience of confessing was enjoyable, pleasurable, fun. So much so, both have become addicted to their preferred technologies of confession. Why should this be so?

Part of the reason that the public display of emotions, in a mass-media forum, is experienced as energizing by many people today is that it has become a largely open-ended, ongoing process in need of continual revision. American media theorist Mimi White argues that postmodern popular culture has given a novel twist to confession, switching confessional speech away from a singular expert (the therapist) and toward a whole host of possible audiences, including listeners, viewers, hosts, experts, and so on. Moreover, we might say that the act of confession itself is becoming increasingly liquidized and multiplied. "At the heart of the new therapeutic culture," says White, "everyone confesses over and over again to everybody else." Psychotherapy is only one very particular model advanced by our globalized confessional culture. Twelve-step therapy programs, personal counseling, memory-recovery experts, addiction management programs, Gestalt and behavioral therapy, phone and cybertherapy, peer counselors, Internet analysts: the list of therapies today continually crosses and multiplies, producing hybrids and new techniques and models for public confession.

But if living in a confessional culture opens new possibilities for forms of self-expression, self-definition, and self-reflexivity, it is also the case that today's revised individualism is shackled with new burdens. Many critics of the rise of confessional culture are correct, in part at least, to dismiss aspects of the therapeutic turn in public life as apolitical or trivial. It is true that the spread of confessional morality has contributed, at least for some individuals, to a retreat inward, toward privatism. Eva Moskowitz's *In Therapy We Trust: America's Obsession with Self-Fulfillment* puts this point forcefully, arguing that therapy culture "focuses our attention on the private life, blinding us to the larger, public good." Two points should be made in this context. Confessional culture, to be sure, can promote a narrowing of the arts of public political life, but it needn't. The public confession of private sentiments can, in fact, work the other way—as we have argued—and involve an opening out of the self to an increasingly interconnected world. But sticking with the concern of critics over people's retreat inward, away from the public sphere and toward egoism, the second point to be made is that the consequences of all this are more pervasive than has thus far been represented in academic and popular debate. For confessional culture, and its impact upon individualism, isn't just about shifting boundaries between the public and private spheres (though it does certainly touch in a profound way on these realignments); it's also about the changing locations through which individuals encounter each other and come to reflect on their own lives.

These locations now consist increasingly of *privatized spaces*—the typing of Internet exchanges on personal computers, the regular use of mobile phones in cars, the enjoyment of mass-mediated spectacles in the comfort of "personal cinemas" at home. As people have necessarily become more sophisticated in the use of new technologies, including laptops, video cameras, and wireless connections of all varieties, more and more often it is through such technologies that individuals launch their engagements with others as well as reflective considerations about their own lives. This is not to say that public space has been swamped, or somehow eradicated, by the privatized deployment of new technologies. It is, rather, to make the point that new technologies play a key role in the increasing privatization of individualism today, so that people approach and enter into the broader political sphere through the public display of private emotions as well as the public confession of private sentiments.

"Ours is a society," writes Susan Sontag, "in which secrets of private life that, formerly, you would have given nearly anything to conceal, you now clamor to get on a television show to reveal." The freedom of new individualisms is that people have at last been discharged from the Freudian sentence of ever-intensifying repression, denial, and guilt; the burden is that the new, desperate search for self-expression takes place in a world suddenly devoid of common reference points for public discussion, not to mention the immense difficulties of investing public debate with life from the isolated and isolating location of privatized spaces, of identities privatized. Simon and Ruth reflect all this, perhaps only too well: they enjoy everything and anything in their privatized engagements with an increasingly interconnected world of global communications; yet both sense that sinking shallowness that arises time and again from the only ever-vague friendships, connections, and encounters that they forge through new technologies day in, day out.

FIVE

THE SELF AND OTHER ETHICAL TROUBLES
Ethics, Social Differences, and the Truths of Multiculturalism

NE OF THE more inconspicuously common words of daily life is "self." As in "I'm not my*self* today." When a person says such a thing, she is saying, in effect, something is wrong with who I am today. "I'm not myself *today*." The "today" is more important than it may seem. To distinguish between the my*self* of one day and any other day is to assume that there is a particular *Whoness* to (again the word) our*selves*.

Thus deepens the mystery of this tiny word. The very utterance of it is fraught with possibilities that pass under the radar of consciousness. "*I'm* not myself today." The saying requires another person or persons—presumably those likely to have noticed some slippage from the individual's presumably more normal and better self. To say "self," however unobtrusively, is to refer to one's *Self*, an ill-defined but apparently true center of one's individual character—that which, in principle, certifies one's difference from all others. The uniqueness of this difference thus comes to attention, more often than not, when it is at odds with its authentic nature, a disparity the possessor of a self supposes may be discrediting in the eyes of another who may have noticed the slip (and noticed it because that other has her own Self, considered by herself no less a special wave in the sea of selves). "I'm *not* myself today." It is possible of course that the locution can be muttered in private, as in "Damn it. I hate myself when I do things like that." But, even when we catch ourselves complaining to ourselves about our Self, we are not so alone as at first it appears. Self-talk is usually prompted by the abrupt realization that some recent behavior was not up to snuff—as upon awaking in an empty bed from which the night's lover had fled in the dark without leaving a name we would have been too drunk to remember, thus joining the company of those who came to and in our beds, only to pass on from whence they came.

Thus, it happens that this most inconspicuous of words carries the weight of the worlds of social participation. When speaking to our*selves* about our Self—an exercise without which we might cease to be—we are in the company of quite a crowd, a crowd comprising the many appearances over time of Whoever it is we suppose ourselves to be, along with all the others from the past of whom the last one we were was but one self among the many that come and go in the Self's daily round of interactions. When we speak reflexively to and about ourselves, we are in a company of others upon whom our Who-ness depends. Had we remembered the name of last night's lover, it would have been given to us only upon inquiry. To ask the name of another is always the opening move in a possible game that could lead, if you find reason to stay with it, to the question "Who are you, anyway?" In this, when we interrogate each other, we are trying to find out whether there is anything about that other Self we might find interesting, useful, or otherwise attractive.

This, of course, we do only by comparing whatever we learn upon inquiry to whatever we take to be familiar and appealing to our own Self. *What's your name? Where are you from? What do you do?* If the answers are "Kenneth from Boston, a surgeon," we will assess the value of the other to our self differently than if the answer were "Luigi from Naples, a cameo hustler." Depending on *whom* we imagine ourselves to be, we will find the other more or less worthy of pursuit. But we should not assume from the outside that we know how any one Self will assess the difference. Somewhere there is an Yvette from Neuilly, a nurse, who prefers a Dominique from Lille, a truck driver, over Alain, a surgeon from rue de Varenne. It is not for others to ask why and how this might be. We can ask, of course, but the truth will make less than common sense because the mystery of the ways of the Self are opaque to those on the outside.

Yet, as we go about our interactions with others, we trust ourselves to recognize the Who in those we come upon sufficiently well at least to know when we are or are not in danger. We are often wrong, of course, as when people end up in the dark with strangers who hang around for breakfast when all we wanted was the comfort of his caress. All the rest was the price one pays to relieve the cold and lonely life.

To speak of ourselves is to speak of the riddle at the heart of social interaction. The practical idea that we can be different or similar from one day to the next is ultimately the idea that there is, somewhere within, a true Self that we and others will recognize as the gold standard for just Who exactly we are, or want to be.

In many ways, all the worlds of social living are contained in this riddle that still has not been better put than it was by William James. While he was hardly the first to contemplate it, James was an important founder of American pragmatist philosophy as well as of theoretical psychology because he saw that the puzzle of individual self-understanding could never be viewed as a private matter. Practical psychology cannot avoid the sociological dilemma that the Self is necessarily social. Again, James's famous line: "A man has as many social selves as there are individuals who recognize him." To which he juxtaposed the other horn of the dilemma of self-understanding, that of personal identity, which is, in effect, who am I if there are so many of me? In the years since James wrote in 1890, a very good bit of professional academic social psychology has been devoted to overcoming the dilemma. But that fact should not alarm us too much, because much of the energy of everyday human consciousness is spent on the same dilemma. If our inner Self is social by virtue of the recognition of others, then how do I recognize myself today as identical with the self I was just before? To say "I am not myself today" is to say "Today I do not recognize myself as the same as I ought to be"— which entails, of course, the fear that others will not recognize us or, at the extreme, we will cease to belong to the company of friends and strangers upon whom we rely.

The Self, if there is one, is that aspect of who we take ourselves to be that is always, without relief, forcing us to reflect and react to the standards we set for ourselves. It is thereby the one constant and never-ceasing source of ethical trouble. When people talk, as in many local pubs they do, of the decline of ethical standards, the deterioration of family values, the corruption of public figures, and all the rest, they are doing little more than what we do to ourselves most days of our lives. Living with ourselves is a bother without which we would not likely bother living. *Can't live with them. Can't live without them.*

Ethics, most simply put, is the bother of assessing the realities before us by the measure of a higher standard; or, in formal language, ethical reasoning is measuring the IS by some or another OUGHT, which is exactly what the individual does when she judges herself not to be Herself.

It would be a fine thing if it were plain to everyone just what we ought to be and do. But the days are long gone when the priest or rabbi could effectively define the standards for the well-behaved selves under his authority. People still believe in souls, as well they should. But the force of this belief declines in proportion to the waves of change against the shores of divine or natural authority. One sympathizes with those who bemoan the decline of traditional values. In fact, since Max Weber and Emile Durkheim, contemporaries of William James, social thinkers have joined the chorus of concern for which nostalgia is a futile solution.

In our time, well more than a century later, there is little choice but to take head-on the troubles of which the interior dialogue of selves with themselves is but the more local instance. At the dawn of the twenty-first century, social differences are so acutely evident that it is impossible to imagine any one set of values or ethical standards serving the whole of humanity. The troubling ethical dilemma of self-understanding has now been writ large. Self-reflection is even replaced by reflexive modernization—the action of social, even global, wholes acting back on themselves, creating an ever-more-troubled process.

And none of these phenomena concerns people more than multiculturalism.

IF MANY SELVES, THEN MANY WORLDS?

Multiculturalism, like sex, has a way of raising its ugly head in the strangest times and places. Much like other irritating subjects of the times—postmodernism, globalization, terrorism, among others—the very idea of *multiculturalism,* the ideology, disturbs out of proportion to what in fact it may be. The reality is that the world in which many people suppose they are living is actually plural: world*s, many of them,* through which we pass whenever we venture out the doors of what homes we may have. Yet, strangely, in a time like the one prevailing since the 1990s when a growing number of people begin to profess *the* multicultural as a way of thinking about the worlds, their professions are often greeted with dismay.

The surprise of it all is in a fact that most social scientists recognize to be true (or, perhaps better to say, true for their science as opposed to their practical lives). The fact (which, come to think of it, may be more like a strong impression) is that, on average, people will endure in their daily ordinary lives what they cannot bear once the reality is described in so many words. This apparent fact of life, sometimes (not necessarily accurately) called "false consciousness," is one whose likelihood is ignored at all costs, very often at the risk of foolishness. The elegance with which people commonly ignore the obvious in favor of some or another impossible-to-prove ideal theory of how the world *ought to be* is one of the more astonishing illustrations of the self-deceptions to which we resort when reality is at steep odds with what we would like to believe.

The truth is that, far from being a unified and unifying world of common comfort, the worlds turn in all manner of directions on the most precarious of assurances. They turn, when they do, on the assumed capacity of individuals, as individuals, to enter some common understanding of what is going on. The assumption is at best dubious. In the reality there before our eyes and actions, it is plain that we and the others ignore, for the moments of our interactions, the many improbabilities of human nature that we could establish even the most temporary of agreements. Our ignorance, it seems, is a requisite that we produce in order to go about the business of getting by. The reason that marriages are so hard to hold on to—and political power or institutional authority next to impossible—is that over time individuals change their minds, thus to become ever more different and difficult than they already were. People enter relations of all kinds on the unwarranted faith that they end as free individuals fully able to know themselves and their wishes, thus to fashion the myriad of microsocial contracts without which there would be no worlds at all.

The prospect of there ever being, or ever having been, One World is, in the light of this foundational innocence of practical social things, preposterous. Yet, it is held to ferociously. Even more remarkably, it holds as if the relations entered will endure forever. The failure of a marriage and the collapse of a political regime may appear to be tragic when in reality the astonishment should be shifted to the other aspect. True, children and the poor suffer all the more terribly when the social contracts of family or political life collapse. But this should not keep us from realizing that the unbelievable here is that marriages and states, much less other social things, endure as long as they do.

In this we come to the crux of the problems associated with the idea of the multicultural. As a word meant to refer to realities, *multicultural* is banal to a laughable degree. The joke is in the facts of the realities. Who could possibly deny today that the worlds amid which people live are many—that, therefore, the cultures vying for the attention of new and old members are just as many? Yet, the fact of the worlds is that just as many people hate the idea of multiculturalism, with a passion. The concern is that unless we believe that *we* are One (or, at least, can possibly be One, one day) we will lapse into a hell of relativism. But anyone who is honest with her inner sociologist of the daily round must admit that, whether a hell or not, the worlds of our experience are seldom seamless. Indeed, the odds at which they conflict seem to correspond to the parallel problems associated with our ability to understand ourselves—understand, that is, the self within to which we attach so much importance.

It truly is bewildering, this question of how men and women communicate and act more or less cooperatively against all the odds. As fathers of children who at the time of our writing, if not of your reading, are still quite young, we are more than keenly aware that the communication of effective understandings between sentient humanoids depends on little more than a passing willingness to pretend that things are not what they are. This pretense permits the moments, or the years, of social contract to endure passably enough such that, when all the silly little deceptions of all the countless individuals who step out with others are combined, on the normal day the worlds turn.

Of course, they cease to turn when some with little power tear down our biggest buildings or others, with more power than any small group should have, burn the cities where the people who tore down their buildings are alleged—without any proof whatsoever—to live. These surprisingly rare moments of global terror are said to be the exception that proves the rule, when in fact they are the rule to which there is no exception. More often than not the worlds turn in spite of the fact that those who turn it seldom have more than a modest clue as to what and why they are doing what they are doing under the cloak of a grandiose credulity.

This is well known when the incompetence of individuals to enter into social contracts is considered in respect to the very young who are, generally (though decreasingly so), given immunity from prosecution for their ignorance. Up to a certain age, children will play with each other, or with adults willing to stoop to them, without the least understanding of what is going on. Child's play can go on for hours on end, without more than an occasional nod to clear and precise conceptual language. Children will, in fact, even play in this fashion alone or side by side with a mate, apparently content with their inconsequential accomplishments.

Annie Lemert, when just shy of her sixth birthday, began to crawl about on all fours, barking like the puppy she wanted to have. Or was it that the puppy-life had her? After a while, her father guessed that the barking meant something. So he entered the game, suggesting a code wherein one bark (*Ruff*) meant yes and two meant no (*Ruff. Ruff.*). The game led soon enough to daddy asking Annie if she were being a puppy for a reason. "Ruff." Was it, he asked, because she wanted a puppy. "*Ruff. Ruff.*" Could you just for a minute, he asked, use little girl words to tell me why you have become a puppy? "Ruff. . . . Because it is easier for me to obey because puppies obey their owners . . . and you're my owner." *Ruff*— indeed! Thus it appears that a little girl of ordinary oedipal feelings—a child no different in affect and manner from others her age—is already very much an articulate member of human society, one able against the odds to use dog barks to bring her daddy into a world of her own feeling-filled invention.

Annie's father happened at the time to be living, with Annie and her mom, in a country whose political leaders at the highest level communicated to their public in a code not much more refined than dog barking. At least the little girl told an inner truth. They, the political leaders of the United States in 2004, told few discernible truths. A proud father wants to think his little girl is a genius of some kind, or at least a striking individual, when, more likely, what she feels is a need to find the words to tell the world what she is feeling inside and does not fully understand.

That, one supposes, is the way of the worlds in the normal course of social things. Competent individual members of the social whole get by even when they do not speak the same language, have the same understandings, or share more than a thin idea of what they are doing. We individuals, as individuals, certainly do not have the same needs and desires. We do not experience even what social things we experience in common in the same way. And when it comes to social things people could not possibly experience in like manner—things like globalization or international capital or the American government—the remarkable fact of social life is that they will pretend to understand their differences with a degree of similarity almost impossible to be true to life.

Yet, we, if there is a We, get by—far better than the realities (as opposed to the beliefs we have in what is going on) would lead us to suppose we might. We are all, if there is an all, more like children than the adults we wish to be—barking our way to some workable world that endures but for the time of our transactions.

ETHICS SPILLS FROM THE LIQUID GLOBE

Therein lies the multicultural dilemma. We are all mixed up with each other in an orgy of experiences, from which we awake in the morning trying to remember the names of those with whom we were embedded. After first coffees, we realize we may not—or in some cases should not— see one another again.

Multiculturalism—the theory of how things may be—is a bed we all have made but don't want to lie in. The worlds, as they truly are, are a jumble of partners who pass and push, touch and avoid each other with, in Zygmunt Bauman's word, liquidity. The question, though, is whether liquid modernity is new or not.

From an angle of vision outside current debates among social analysts, the liquidity question can be said to turn on assumptions about whether the worlds of the early twenty-first century are coherent—whether, as we said earlier, it is any longer possible to speak of One World as though there were a given, stable, encompassing sphere of human order on the surface of a physical globe of known cosmic address.

The One World idea is, of course, an assumption many still hold dear—and none hold it so dear as those with economic power over global politics. It is in effect the foundational value underlying the principles of economic development by which the global powers assess the failure of the poor on the global margins—the alleys of Calcutta, the deforested villages of Haiti, the chaotic streets of Kinshasa. The peoples of the so-called underdeveloped world are considered, in effect, failed Norwegians. Their social and economic miseries devolve from their having thus far failed to join the modern world. The One World dogma is just as present, however, in the boosterism of those geopoliticians who think of globalization itself as a wonder of hope and a promise of human progress. They overlook the fields and valleys of Somalia and Vietnam, of Iraq and Afghanistan, strewn with the rusting remains of high-tech armaments brought down by the clubs of ancient warlords.

Yet, the faith of the global modernizers that the world, if not yet one, can still be holds very little water when their world is measured against the prospects of the poorest. For them, *globalization* is an abstraction from which trickles little more than spoiled water and parched earth. For them, the modernized nation-state is but a prison house they flee, when they can. For them, *progress* is a cynical rhetorical boast of those already well ensconced in the comfortable suburbs of Geneva and Bombay, from which the comfortable, holding their Bombay Sapphires cold to the cheeks of arrogance, complain of the failure of the poor to be good enough human beings.

Among the social analysts, the subject of the moral nature of the worlds is, to be sure, given a less self-satisfied consideration. Still, the debates turn for the most part on the question of whether or not it is necessary to consider the world as worlds, which is to suggest that the One World is something more than merely transformed in style and structure—that it may not be One any longer and thus that the larger realities that the world of the well-meant imagination once embraced are now shaken down to the reality of its many incommensurable worlds clashing before civilized eyes. This is a prospect that goes beyond theories of, say, Ulrich Beck's "second modernity" or Anthony Giddens's "reflexive modernity." It may even go beyond Zygmunt Bauman's much more daring idea of "liquid modernity."

Liquidity, if we are to take it seriously, is rather more than lightness of social being. The mixed metaphor that accompanies the idea is perhaps a necessary end to which social criticism comes when one attempts to preserve even a remnant of the original hope for the modern world, which was, in short, the hope (or was it a wish?) that all men could be one because all men enjoy a common humanity. The ideal is about as appealing as any ethical principle could be, even when it leads to trouble such as, most notably, the necessity of bringing women (if not children) into the formula. The formula, even then, becomes quite plain: *The* world is the imaginary place in which the history of human progress unfolds. Such a world is One in principle (if not *yet* in reality) because progress is the admittedly hard and painful work of discovering and encouraging the common humanity that unites us all.

When put in common parlance, the classic liberal principle refuses to recognize what Richard Sennett has called the troubled pronoun or, more practically, to recognize the ubiquity of the *Whose we?* problem. It may seem a stretch to leap from questions of the nature of the world to such particulars as the language we use in our daily and very well meant attempts to bring each other into our conversation. But, in truth, the leap from world to the *Whose we?* is the only way to resolve the prior riddle of how the worlds of selves can be thought in the microdifferences of self-talk that we wash away in the presence of others, sometimes at the cost of criticizing ourselves. "I'm not myself today." Think of it this way. Those who assume there is a common humanity (even if their assumption is held in the cortex of preconscious mind, thus seldom exposed to scrutiny) will quite naturally speak of themselves in relation to others to or with whom they are speaking or writing as if they together constituted an unassailable *we*. It is a perfectly natural way to speak—or is it?

Or, think of those who might find the embrace of a dominating *we* offensive, even excluding. Think of women in the workplace whose supervisors suggest that "we could just work late tonight to finish this project, then I'll treat you to dinner and drinks." Quite apart from whether the suggestion is a sexual play, think of its ignorance should the assistant be a mother of small children. *Whose we?* is about not being able to join the dominant common humanity because, in point of practical reality, there are babies to feed or pick up at day care. Think, too, of those whose conflict before the assumption of common humanity may be even more acute, if not different in kind, than that of a working woman. Think, that is, of those who have no work and are beset with all that causes and accompanies the lack of work. They could be children begging in the wild streets of São Paulo or they could be guest workers packed ten to the room in *bidonvilles* on the dusty outskirts of the *grandes villes* of the Western world—those, that is, whose search for work leads them to scraps of employment unlikely to purchase the hope they need.

The poor so poor as to beg, like the poor employed so poorly as to suffer the worst indignities, also suffer from the injustices wrought by the naïve faith in One World so that the *Whose we?* query does not arise. The poor and miserable in this world are far from stupid, even though they are unlettered. The other side of globalization is that the full and many worlds are there plain to see—on the sheets of newspaper they use to cover themselves against the cold, in the indifference of those who ignore their pleas for coins as they pass by in the Underground, in the flickering sounds of their cell phones calling who knows whom, who knows where for some excludingly serious business.

THE EMOTIONAL COSTS OF SOCIAL DIFFERENCES

Consider, then, Norman Bishop of Middletown, Connecticut, a smallishly plain city in the urban Northeast of the United States. In 2004 Norman had celebrated fourteen years clean and sober. But his day-to-day program of recovery from corrosive effects of his addicted self is the least chapter of his story. He is also HIV positive. In fact the diagnosis of his infection, probably by bad needles if not a sexual encounter, was what led him into a state-sponsored rehab facility, then to Narcotics Anonymous, which he attends several nights a week. Yet, even the infection is not the full story. Though neither addiction nor infection respects social differences, they do find their way into the systems of the poor and economically marginal with uncommon frequency.

This is how Norman tells the story of his life since the days he lived in New Haven, then one of America's most economically and socially dangerous towns:

> As recently as 1990, my life was organized around hustling the money to score the drugs I felt were the only way I could live. And, because of the life I was leading, I was already HIV positive.
>
> Before my life had come to this, I was living in Brooklyn, New York, as a street vendor. In the early 1980s I was a peddler, selling junk clothing and jewelry to people on the run. I knew how to sell and market—and to hustle. But when I tried to reestablish my little business in Connecticut, things turned bad. The street business failed. Because I am an experienced draftsman and a skilled glazier, I was able, somehow, to find and keep work. But the drugs took over my life. Things were so bad that I can hardly say exactly how I was exposed to HIV. Probably it was the needles. Whatever, . . . the infection . . . will always, from now on, be a factor in my life.
>
> Yet, by the grace of God, I was able to turn my life around. In 1991, I checked into a rehabilitation program at a nearby veterans hospital. When I got out, I decided to change my life. I knew enough to avoid the old life in New Haven. So, I found work as a glazier and moved to Middletown. Then my new life began.

And what a life had begun. Today, Norman Bishop is known and respected wherever he goes in his new home city.

Yet, this is not the end of the story—the stories of those infected by the HIV virus, like those of the recovering addict, are life stories that never end. As he says, Norman lives each day with the disease that likely will kill him one day—though not any day soon. At fifty-eight, after the better part of twenty years infected, Norman has already outlived an infection that in most parts of the world each day kills children and young men and women by the hundreds and, in some places, thousands. The difference, of course, is that in the Western world, even in the more socially conservative nations like the United States, social benefits are available for the medical and pharmaceutical treatments that prolong life. So, in one way, Norman has benefited from the good luck of a draw at birth. Had he been born in Uganda or the Sudan, his new life would not be so promising as it is.

Don't, however, get Norman wrong. He is not one to play on sentiment, much less dismiss his old life as a tragedy of the racism and social indifference that pervades even (and especially) American social policies on health care, poverty, housing, and much else. Nor is he one to celebrate the good fortune of the access to treatment his nation now provides after it overcame the scurrilous indifference to AIDS associated with the Reagan-Thatcher political climate of the 1980s.

Many who know him want to treat Norman's story as a heroic tale, which, with respect to the new individualism, might be construed as a morality play of just how brilliantly the ordinary person can compose his individual life. In fact, Norman Bishop (who gives us permission to use his real name and has helped us tell his story) is *not*, and most decidedly not, a golden boy of postmodern success. Quite apart from the dark black of his complexion, he simply does not strike one as golden. Truth be told, conversations with him are slow and halting. His speech betrays the relative lack of education that may have contributed to the failures of his previous life. When he smiles, he is charming, but the smile is not what one would call infectious. He smiles, when he does, from the inner awareness of the real worlds. He is alarmingly steady in manner, kind but not effusive. If some think he has a fault, it is that he does not easily thank people for their work with him. And this is where the plot of man's way thickens. One supposes that Norman does not express sentiment readily, nor offer a profusion of cheery thank-yous, because of his understanding of himself as member of the worlds through which he has passed, trying to get by, now to live.

If his former life was a life of hustling on the streets to score the drugs that bought him infection, addiction, and poverty, then his present life is no less a hustle. But now it is a hustle to save his life in the only way men and women in his precise situation can. The HIV-positive life revolves around unyielding facts. The realities are never far off.

Imagine that whatever else you are doing in your life, you must, without fail, make regular visits to your physician, then to the pharmacy to renew the prescription for the medications that prolong life—not to mention other health issues wickedly associated with the life; in Norman's case, diabetes. First of all, part of each day is spent testing blood-sugar levels, taking medications, and generally monitoring the body's hidden messages. Then, in addition to the time spent in medical self-care, a good bit of one's time goes to the healing necessity of Narcotics Anonymous meetings; then there are the regular visits with caseworkers on whom one depends for eligibility for social and medical benefits.

Remembering the woman asked to work late by a boss who took her to be a *we* when in fact her babies made her an Other, you can suppose, in this day and age, that the woman would likely be excused, in the short run at least. By contrast, imagine being HIV positive and economically at risk and then asking for time off in the middle of a workday for a doctor's appointment. You may be excused the first time or two, but in time surely a supervisor will demand to know just what is wrong. Then what do you say? Like Norman, you may not be ashamed of your HIV status, but the world is. Still today, a good quarter century after the first AIDS case was diagnosed in 1981, very little social progress has been made in overcoming the public's lack of understanding of the disease.

Even though, worldwide, HIV infection is growing most rapidly among heterosexual women with no particular history of needle exchange, most people (even those who pretend to be tolerant) assume that the infection is the victim's own fault. Gay men (more even than women) and drug users (more than the poor) are considered moral undesirables. They are stigmatized as having what the American sociologist Erving Goffman called a "moral blemish." In his brilliant 1967 book, *Stigma*, Goffman pointed out that most people most of the time are in a position where something about them, if found out by others in their lives, would discredit them socially. Yet, most people, even those whose secrets are quite grave (like a history of prostitution), can often pass in the general public. Still, there are those who are subject to multiple stigmas, as Norman is—those who cannot cover the markers that set them apart as, in a word, different.

For one thing, Norman is black in one of the world's more race-conscious societies. He is marked thus by what Goffman called rather inelegantly a "tribal stigma." He belongs to a group people don't understand and often do not like. Plus which, he is in addition marked by poverty and reliance on social benefits in a society that despises economic failure and generally hates to pay the bills for those who cannot succeed economically (the latter being those whom the genially cruel Ronald Reagan labeled "welfare queens"). Then, on top of it all, he is sick with a disease that is assumed to have been contracted through one or another immoral behavior. Take your pick: gay sex (or any other kind of sex, for which gay sex is prejudicially taken as the prototype of sexual promiscuity) or drug use. It hardly makes a difference if, like Arthur Ashe, you were infected by a blood transfusion or, like women in Uganda, by infected husbands who refuse to wear condoms. HIV is *the* disease of moral failure. How many stigmas would that be? Black, poor, and then finally HIV positive—the all-purpose stigmatizer of the black and poor, especially.

Then, coming back to Norman's new life, one might ask again, What are you to tell your employer when you suspect that he might have hired you in the first place either to demonstrate his race blindness or to "help the poor" (and for either, he may have gotten respect and/or tax credits), when you, on top of it all, are known to be sick without *appearing* sick with a disease considered to be caused by your own moral failure? What exactly would you do? Out yourself, when, if you were so fortunate as to have a job that would pay the enormous costs of medical treatment, you know that losing the job means falling back into the grip of dependence on social programs?

To some this may sound like a sad story. But Norman's life is not sad. It is a struggle, to be sure. But he learned soon after beginning to deal with the addiction and the disease that he had to find a way to live meaningfully. Survival was not enough. He knew that in the worlds dominated by modern One World thinking, the key to the door of self-respect is the respect others give, if only begrudgingly, to those who hold a job that pays their way to accredited membership in society (which usually means not some society of citizens so much as productive labor in the society of economic utilities).

Hence the double bind of individuals in Norman's situation. Life is meaningful when others recognize us as working and productive members of the social whole. Yet, there is not now, and never will be, productive work for all, especially not for those, like Norman, whose medical needs would cost the better part of $50,000 were he to pay for them himself. Admittedly, had he been born in Norway, he would not face the same difficulty (then again, had he been born in Uganda, he would likely have died by now). In the United States, and to lesser degrees elsewhere in the modern world, even if the state covers medical expenses for the disease, no state-managed economy is likely to provide jobs with income sufficient to afford a dignified life. In Middletown, rent for a modest apartment in 2004 was, on average, $750 a month. Norman gets by with a small studio for much less, but still the $500 he pays each month for rent is more than half his government check. The double bind is what passes for normal with the poor, and it is much more than merely a double bind when they are infected and have only to offer the market economy experience in street vending or skills as a glazier.

What Norman has done to earn for himself the right to understand himself as a dignified individual by the harsh and impossible standards for so basic a recognition is to devote his life to helping others find work. This, in turn, has made him a productive worker in the world. He founded Positive Solutions, Inc., a nonprofit organization designed to provide work experience for the HIV-positive poor; hence the name: a positive solution for a negative reality. The organization he started now offers part-time work for seventy individuals each year. They make little money in the light assembly piecework they do for a local manufacturer, but the participants begin to go into the world, to experience themselves as productive, and relearn or learn the essential discipline of a work life. To support the project, which cannot cover its expenses through the outsourced labor the workers perform, Norman has also established a shop on Main Street that sells African and African American crafts and fine art. Here he uses his skills in sales, but even more important, when he is working in the shop, he spends the time answering the questions of people who come by to find out just what Positive Solutions is about. There they learn, and spread the word, that people like Norman with HIV are not terrible people—far from it. Norman himself still depends on government programs for his health care and basic income. He takes only a small stipend each month to cover the necessities of a decent life. He has no intention of enriching himself, which, even in a liberal college town like Middletown, one would never do selling what he sells.

What does Norman Bishop's story have to do with multiculturalism? In short, it helps to dispel the liberal and well-intended notion that the multicultural has to do with celebrating all the varieties of selves who live in your town, not to mention those who may live under your skin.

True, Norman deals with people of all social and economic ranks, all colors and ethnicities—from the city's mayor and its physicians and judges to the city's homeless and marginalized. He would not be able to deal with them—and deal in ways that make them want to come back, even to give time and money to his work—were he to put forth the poor-me face or play the guilt line about helping the less fortunate. People do not respond over time to this kind of thing. This may be one of the reasons why Norman is neither a glad-hander nor a cheerleader, but a plain-spoken man of the streets. He wants others to join in his work. But he wants them to join of their own accord. So he asks for help. Let others decide. He may ask again if necessary, but still he lets them decide. And when they decide, they do so not to join a hero to bask in his glow but to join with others who suffer the same exclusions that once meant a dead-end, possibly death itself, for Norman.

Multiculturalism, the theory and ideology, is frightening to those in the more secure positions because they realize that all social differences are not equal. Yes, it is true that the variety of cultures that present themselves even in small and plain cities are rich and compelling, and certainly valued by those who draw their lives from them. The liberal multiculturalist may even let himself get carried away demonstrating with apparent goodwill his sense of respect for these cultural differences. Who does not like South Asian food? Who does not know a Chicano gardener? Who does not respect Kofi Annan? But as W. E. B. Du Bois once said, not long after William James defined the riddle of the social self, one grows weary of the white people who come up to announce that they knew a good colored man once in the war. In this respect the reactionary is the more honest when he says, "Oh, he's a Jew, what do you expect?" Or "Those liberals, they'll ruin our values by watering them down with all this gay marriage evil." And so on.

The multicultural—the reality as opposed to the theory—is about nothing more or less than the facts of life in the different worlds. There is no One World outside the stark denials of ideology because social as well as cultural differences are real. To say that they are real is to accept the realities (not the prejudices) as real in fact, which means not necessarily available for melting in your pot, or mixing in your salad bowl, or enriching the education of your bourgeois white kids. Social differences are about differences—hard and given. It is more than sham to say, as some do still, that if we take social differences too seriously, we will undermine our common humanity.

Of course, human beings hold social things in common. We, if there is a *we,* surely recognize fundamental aspects, including values others may hold. But we recognize them especially well when they agree with our own prejudices. Americans may all (or mostly) share a commitment to the dignity of hard work at productive jobs. Norman does. Western Europeans may still, to some degree, recognize the responsibility of the state to provide basic social benefits to most (excluding the guest workers, of course). Yet, the *we*'s of such places are markedly less inclined to respect the cultures with which they associated (with notably little appreciation) people who seem to look the other way when people saw off the head of an innocent. And those in Europe and America who cast aspersions on people of Middle Eastern cultures seldom consider the figurative heads they cut off with the flight to suburbs, their gated communities, their silence before the migrant workers without whom they could not live.

Multiculturalism is, as we say, not about celebrating, even merely "respecting," social differences. It is about the hard work of living in the real world with both eyes wide open to the seriousness of those differences. The problem, of course, is with the word, after all. When we speak of "multiple cultures," we invite the reduction of social differences to the flags people wave, the costumes they put on for holidays, the songs they sing, and the dances they dance. These things have their place, but they do not relieve the responsibility for prior realities. People kill in the name of Old Glory, they hide behind burkas to carry their bombs, they dance their salsa to relieve the misery of hard workweeks at little pay. Under the cover of cultural expression one finds the one true and essential humanity there is. And that would be an essence of differences.

THE INDIVIDUALIST AMID THE HARD DIFFERENCES

The essential social difference of what common humanity there might be is that, whatever we do in each other's company to get through the day, we are not the same. And this, of course, is where individualism the ideology (as opposed to the hard reality) comes back to haunt. Individualism can be, as the social critics say, any number of things. It can arise as manipulated and manufactured individualism (as the German critical theorists have it). Or it can be the agony of isolated privatism (as American social critics like Bellah and Putnam may deem it), or it can be institutionalized individualization (as Ulrich Beck and others in Europe believe). But all that these theories of its nature may mean—even granting that there is something new about individualism in our time—is that the status of the individual in relation to her worlds is a source of trouble without end.

We should never forget that individual*ism*, like multicultural*ism*, is first and foremost a value; hence, an ideal; thus, also an ideology. True, it was a powerful and effective idea—one that lay at the foundations of the modern world beyond what Eric Hobsbawm calls the "dual revolutions" of the nineteenth century: the revolution that led to the modern democratic nation-state and the one that produced what Max Weber called the "tremendous cosmos" of capitalism. Both republican politics and entrepreneurial capitalism were established on the principle of the free individual pursuing his (*sic*—still!) enlightened self-interests in the marketplace while protecting his rights to voice (and of course private property) in the democratic polis. As fine as these values might be in the world of ideals, as much as they may have made the world better for our children and millions of others, there is no real evidence that, as values, they are fixed in the nature of things. In fact, when one looks at the hard evidence of the human condition after several good centuries of liberal values, it would seem that the highly esteemed ideals of the free individual have, in fact, led not to an amelioration of human suffering but to its opposite. As time goes by, the reality is that a hard look at the state of free individuals is most discouraging.

Individuals left to their own devices will, over time, fall into differing social groups—groups that may still have a flag to wave, or children well enough to learn the songs, or traditional dresses left from the fires of civil strife and rape. But when measured by the standard universal measure of the modern world—that of economic prosperity—the social groups of the world are growing rapidly apart. The rich are richer in proportion to their small numbers. The poor are poorer as their numbers grow. And the poverty of the poor is not the genteel poverty of the feudal countryside, where the miseries were at least held at bay by access to wood for fuel and the land for food—when, that is, the royal guardsmen did not chase down the poachers of private property and the land had nutrients enough to supply raw potatoes.

Social differences are not merely economic, nor are they merely cultural. But economic differences are, as they always have been, the final test of the values different people hold. No matter how colorful the flag, the costume, or the song, when millions die of starvation in lands grown arid as the forests and water sources are pillaged by the captains of global industry, cultures can die. Think of the Democratic Republic of Sudan, which for those who fled to Chad from Darfur is a state in name only. Imagine the Amazon outback of Brazil in a century or less, or the already denuded forests of the Philippines and Haiti. Think, for that matter, of the North End of Middletown—an otherwise comfortable if dull city with its own corners of human despair.

Norman Bishop, not the hero, but the man who puts one foot in front of the other for meaning and life itself, is what the multicultural, the reality, is about. His values are rock solid, confirmed in the teachings of the African Methodist Episcopal Church, supported by the work he does with the National Association for the Advancement of Colored People, advanced by the discipline of twelve-step recovery meetings, enriched by the dignity gained from work in the world with and for others. All these are fine values. But, though he may be a saint, he is not a hero. The hero is the mythic individual of Western drama—the grand and conquering man of war or some other struggle along life's way. The saint, if that is the word, is one who takes the vow of poverty, sits under his tree till the reality sinks in, then goes about the business of accepting life as it is, with all of its differences in tact.

The world is multicultural. The differences that make the world *worlds* are real. They are real because of values, to be sure. But the values that aggravate the differences are always a question of material differences. Cultures are economic. Economies have cultural consequences. To divorce the two is the height of foolishness, and especially so in worlds like the present ones where the new cultures of global communications are themselves technological marvels that produce economies of time and space so astonishing that economic realities are virtually indistinguishable from cultural ones.

Today's two cultures are no longer those of C. P. Snow in 1959, humanist and scientific cultures. A half century and a new millennium after, the global elites are neither the literary nor the scientific but those connected to the World Wide Web. Cultural privilege is indistinguishable from economic value and is reserved for those who understand the language of electronic connectedness and are willing to subject themselves to its demands. Call for help from Bristol; get an answer from Bombay in a voice trained to eliminate differences of English-language accents. This is what the One World has come to—a world that excludes those without access to digitalized realities, without which whatever local worlds that may remain will shrivel. The relative few who are privileged members by competence of this elite scarcely imagine that the greater half of the globe is inhabited by those to whom they are connected at most at televisual remote. Those who are excluded are not, however, excluded simply for want of a terminal. Even in the Nubian Desert there is a cell phone or a work station somewhere. Such things may be nearby, but they are in other worlds for those who scratch the hard surface of the globe for another day for the sake of their children. Everyone who knows these things knows that the global culture of electronic communications can and does go everywhere, or nearly everywhere. Women in Bangladesh sell their crafts on the Internet with the aid of microfinanced loans. A solitary woman in a Vermont farmhouse won a Nobel Peace Prize for her work in mobilizing the removal of land mines—work Jody Williams did largely from the personal computer on her kitchen table. The two worlds of today are not so simply distributed geographically. Or, better put, the social geography of economic exclusion is a geography of global miseries found just around a corner the privileged seldom turn as they pursue their enlightened interests. All the worlds could be connected at relatively little social cost. But most of the world is not because the larger half of its peoples suffer AIDS, malnutrition, civil strife, displacement, homelessness. They live in camps and tents, cardboard and tin shelters. They drink nasty water, scratch or beg for food, resort to eating weeds and shoe leather. They shiver the nights away on deserts of despair the connected cannot or will not imagine.

The new cultural divisions strikingly obliterate the old-fashioned nineteenth-century debate over the causal force of cultural or material factors—between, that is, cultural idealism and historical materialism. Today's two cultures, when mapped on the surface of the globe, would overlay almost precisely the social differences of material hope. The map is drawn, no doubt with the ink of global economic greed—with the dirty hands of industrial and postindustrial capitalism's half millennium of conquest and pillage of, in Immanuel Wallerstein's term, the periphery of the world-system.

Viewed in light of developments such as these, the very idea of individualism, however defined or interpreted, is jargon of an ancient world of tired ideals. The classic values of individualism—even the new ones that may be manipulated, isolating, or individuating—are in many important ways the symptoms at least, and often the cause, of the present world's sharp two-culture divisions. Hence the irony, the cultural divide between those with access to the electronic world and those excluded from it is the midwife of a widening recognition of the multicultural facts of the worlds. Those with the power of the Web can and do see the world. June 18, 2004, at 1400 eastern standard time: just this moment word comes from Riyadh of another beheading. The word flashes on the screen within minutes of the event. The pictures of this horror are said to be available on the Internet. At the same time, in Atbara, Sudan, at 2100 East Africa time, the temperature has just begun to dip below 40 degrees Celsius as dust storms whip from the Nubian Desert through the city outskirts. Further to the west the dust storms blow on children fleeing the militia in Darfur. The word of the beheading of a stranger, while not a matter of indifference, does not rise to the level of news. Off the screens of teleconsciousness, people see decaying heads along the dusty roads to safety. In global terms Riyadh and Darfur are virtual neighbors, just across the Red Sea from each other. But for the connected and the unconnected they could be different planets. In Riyadh one can see the beheading of human decency. In Darfur one turns away from the storms that kill ever more slowly.

Back in Middletown, Norman Bishop, just weeks after hip-replacement surgery, is lifting boxes and tables to move Positive Solutions to a new home. The larger space was required. Why? Because, among other reasons, he realizes that the cottage industry that serves the HIV-positive poor will run its course and that selling African art will go just so far toward paying the bills. He needs the space to develop the organization's computer training program, hopefully then to train people to serve a new data storage business he hopes to establish. Norman Bishop is no fool. He uses the teleworld and knows others must too. He sees the impossibility of getting by among those in his town who will remain on the margins of economic life until they get connected.

ETHICS ON THE DESERTS OF THE MANY WORLDS

The multicultural realities require a new individualism—and require it mercilessly. The new individualism is, thus, about whether people in the worlds on the globe will or will not accept the social differences globalization professes to eliminate. The new individualism does, indeed, involve an understanding of the individual as a manipulated, isolated, institutionally produced self. But the demand to accept honestly the harsh social differences is more than troubling the ancient verities of the moral individual.

Multicultural realities are, it is true, ethical trouble, but not of the kind that disturbs the cultured despisers of the celebrators of multiculturalism. Ethics, strictly speaking, is the thinking through of the differences between the IS and the OUGHT of social worlds. Ethics, at least in times such as these, are always social ethics—a continuous, unending dialogue between a sociology of the worlds as they are and an honest idealism of the worlds as they ought to, and can, be. In earlier times, ethical oughts were drawn from some other world—from the gods, from theories of natural law, from contextual or utilitarian analysis of the right or the necessary. The now questionable ideology of common humanity is in a state of collapse because, in the end, it was little more than a thin utilitarianism—the idea had come to be, if there is no common human, there can be no One World, whose loss means the loss of liberal humanity itself.

If, however, the IS of social realties is that of worlds, then the IS is a troubling ARE, which can only mean that the ethical OUGHT must be OUGHTS. To those clinging fast to the old ethical world, this is a tragedy. For those, like Norman Bishop, willing to live in the new order, there is no tragedy. For him, there is bad news but few tragedies, because he and those with and for whom he works live with a tiresome tragedy every day of their lives. With each dose of meds, they cannot help but think of an earlier life that led them to illness, and all that goes with it. Like children in the dust storms from the Nubian Desert, the poor with AIDS can hardly stop to ponder tragedy. They understand very well that the worlds in which they live are, in effect, under ethical judgment. They know very well, in the Old World, that they like all others are sinners facing an uncertain end. The decision to live is a decision not to wallow in the terrible, which to them must become mere bad news. Their ethical decisions are ones that turn on life itself. They, above all others, cannot deny the realities before them. They cannot choose to hate (though certainly they have this feeling) those who deny them or those who have what they never will.

To be an individual in such worlds is to be willing to accept what cannot be changed in order to change what can. This ethical wisdom of Reinhold Niebuhr's famous serenity prayer is the wisdom of realistic discriminations—of knowing the difference between an OUGHT that can be achieved and one that cannot. It may sound like resignation, and this may disturb the old liberal values of the heroic agent of social and moral change. But, in the end, to be human is to face one's finitude. It makes little difference whether the end of one's life comes from so-called nat-ural causes, from AIDS or cancer, from starvation in the ever-expanding deserts of a deforested world, from machetes at the hands of ethnic des-peradoes. In such a light, there is relatively little room for darkness. Yes, the night comes. Yes, one celebrates the light of another day, even if it promises little more than another day's begging. But the important yes of the honest new individual is that she does not insist that her personal rights are special. Hence the irony of the new individualizing ethics. Founded on the factual reality of social differences, mediated by the com-mon humanity of death one day, ethics such as these give people like Norman Bishop, of whom there are millions the world over, the serenity to accept the differences upon which the worlds turn amid the starts and stops necessary to haul away the debris of human terror.

CHAPTER SIX

SURVIVING THE NEW INDIVIDUALISM

Living Aggressively in Deadly Worlds

I NDIVIDUALISM has become so prevalent in talk among modern people that many will be surprised to learn that the word is of relatively recent vintage—not much earlier than 1835, when the great French social thinker and observer of American life Alexis de Tocqueville, in *Democracy in America,* gave the word a still-cogent meaning:

> Individualism is a novel expression, to which a novel idea has given birth. Individualism is a mature and calm feeling, which disposes each member of the community to sever himself from the mass of his fellow-creatures, and to draw apart with his family and friends.

What was novel about the idea and the word in the 1830s was that Tocqueville, himself quite a serious individual thinker, was commenting on the social consequences of a moral and political principle that gave rise to the modern world. The idea was that the proper and primary condition of the human individual in society is a state of composure within and comfort without among those few to whom one is most closely bound. To achieve this idyllic state the individual must "sever himself from the mass of his fellow-creatures and draw apart."

Tocqueville's definition begins to suggest the degree to which, prior to the modern world, individualism was far from a normal first consideration when people thought about the purpose of their lives. Individualism, as a commonplace moral ideal, was not just unique to the modern world. But in many ways its prevalence has been one of modernity's identifying social facts. This is why, years later, we recall Tocqueville's nineteenth-century observations with interest and why the fate of the moral individual and his freedoms (or lack thereof) were long a worry of social critics in the twentieth and twenty-first centuries. Yet, the story of the concept's origins, like those of all important social facts, is not entirely clear.

Prior to the revolutions of the eighteenth century, all persons thought of themselves as mere particles of a mass of social order. Certainly, those of the noble classes gave evidence of an extreme confidence in their subjective worth; and long before that, men and women like Aristotle, Augustine of Hippo, the biblical Ruths and Marys, and many others, knew how to think for themselves. We have seen how the concept was put into practice before the word was coined, in the thinking of eighteenth-century revolutionaries like Jean-Jacques Rousseau and Ben Franklin, among many others.

What distinguishes Alexis de Tocqueville's definition of individualism in the complicated path of the word's prehistory as a political and moral ideal is one important, but little-noted, aspect of the work that led to *Democracy in America*. Tocqueville was not engaged in philosophical work so much as an early form of sociological observation. In the 1830s the line between the two was fine indeed; still, there is something to be said for an idea that begins not in logic but in systematic observation. The individualism Tocqueville defined was a social phenomenon as much as an idea—and one that was already widespread in North America in the early generations that grew up after the French and American revolutions. And in the nineteenth century, nowhere else was individualism more in evidence than in early modern America, where, long since, it still finds its most acute expression.

This being said, it could well be asked, *So, what then, is all that new about the new individualism?* In one sense, the honest answer would appear to be, Not all that much. The theories of the new individualism we have presented throughout the book still exhibit traces of a search for a "calm and mature" state of individual life apart from the unsettling complexities of society. The differences over time are in the changing social realities faced by individuals.

When the word came into use, in the 1830s in North America especially, but also in Europe, the modern societies were, by contrast to today, anything but complex; nor were they utterly simple for all social classes, as we know from the fiction of Charles Dickens. Life was hard for many in mid-nineteenth-century Europe and America where the early factory system brought misery upon misery for those forced to leave the worlds they knew in search of what living they could earn from long days pressed against the machinery. Still, this was a world in which individuals (so-called after the fact) could imagine themselves enjoying a private life cut off from the public sphere. It is true, we must say immediately, that the individuals who in fact enjoyed the freedom of a mature and calm individualism in a settled life among friends and family were, with rare exception, white men, and men in particular of the middle and upper classes. The people in Jane Austen's novels who enjoyed their luxuries in estates in Bath were people of privilege. Yet, as we also know from the great nineteenth-century novels of English literature, if any among the landed classes were deprived of a sense of individual self-composure, it was women like Jane Eyre of Charlotte Brontë's imagination. No Creoles, and certainly no blacks, needed apply for the status, save for the now famous madwoman in the attic in *Jane Eyre* and other accidents of the colonial system. Nor did it happen that the poor—those today we call the working poor—had much assurance of the benefits of individualism as a way of life. Yet, we know very well that they understood the principle and aspired to attain it. This we know from the ease with which former slaves and subjects of the world colonial system were able readily to adjust to the trappings of the bourgeois life once they gained their freedom. Late in the nineteenth century, men like Frederick Douglass and women like Anna Julia Cooper, both born into slavery, lived their adult lives according to the principles, if not the exact social realities, of the bourgeois individualism that then prevailed in the dominant white middle and upper classes.

What, then, is new in the new individualism? Well, first and foremost, it helps to realize that individualisms of all kinds, new and old, are moral and social codes before they are concepts. This is the conclusion we draw from the origin of the word at a certain time in the early evolution of a new form of bourgeois civilization in the modern European diaspora. Social ideals (even after they become concepts of various kinds) are always linked to what the great German social thinker Georg Simmel called "social forms." The ideas men and women live by necessarily must fit to an efficient degree the society in which they intend to live. Otherwise, as monks of all kinds will tell you, they must quit the dominant social order to find another that will tolerate their peculiar ways.

This is an important point to keep in mind as we consider the question of how one survives the new individualism. And one of the best ways to keep it in mind is to note, and remember, that each of the three expressions of the theory of new individualism we have described arose in a specific social setting. While there were variations on the theme of Tocqueville's definition in the century or so between his definition in the 1830s and the 1930s when in Germany critical thinkers revised the term's meaning to suit the times, the old individualism remained, for the most part, a near, if not perfect, constant. The century from the 1830s on was the period when in the West (and in selected quarters of its vast colonial system) the bourgeois class rose to the prominence previously reserved for a nobility. In business, the arts, and literature, as in the values in which they were formed, the new bourgeois class lived in families among their kind. Even Marx in London, poor though he was, and the most radical of critics of the bourgeoisie, aspired to live a bourgeois life. He withdrew from the public order for great periods of time to write and think in the British Museum—and was afforded this luxury by the generosity of his wealthy comrade Friedrich Engels. Marx's detested bourgeoisie, like Jane Austen's more benign class of a certain cultural refinement, was a new and original social class, one as different in kind from the nobility of old as it is from the so-called middle classes of today.

DEADLY WORLDS AND THE MANIPULATED NEW INDIVIDUALISM: AFTER THE 1920S

The first of the three attempts to understand what has come to be called the new individualism was, of course, the theories of the German school of critical theory that had their roots in the terrors wrought by Hitler's rise to power in the 1930s and the war and genocide that followed. There can be no doubt that the evil of Nazi fascism and the slaughter of innocents to which it led was the foremost spectacle that led German social thinkers to realize that social theory had to reevaluate its classical assumptions, in particular those of pure science as the basis for social progress and of the moral individual as the engine of social history. The Nazis themselves used the language and practice of scientific knowledge to execute their final plan of racial purification, which among other of its terrors demonstrated just how vulnerable the moral individual is to the influence of wicked authority. Yet, as terrible as the Holocaust was, there was another realization, widely shared in Europe especially. The unresolved political and economic crises that followed the Great War, as Europeans still call the First World War, led soon to the recognition that the old days of nineteenth-century faith in the ideals of individualism were passé if not gone forever. The moral individual, however fine an ideal, had, in effect, failed to serve as a sufficient moral glue to hold the social whole in place; on the contrary, exaggerated individualism was widely thought to have been not only futile before the gathering social storms but even partly responsible for the catastrophe, at least in the sense that individualism did little to hold off the wars, market collapse, and political terrors.

In this regard, the horrors of the First World War were decisive. All across Europe, where the Great War was fought so visibly, social thinkers of all kinds began, soon after in the 1920s, to reassess the social and political theories of moral individualism that Tocqueville observed a century before. But in Germany the situation was different in important ways that affected the ability of its leading intellectuals to reassess the traditional as freshly as, even in France and the UK, it was possible. Germany had experienced its defeat in the war with abiding bitterness at the price the allied nations imposed, which led to political and economic instability as it faced the impossible task of social recovery under the financial and political penalties excised by the Treaty of Versailles in 1919. Instability is always the seedbed of political trouble, especially in democracies as ill formed as Germany's. Hence, Hitler's rise to power and the nightmare that followed. These events are not so easily summarized into a neat causal nexus, but they begin to explain why social theory turned sharply critical of the nineteenth-century values of the knowing and powerful individual of bourgeois culture.

The early founders of the German tradition of thought from which Jürgen Habermas today has descended were forced to flee Germany.

Many settled for a time in America, where, like Tocqueville before them, they no doubt saw firsthand an old individualism that, in their land, was no longer possible. What Habermas calls the colonization of everyday life by the larger social forces is itself a critical theory directly related to Theodor Adorno's deep mistrust of what in the 1940s were the new mass communication cultures created by radio and the new wave of Hollywood cinema. He had seen firsthand how Hitler and the Nazis used these media essentially to manufacture a goose-stepping mass culture of obedience to authority.

These, then, were the social realities that led to the widespread idea that the old individualism had given way to a new one in which the social individual, once the ideal of independent calm cut off from "the mass of his fellow-creatures," was now, under different conditions, the tragically helpless individual produced by a culture of *manipulated individualism*. The single most striking image of the manipulated individual emerged well after the Second World War, in the 1960s, when Herbert Marcuse wrote his celebrated book critical of the mass (now mostly televisual) culture. The book was *One-Dimensional Man*, a study of the systematic deadening of the free individual's cultural and political independence. The remaining, shriveled dimension, according to Marcuse, was the mindlessness created by the pervasive intrusions of mass culture. Marx's "rural idiocy" had become Marcuse's "urban imbecility." The once proud, if arrogant, mature individual of the nineteenth century was now the shell of his former self, with all the individualizing qualities eroded by the steady drip of lowbrow culture. *I Love Lucy* and *The Brady Bunch* did the work once done by Hitler's tirades—creating the hollow men T. S. Eliot had foreseen in 1925 when the trouble of the first war was already coming to the fore. From these social experiences—ones by no means absent today—came a first important step toward rethinking the old individualism as a new and far from comforting manipulated state of moral life.

THE EMOTIONAL COSTS OF ISOLATED PRIVATISM: AFTER THE 1950S

The second theory of the new individualism emerged in the years when critical theorists like Marcuse and Habermas were refining theirs, and it came, predictably, from American social theorists (or, at least, social theorists who, in contrast to Marcuse, both lived in America and thought *as* Americans). The time of the first foray into this second theory of new individualism as *isolated privatism* was early in the 1950s. Ironically, this was a time when, so soon after the second war in Europe, the United States stood tall in a unique global position—a posture, if anything, more strikingly unique than even today when it stands as the only remaining superpower. Yet, already by 1950 it was evident that the United States and the Soviet Union were at odds, odds that were dealt in the unsettled peace at Yalta in 1945 in which vague agreements entered into by Franklin Roosevelt, acquiesced to by Winston Churchill, and eagerly sought by Joseph Stalin ceded to the Soviets a considerable chunk of Europe's real estate. It would not, however, be fair to say that the Soviets had no claim on Eastern Europe. They had in fact made the crucial difference in the defeat of Hitler on the eastern front (a fact that American and British generals resisted mightily). Still, among much else, this gave the Soviets a considerable buffer against the West, including half of Germany. This fact, combined with their military, scientific, and technological capacity, made the Soviet Union a rival to American dominance in real political terms, if not economic ones. The Cold War thus was both an iron curtain dividing the world *and* a wall that cast a long shadow over Europe and the United States.

In the United States the situation was, in some ways, absurd. America, easily and without question, was the mightiest nation on earth, especially economically, because, in addition to having mobilized its industrial capacity in the war effort, it had once again avoided war on its own land. As a result, Asia and Europe, even the Soviet Union, had suffered the ravages of land and air warfare, leaving their economic infrastructures either limited or, in the cases of continental Western Europe and Japan, all but destroyed. Still, because of the perceived threat of Soviet communism, American economic superiority came up against its geopolitical limits. No economic rivals in the one aspect; a dangerous and powerful rival in the other. The Cold War remained cold because of this global imbalance of power, which left the door open through which a Siberian draft crept, chilling the moral bones of the Americans. The theory of military containment had the further unanticipated effect of containing the domestic vitality of American society. The rivalry, as instituted through the Cold War, was founded on little and led nowhere, as we now know—nowhere, that is, but to the Soviet gulags and America's anticommunist terrors.

It may be that the suffering visited on innocents—including in Korea and later Vietnam, where millions died in the name of this Cold

War—was the consequence of the contradiction in the global situation. People, including whole nations, feel disaffected or alienated when their worlds make no sense. This was Emile Durkheim's far more elegantly put idea of anomie as a cause of personal violence. America in the 1950s, when the televisual culture that so infuriated Marcuse was coming into its own, was a very strange mix of silliness and outright evil—the silly humor of Milton Berle and *I Love Lucy* and the evil of the two gulags (including the American one in which thousands were banished from public life by unfounded accusations that they were communist fellow travelers). Underlying both the silliness and the evil in America was its exceptional level of affluence.

The 1950s in America was the period when an economically more modest middle class replaced the traditional bourgeoisie as the social standard of the Good Society. And this middle class—populated by returning veterans of the war and their new wives and children, under-written by a booming economy with jobs aplenty (at least for whites), and enhanced by a cornucopia of cheap homes and cars cleaned and ser-viced by a then astonishing array of new gadgets—this middle class was the avant-garde of a new social world.

This was the golden age when, in America at least, experts thought that finally the old values of human progress would become manifest. The idea was simple. If the formerly marginal economic classes of men and women—those once consigned to the uncertainties of the working class—could own homes in Levittown, drive one or more cars, take vaca-tions on their boats, spend hours at leisure bowling with others, leave the housework to home appliances of all kinds, invite Elvis and Uncle Miltie into their homes by TV, what more could they want? The prob-lem was that the women and their children left in empty suburban towns with no particular cultural life did not enjoy the routine drone of their lives in houses that looked all the same, with neighbors who aspired to do what they did—far from it. Films like Marlon Brando's *The Wild One* in 1953 portrayed the rebelliousness of the new and young middle class. Middle-class affluence put money in the pockets of children, who became economic factors in themselves, which in turn led to the creation of what was soon called "youth culture"—young people with enough money to own a motorcycle (or, later, to shop at the malls), cut loose from stultifying (one-dimensional) suburbs to rage against the world. Their moms were, at the time, quieter about their anger, which did not emerge until the women's liberation movement a decade later. Meanwhile, the husbands and fathers of the middle class were off at their shops and offices, or on the empty road we know from Arthur Miller's *Death of a Salesman*. Say what you like about male privilege (and there can be no doubt that, compared to their wives, the men did enjoy freedoms), these men worked hard. In their minds they had fought the war that gave the freedoms, and now they worked hard to enjoy their cars and boats, to keep the kids and wives happy. They too had their doubts.

In fact, in the 1950s in America there was plenty of doubt to go around. At home in suburbs, or in the crushing conformity required in the workplace, there was doubt as to why the newfound affluence did not lead to personal happiness. Looking out on the world, there was doubt as to why a good America, which had defended freedom twice in the century and now was rebuilding both Europe and Japan, was not respected as the supreme world power—a status many thought America had earned and proven, but which the Soviet and Chinese communists defied at every turn. Thus, while the urban imbecility spawned by tele-visual culture created a veneer of fancy-free living, those who looked closely at Elvis could see Marlon Brando's wild one—a connection that had not escaped the young. Rebellion, when it occurs in cultural (as opposed to political) forms, is a sign of something wrong, usually a con-tradiction, often a repugnant cultural expectation, sometimes no more than a vague interior uneasiness that something is broken in the world. One of the more memorable early books on the problem was *A Crack in the Picture Window* in 1957. All the modest splendor of the new lives and homes with picture windows meant to invite others to see the affluence within was somehow a broken image.

But where does isolated privatism come into this strange mix of the American 1950s and after? Today, Robert Putnam writes of bowling alone and argues that this once most social of leisure-time activities has now declined into the pastime of a stratum of the new individuals. While critics argue with Putnam's evidence, what remains is that for a long time, since at least the 1950s, American social critics have worried about the loss of the old individualism of Tocqueville's day. One of the first and most sensational of the critics was David Riesman, who with col-leagues published *The Lonely Crowd* in 1950. The title says all that needs to be said. On the surface of the 1950s everyone was crowding together— wearing the same gray flannel suit to the office, living in the same or similar picture-window tract homes (even the well-off), seeking out the routine gossip in neighborhood coffee klatches, looking down the high school hallways for the latest fashion fad or new lingo. All ages among the new and rising middle classes in America were, indeed, caught up in crowd behavior. The new word was *conformism*, but what was meant was conforming too much to Tocqueville's "mass of fellow creatures." The concern on the part of social critics like Riesman was that behind all the crowd behavior lay a loneliness that represented the surface emotional state of the character of individuals. In his language, an empty *other-directedness* had taken over the personal lives of men and women who had once been *inner-directed*.

Naturally, Riesman, like other academic social scientists in his day, was not writing a popular essay (though, remarkably, this very academic book quickly became an all-time best-seller among books of the kind). What he and many others saw was a fundamental transformation in the social character of modern man (as they used to say in those days), a transformation that threatened to erode the economic and social achievements that had produced all that was good in the modern world. Who were these two "characters"? The inner-directed man was none other than the man of nineteenth-century individualism, but a type of individual who, late in the nineteenth century (and well before the new middle classes arose after the Second World War) was no longer free to indulge in the lofty bourgeois comforts of Tocqueville's individual. The individual had already been transformed into the self-starting entrepreneur, a man with little time to enjoy the comforts of private life because he was so engaged in the business of hard work, producing for profit in the burgeoning capitalist system. This man was none other than the ideal type the German sociologist Max Weber illustrated in his description of Benjamin Franklin—the modern man himself: frugal, self-motivated, goal oriented, hardworking, disciplined, and set upon a life of capital gain, which he saw as a way of contributing to the building up of the modern world. Weber published his famous essay on this modern man whom Riesman would come to call inner-directed. *The Protestant Ethic and the Spirit of Capitalism* appeared in installments in Germany in 1904 and 1905. Ever after, social scientists took it as a truth of social psychology that the modern person was modern by virtue of his individualism, an individualism that thrived on an inner-directed self by work in and on the exterior world.

By 1950, Riesman and others, having been taught to take Weber's description of modern man as gospel (and not unreasonably so), saw a very different sort of character—the conforming individual who gave his life over to hard work, yes, but a half century after Weber, the hard work that postwar social critics observed had become, they thought, the work of performing as a team worker—as an individual who supported the company goals, as one who could be counted upon to live according to the conforming values of the culture, as one whose wife and children were "normal" in number and kind, and so on. Believing as they did, social critics of the American 1950s had every reason to be concerned. From all appearances the affluence of the time had yielded a comfortable physical life, with enough leisure time to play, thus to work less, and enough surplus cash to spend, thus to buy and consume. Where Weber saw a producer, Riesman saw a consumer—and he was not wrong. Americans did have money to spend, and they spent it with a vengeance on cars, clothes, trinkets, just plain stuff that could magically adorn their homes and bodies. There was truth in the observation. Something was changing, as we now know, as the great American commercial invention of that day, the shopping mall, has spread about the world. Postmodern man is, first and foremost, a shopper! He, or she, may hate the attribution, as much as she or he hates the credit card debt that grows beyond repeal, but it is very hard to deny.

This, then, is where the concern over isolated privatism first arose. The American social critics were, in a sense, not all that different from the German critical theorists. In the 1960s Marcuse was living in California. He saw and experienced what Riesman and others had been commenting upon. The difference was in the causes to which the effects were attributed. Marcuse, with his German sensibilities, saw a one-dimensionality imposed from the outside by the evils of mass culture. Riesman and others, notably the sociologist Erving Goffman, put the blame, or the responsibility, on the individual for what Goffman called being a self who presents himself in social settings by means of a native skill at impression management. In this respect (though not in others) the American theory of isolated privatism and the European one of manipulated individualism were (and are) two sides of the same social coin, deflated by a decline in the market value of the old individualism. For the European critical theorists the threat to the individual was evident and out in the open—the fissures in European social and political structures aggravated by wars and depression, brought home metonymically by Hitler. For the Americans the threat was subtler, but just as devastating. Abroad their national power was, if not weak, at least vulnerable to challenge; at home, all the affluence in their domestic worlds could not keep the kids, then the women, then the men from rebelling, rebellions ironically wrought not by deprivation but by an excess that remained (as their older values taught) unsatisfying. Come home from a day at the mall and what do you have? Tired feet, unbearable debt, and (more often than not) worthless stuff bought on sale that in the dulling light of home is fit only for consignment to the back of the closet. This is hardly a holocaust, but it is in its way a kind of interior terror that can erode the individual's self-confidence.

Worn-down shoppers, like today's couch potatoes, cannot even begin to think of themselves as the source of moral and political power in the world. This was Marcuse's main point. Thus, leaving aside the fact that, when push comes to shove, Americans tend to see the individual as the source of social action (as Europeans tend to see the social as the source of individual power or its loss), what remains is that today's theories of a new individualism in America descend from a uniquely American social experience that was undeniably (if temporarily) different from Europe's. In the 1950s the Americans were building miles and miles of highway on which lonely individuals fled from block upon block of tract homes, while Europeans were, literally, rebuilding society as a whole. No wonder that on the European side of the Atlantic the new individualism was thought to have been manufactured by an evil that had to be eliminated from the social structures in which it grew, while on the western side of the sea it was a failure of American moral will.

THE GLOBALIZED INDIVIDUAL, RISKS AND COSTS: AFTER THE 1990S

The third of the three theories of the new individualism has its roots, no doubt, in many of the same histories that led to the first two. By the late 1990s proponents of the first two theories of the new individualism were either dead or retired and aging. The third group of social critics, mostly European and mostly British (either by birth or by immigration), is of a younger generation (even though they themselves are no longer young). They are of the generation Americans call the baby boomers, a kind of shorthand for those brought up in the false affluence of the 1950s—too young to ride with Marlon Brando's wild bunch, but old enough in the 1960s to see their mothers turn into feminists or hear their fathers talk of Woodstock or Selma. The experiences of this generation were different in Europe, where a definite seriousness of social purpose was necessarily more the order of the day. Yet by the end of the twentieth century, what Europeans and Americans saw and heard (however differently) in youth simultaneously prepared them for dramatic changes in the world and failed even to begin to describe the transformations that set in in the 1990s and into the twenty-first century. The speed at which globalization—both the concept and the reality—transformed daily life made the events of their youth look like buggy rides by contrast.

Early in the twenty-first century we do not yet know how far and how fast globalization will take us, nor even, when and if it comes to a rest, whether the inertia will throw us down on the murderous rocks of social collapse or let us down on a soft cushion of economic comfort. People argue both sides of the story. They agree only in the word they use to name it—*globalization*—which may turn out to be unwise, if only because the worlds they describe so differently seem so utterly incommensurable. Yet, in one additional respect, the two views (and the countless variants between) do seem to agree on two things: that the world today is risky (who could deny it after 9/11?) and that the risks, being beyond the control of our familiar national cultures, require us, as individuals, to adjust—a small accord, but interesting just the same. Whether some are right to call this adjustment *self-reflexivity* is itself another matter. What we at least, if not all the disputants, can agree on for now is that globalization requires a new way of being and behaving in the world.

Richard Sennett (actually more of an isolated privatism theorist in spite of his recent ties with the British proponents of risk society) has said in *The Corrosion of Character* (1998) that the fathers of his generation normally took and kept the same job with the same firm or institution all through their adult lives until retirement, while their children grew into an entirely different world. Today in the West that ideal is gone, and it is deteriorating even in Japan, where corporate loyalty is a matter of honor. From about the 1970s on, when economic crises arising from the manipulated costs of petroleum hit hard the then still industrial world, men and women (and note too that in the United States it had become necessary even for middle-class women to join the workforce) began to have several careers. For many women, it became a matter of living as a homemaker during their twenties then going back to school to train for a new career that, once entered, led from place to place—from teaching to real estate, from law school to corporate management, from medicine to academic research. This of course was a pattern already flourishing among the men—one that has in the adult years of the baby boomer generation become standard, and for many tragically common, as globalization sent capital and jobs abroad, leaving many workers in their fifties without employment. Whether the global traffic in jobs, constantly shifting in search of cheap labor, leads to the tragedy of unemployment and an early death (as it has in far too many cases) or to distraction of the kind we saw in Larry and others, or to a reinvention of self as we saw in Norman, there can be little room for doubt that to survive or thrive in a global world, the individual must think differently about himself.

When social conditions require individuals to think differently about their lives, they must begin with thoughts of who they are and who they wish they were. They must think of themselves as individuals who may be, as Norman was while suffering the addiction that led to HIV infection, lost in a world where, whatever their skills, they cannot find a decent job, much less a decent life. For an individual to adjust to changed social conditions (even ones that seem so routine as the decline in the industrial sector in which one has worked for years), she must *reflect*— look back, that is, on the self she has been inhabiting. This, in a word, is the self-reflexive attitude of the new individualism as it has come to be early in this century; and, it hardly need be said, self-reflexivity will be all the more intense and essential when the changing world all about is filled with risks—risks that prevent any life, even among the well-heeled, from reclining into self-satisfaction. In a sense, social life has always been, and will always be, a matter of risk. Individuals, whatever comforts they have or desire, cannot and do not control the larger social realities. Many of the bourgeois old individualists of the 1830s saw their sons or grandsons off to death in the Civil War in the 1860s. Yet, as terrible as civil and world wars may be, the long run of history has shown that in time they relent, and peace, if not always prosperity, returns.

THE DEADLY COSTS OF GLOBAL VIOLENCE

The question we would ask of today's world is whether individuals, new or old, living in this new century can reasonably expect war and violence to disappear from the global scene. A century earlier, the Great War was fought, according to the optimistic, as a war to end all wars. The record of the intervening century, however, is one of nearly continuous war. And, to make matters worse, even when the wars are more regional than global, one can hardly look forward to a moment when peace might reign. The globalized worlds seem to be ones in which social and economic violence is more, not less, in evidence. It may be, some would say, that with our brilliant new information technologies, it is not the violence that is greater but our capacity to know about it instantaneously and thoroughly, in more cable-televised detail than anyone with a life could want. This of course is a possibility whose truth only time will tell. But it is also possible, and just as likely, that the pattern of war and violence that grew across the twentieth century has now became commonplace.

It is certainly true, though its enthusiasts deny it, that globalization has led to deeper and deeper cleavages between the world's haves and have-nots. While parts of South and East Asia have joined the land of the haves, Central and North Asia, southern Africa, much of the West Indies, Central and South America, the Far North of First Peoples in Canada, and economic refugees in Russia have become the lands of the have-nots. And the gap between the two has widened in near exact proportion to the appalling wealth in the lands of the haves. It is a topic of much discussion among policymakers whether poverty incites violence. What is hard to deny is that when the poor see the wealth from which they are excluded, they have confirmed reason to feel anger and much else. In Dickens's day the poor in East London, lacking television or radio, even telephones, had little direct knowledge of the rich in Kensington. Today those fleeing Taliban warlords knew that some in Kabul had a better life, as even those in border camps in Darfur or makeshift shelters in post-tsunami Indonesia have contact, perhaps even televisual, with the trappings of affluence that were, until disaster struck them, comforts they themselves had tasted.

Whether it is actual warfare, civil strife, the spread of AIDS, the sale of children into the sex trade, grinding poverty, or sewage flowing in front of the doorway of a shanty, violence is present whenever those with the means use their means to protect their privileges against those who want a share of them. And, to come to the unique feature of globalization, when money and time move as rapidly as they do today on the wings of a digital bird, *everyone* knows that he or she is at some risk— even those most securely ensconced in their gated villas.

The global worlds are risky in ways that go far beyond the historically normal risks of famine, drought, and warfare. The risks now are ones from which no one can be assured a free pass and into which millions upon millions tumble day by day. The very idea of a mass society as an imposition on the individual is eclipsed in such times as these by the mass of human misery. It is true, of course, that those who wake to the smell of sewage are very much more at risk than those no longer able to find good help to clean the apartment. Yet, what ties shit on the streets to the inconvenience of dirt balls under the sofa is that the shit is likely to have been left, in shame and mortification, by the woman no longer able to travel north far enough to find meager work cleaning the master's shit from the master's toilet. In a global environment everything is linked to everything else. A principle that was for centuries a matter of Buddhist belief has become a hard social and economic reality. No one sees the butterfly that sends an economic or social tsunami our way. No one believes that the wave of global flooding can rise up to the penthouse. But it can, and it has—today with ever so much more regularity. And whether you fall asleep plotting a way to slip across the border to San Diego or feel the backache from doing your own cleaning for a change, the one inevitable fact of life today is that everyone must think— and think about herself, deeply and seriously. Some like Norman will adjust and make a new individualism. Others will not because the risks are too real and their resources too few.

These, more or less, are the conditions that define the new individualism. And now we can see how these earlier traditions of social criticism were driving at much the same thing as came to be in the recent thinking on the reflexive individual in a risk society. It is plain to see that writers like Ulrich Beck and Anthony Giddens are building on earlier traditions of social criticism. Beck, being a colleague of Richard Sennett, surely knows the isolated privatism theory of individualism (as Sennett, since moving to London, has begun to think more in the language of risks). And, too, it is evident, as we've remarked, that as early as the 1950s American concerns over the new, other-directed individual were parallel to those of the German critical theorists over the manipulated individuals.

The movement toward both the theories *and* the realities of a new individualism is, we repeat, not really a theory (even when it is expressed in theories). The movement is a movement in the history of the world— one that began in the shocking violence of the world wars, that was aggravated by the threats of late modern commercial and conformist society, and of course one that appears full-blown in the speed of change and disruptions visited upon people whose parents told them as children, Be patient, your turn will come. Today one's turn may not come. This is the risk that evolves over a long trajectory of social change that has eventuated in the new individualism—an individualism, not of those cut off from the mass, but of those with little option but to confront the mass of society and in ways far more complicated than the earlier idea of making the world a better place. For many it may be enough simply to get by. The new individualism can also lead to a new, more robust individual, a woman able to multitask without lapsing into multiple personalities. Whatever one thinks of it, the new individualism is the outcome of the inevitability that those who survive or thrive in risk society are required to juggle. It was once thought that the individual was of a separate order from mass society. But that, we see, was at best an artificial analytic distinction, available in practice only to those of means. Today, the story of the new individualism is a cautionary tale with an uncertain resolution.

If we have reservations about some in the British tradition of the new individualism, it is over the all too easy assumption of the play of *reflexive individualization* in the face of risk. Is not *risk* too gentle a word in a world where many are so caught and violence so prevalent? Those who suffer most grievously the effects of the dangerous worlds seldom have time to respond reflexively. While Norman found his way into recovery and treatment for his addiction and disease, hundreds, even thousands or more, do not. They fall away, dying all too often in the streets or county jails. The worlds today are not so much risky as they are *deadly*, and especially so for those on the social and economic margins.

Deadly worlds are violent worlds. They may not lead immediately to the death of the body, but when violence is pervasive, either in the neighborhood or across the world, that violence is experienced and has its effect. One no doubt feels herself at risk, and especially so if one is a child, little aware of the whys and wherefores of the gunshots down the street. There is a risk, to be sure, but the ubiquity of violence in the world is something more.

Individualisms, whether old or new, are, first and foremost, practical moral principles by which men and women measure their personal worth. They may come to be accepted by, or embodied in, literary or social theories, but before they rise to the level of intellectual curiosities, they are the mundane theories of men and men living, not always well, in the quotidian. Thus began the *old individualism* in the decades and centuries before Alexis de Tocqueville put it into words. What he saw in his visit to America was a then just emerging bourgeois class, a class to which those who, a century later, would be called lower or middle class aspired. It was a social type he had seen fully formed in Europe, where the bourgeoisie had emerged somewhat more by descent from the declining nobility. By contrast, in America the bourgeoisie had arisen rather more

from a yeomanry whose ties were not to the court but to the independent farmers who Thomas Jefferson thought were the promise of
American democracy. Jefferson himself, while a landed slaveholder and a
man of noble culture, lived most of his days as a reluctant patriot and
revolutionary—services that caused him to exhaust his wealth and to die
a man of limited means in the moral debt of those who had covered his
financial obligations. Benjamin Franklin, likewise, began life as a shop-
keeper and tradesman—a printer first, then a newspaperman, and only
then a statesman and scientist. These two extremes were the typically
American old individualists—men engaged in society, but engaged on
the basis of duty not privilege, and men who made their marks by bringing to their callings and avocations unique and individualist talents.
By the time of Tocqueville's observations in the 1830s both were gone
from the scene. Still, as Max Weber would put it, they were ideal types,
historical individuals who represented in practical terms the old individualism Tocqueville saw a generation later spread across the land—the
old individualism that cherished the independence of spirit of being cut
off from the masses. Thus, the old individualism, while aspiring to the
unique calm of the private self, was just as much a product of its social
conditions as were the later new individualisms of the twentieth and early
twenty-first centuries.

Individualisms, old or new, practical or theoretical, are more social
things than psychological ones. If they are to be studied, they must be
studied by the rules of sociology—as, that is, facts of a social kind that
cannot be explained away as having been caused by the impulses of the
mind or psyche. This is why not only Tocqueville but also all the subsequent theorists of modern individualisms were and are either professional sociologists outright or, as in Tocqueville's case, protosociologists.
From Adorno to Marcuse and Habermas, from Riesman to Sennett and
Bellah, from Giddens to Beck and Bauman—all the major theorists have
thought as sociologists. This is not a fact of convenience, but one of
moment. It calls attention to a theme that has always been in the background of thinking about moral principles in social history and certainly about books (including this one) and essays on the old and new
individualisms.

In a word, moral principles of individualism, while they are clearly
of keen interest to actual individuals, are also of broader interest for the
ways they represent practical theories of how individuals at a certain time
think of themselves in order to deal with real social conditions. Older

practical theories of the individual (those of the 1830s) could plausibly define the ideal individual as one who had been able to sever himself from the masses so as to enjoy the calm of the set-aside life. Newer ones, since the 1930s, were individualisms that arose under social conditions when one could not possibly escape the mass of fellow creatures. This may well be one of the reasons that the theories of the moral conditions of the twentieth century were critical theories—thinking, that is, that began in a sense of fear, nostalgia, or cautious optimism that the risks of authoritarian governments, of beguiling commercialisms, of global liquidity must be either attacked forthrightly (as did the Germans with their manipulated individualism) or bemoaned sentimentally (as did the Americans with their isolated privatism) or put forth with low-key determination (as do the gathered British with the reflexive self). These variant interpretations of the new individualism as they came to be in the twentieth century are, with no important exceptions, emerging interpretations of a changing world across a good century—from the meltdown of the world wars to the deep freeze of cold war to the liquidity of globalizing speed. Each stage had its own historical moment. Neither of the first two could have anticipated the third. At the same time, the third would not likely have come to pass as it did without the technological and social innovations born of the mobilization efforts in the world wars, which in turn were converted to peacetime applications, which in turn created a world of unending desire for state-of-the-art gadgets, which in turn led to wonders of all kinds. Telecommunications are miraculous, it is true—miracles that more or less equally allow the Marines to call in the air strikes and the terrorists to signal their suicide missions.

Hence the merciless elegance of the liquid world: The comforts come with the violence; the violence accentuates the longing for comfort; and, in times like these, neither is likely to win the day. These may be days that cannot be won. But they must be lived in because they are the only days we have. This may be why the British theories of reflexive individualism are in their way both cautious and sober, while at the same time less bitter than the earlier German criticisms and not at all nostalgic like the American ones.

SURVIVING THE NEW INDIVIDUALISM

Thus we come to our final question: How does one survive the emotional costs of the new individualism? And how especially can men and women come to terms with such liquid worlds, whose liquidity is the source of their risks and dangers, whose dangers are the source of its deadly violence? As we have throughout, we answer these questions with the stories of individuals, in this case two who are well enough known to us, as they are to many who learned to live and think by their teachings. Had they both lived, they would have been in their eighties early in the 2000s. Ironically, they knew each other for a time in the 1940s, which makes their different paths to individualism so striking. It is not incidental that one was a man, the other a woman.

The man was C. Wright Mills (1916–1962), one of the most influential social thinkers in America in the 1950s. Mills in many ways stood at odds with some of the social critics of that day. While he certainly shared, say, Riesman's concern over the rise of other-directedness, he was unusual for an American intellectual of the day in that he attempted to bring more European ideas into his writing, especially the ideas of Max Weber and Karl Marx. As a result, Mills's criticism of modern society had many of the features of the Europeans' viewpoint. He saw the problems not simply as a failure of the individual to keep a sense of discipline and hard work in the face of consumer culture but as, even more, the result of systematic exploitation on the part of an elite. In one of his well-known books, *The Power Elite* (1956), he systematically, and for the first time in a popular book, described the actual existing relations among business, military, and government elites. The very expression "power elite" then entered the American language, as did the idea that an elite that included people who were elected by no one in particular exercise unusual power over the policies that affected American life. By 1960, Mills's idea was so well known that it is hard to miss its influence on the then president of the United States, Dwight D. Eisenhower, who in his farewell speech upon leaving office warned the American people of the dangers of "the military-industrial complex."

Even more famous, and more important for our purposes, was an earlier book, *White Collar,* which appeared in 1951, a scant year after Riesman's *Lonely Crowd.* This earlier book was less a lament on the passing of the old individualism than a critical analysis of the new middle classes of white-collar workers then defining a new social location between the working class and the older bourgeoisie—those who were more likely to work in lesser administrative or managerial office positions than in factories and, in contrast to the older bourgeoisie, were unlikely to be the owners of their workplaces. They worked increasingly in larger and larger corporate firms that in the 1950s (and since) demanded the very other-directed conformism that bothered social critics like David Riesman. Yet, Mills's purposes in his work were not merely to analyze the sociology of modern life but also to provide the people affected by it the tools to engage themselves in political action that would take power from the elites, power they would then use to participate in the social world both to make it more human and to improve their personal circumstances.

This led in time to what Mills called in the title of a later book, *The Sociological Imagination* (1959). He was nothing if not a believer in sociology. His idea of the sociological imagination was not, however, so much concerned with social science as with the political importance of a practical sociology for ordinary men (he spoke that way) who lived personal lives as individuals but whose personal lives were determined by the history of the larger social structures. Individuals, he argued, tend to see no further than their own noses. As a result, when something goes wrong in life, they tend to blame themselves for their "personal troubles." It was here that C. Wright Mills shared a concern of the other social critics of the 1950s. But putting the concern to practical and political purpose, Mills said (to the astonishment of some) that what these "men" needed to do was to become sociologists. His sociological imagination was the art of seeing beyond one's personal troubles to the larger social structures that, as often as not, aggravate (or create in the first place) the troubles. The wives and mothers of Levittown come home from a long day at the King of Prussia Mall. In their fatigue, they look at their haul, with remorse. They spent too much. They consider themselves moral failures. Being isolated in one-dimensional suburbs, they have little ability to imagine sociologically, to examine their moral failure as individuals in the light of the social issues in the wider culture. They lack, not intelligence, but the intellectual wherewithal to consider that their shopping is prompted by the structures of postwar life—affluence, media, advertising, fads, proximity to others, the malls themselves, not to mention the elites with an interest in manufacturing a consumer mentality. It is evident that C. Wright Mills straddled the critical fences: while acknowledging the plight of the individual (as did the Americans), like the Germans he put the blame on the culture itself. Mills was not alone in his thinking in his day or since. His thinking influenced, among others, the political radical movements of the 1960s, especially the student and antiwar movements. Though he died in 1962, his influence grew in the years after and remains important today.

Just the same, we introduce him here not so much for his ideas as for his own way of living, which in many ways illustrates both the promise and the tragedy of the new individualism, especially for men who came into adult life in the 1930s and devoted their mature years to living in the face of the changes in America in the 1950s.

C. Wright Mills was anything but an old individualist. He loathed bourgeois refinements. At the same time, he was driven from youth to become an American original. Everything about his approach to education and later to shaping a career as what today we call a public intellectual was at odds with the prevailing norms—anything but cut off from the mass of society, so but determined to be the critical individual of social ways. The man was, in his way, the epitome of inner-directed individual and the antithesis of the other-directed conformist. Mills was born in Texas, from which he took the rough-and-tumble, independent ways. Already as a green first-year student at Texas A & M, the most unlikely of places for such a character, he wrote a most literate indictment of the school as feudal, and worse. He quit the place for the rather more urbane University of Texas, where he studied philosophy before undertaking graduate studies at the University of Wisconsin. He was never satisfied with work in one field to the exclusion of others, yet at Wisconsin both sociology and the school's progressive culture encouraged his individualism. Even in this Mills worked at odds with prevailing disciplinary norms by writing a doctoral dissertation on American pragmatism while beginning his work with Hans Gerth on Weber and European social theory—in the United States at the time a rare combination of interests. By the 1940s he was teaching at the University of Maryland, then in 1945 he moved to New York, eventually to teach sociology at Columbia University.

Through it all Mills refused to adjust to the dreary norms of academic sociology or to accommodate its, to him, creepy narrowness and mind-numbing abstractions. He was never accepted as a full member of Columbia's graduate department of sociology, then the leading program in the field. He refused to write as others wrote or think as they thought. His first major book, *White Collar*, in 1951, brought him public acclaim, as did all that followed. In short order, Mills was, in the public eye, one of sociology's most famous writers, while many of his academic colleagues shunned him. He lived his intellectual life as he did his personal life. He dropped his kids off at school on the motorcycle that became his public signature. He loved guns, it is said, but even if this was a rumor from his

Texas origins, Mills thought and wrote and dealt with the world in the style of a gun-toting, quick-draw artist on the frontier of modern life. He built homes and plowed gardens by hand and traveled the world, while reading and writing prolifically.

His travels led him to Cuba and meetings with Fidel Castro and Che Guevara just after Cuba's 1959 revolution. After, Mills wrote *Listen Yankee* (1960), which praised and defended Castro's revolution. The liberal foreign policy establishment rose up against him, as had the Columbia establishment earlier. Behind all the bravado of his public face, Mills no doubt felt the sting of rebuke. He suffered a massive heart attack days before he was to defend *Listen Yankee* in a nationally televised debate. Fifteen months later, while trying to recover his health, he died of a second heart attack. His tombstone in Nyack, New York, reads, "I have tried to be objective. I do not claim to be detached." Mills had lived his forty-five years with speed and audacity, even defiance. All of his important intellectual work was written and published in the nine years between 1951 and 1960. In the same decade he built three houses and one BMW motorcycle. Liquid he was not, but his living was a flash of aggressive speed.

Mills lived in his own way, and certainly his brand of individualism was new, if not settled. His was a life lived with courage, to be sure, but also with insolent protest against the one-dimensionality of modern culture that reduced individuals to empty vessels lacking, in his words, the sociological imagination to resist the power elites. He also protested the mindless conformities of the new middle classes of the suburbs and the shallow privatism that bred the isolating detachment of an individualism cut off from the masses—cut off not by choice, as in Tocqueville's day, but by the destructive forces of the modern world. He did not come close to living long enough to witness the globalizing extensions of these forces. Had he, you can be sure that, while he would have argued aggressively with the British proponents of risk society, he would have taken their point, and especially the basic concept of the reflexive self. Mills was nothing if not a man (too much a man, perhaps) who lived with an objective eye on global realities and a heart engaged in reinventing himself.

Yet, he did not survive either the global realities or his own masculinist style of individualism. Did the very public controversy over his daring attempt to defy the American establishment by praising Castro kill him? It is tempting but facile to think so. It is enough to regret that his heart gave out at a young age—perhaps because of disease, perhaps because of the speed with which he lived, perhaps because of the emotional and physical toll inflicted by his way of setting himself against the dangerous worlds. C. Wright Mills was a new individualist who understood, or would have understood, the entire history of modernity's attempts to come to terms with the cuttings apart and comings together of individual *Character and Social Structures* (1953)—the title of one of his books—and the key terms of his famous idea in *The Sociological Imagination*.

THE PROMISE OF AGGRESSION

How indeed do individuals survive in worlds made deadly by social structures? Mills understood the question but not the answer. The answer may be suggested in the life of a woman of our acquaintance and friendship who, for a time in the 1940s, worked with Mills and whose own professional and personal career was devoted to many of the same concerns, though in a much different way and with markedly different life consequences.

Phyllis Whitcomb Meadow was a survivor, if ever there was one, just as she was one of the more unusual individualists anyone could hope to meet. Though but a few years Mills's junior, she not only lived but lived actively and well until a particularly virulent form of cancer limited her days. Even then, between visits to the hospital for care, while suffering dramatic weight loss, Meadow continued her life's work. One winter day in December of 2004, just weeks before her death at age eighty, Phyllis took herself from the hospital in New York City, dressed herself grandly, and went directly to share the stage in a long-planned public discussion with the world-famous French psychoanalyst André Green. Most in the audience of five hundred were unaware of her illness. Those who were marveled at her energy, as they always had. Phyllis Meadow was famous—and to some notorious—for a level of human energy that would have shamed those about her were it not that she used the energy almost always for constructive purposes that gave life to others.

Phyllis met C. Wright Mills early in the 1940s at the University of Maryland. She was drawn to his intelligence, as he must have been to hers. Still, in one class he gave her a C+, apparently to shock his young student. Mills loathed the University of Maryland. If Phyllis had been a loather, she would have, too, but her style was to embrace where possible, transform where necessary. Soon she became Mills's research assistant. When he moved to New York in 1945, she followed him, taking a day job in publishing while serving as his research assistant for, among other projects, *White Collar*. Late in life, Phyllis recalled her few years working with Mills:

> His main impulses were for work. He once told me he wanted to learn more about literature, so I made a list of all the great works and brought the books to his apartment on West Fourteenth Street. The place was lined wall to wall with books. They soon disappeared. He had the ability to read three or four books a weekend. . . . He died a terrible death at forty-five. He just burned himself out.

She, by contrast, lived on, four decades longer than Mills, working and living every bit as hard and fast as he had.

What accounts for the difference between two people of enormous energy and intelligence, both roughly of the same age and living through the same social times, both conspicuous individualists in several of the new senses of the term? One survives; the other does not. Again, we ask, how does one survive the new individualism, which, as Mills's life shows, can be risky, even dangerous, perhaps even deadly?

It may be too simple to suggest that the difference that led to Mills's early death is genetic. Something was physically wrong with Mills's heart. After the first attack, he did everything one then knew to survive, including visits to clinics in Russia. Yet, Phyllis Meadow may be right that, whatever the underlying illness, he burned himself out in the sense that his human energy, so great and brilliant, somehow did not keep him going.

One might dismiss Phyllis Meadow's remark as pop psychology were it not for the fact that, after her few years working with Mills, she went on to become one of America's most original and important psychoanalysts. In the 1950s she was trained in psychoanalysis at one of New York's many institutes, where she sought out teachers and training analysts who were themselves individualists, people who cut against the grain of establishment psychoanalysis as Mills had resisting the confinements of establishment sociology. After becoming a certified lay analyst (then a rebellion in its own right), Phyllis took a PhD in psychology, partly because she was devoted to learning but just as much because she was smart and knew that in that field, as in others in that day, a woman without an MD had to be otherwise certified. She was nothing if not ambitious, like Mills; but her ambitions led her in quite another, though just as defiant, direction.

Phyllis began her life's work in the 1950s, in a day when in the United States feminism was unheard of, which meant, among other things, that an independent woman faced odds that were, if not impossible, certainly more severe than they would be today. In point of fact, never in her long life did she, so far as anyone we know knows, think of herself as a feminist. Certainly she refused to talk the talk of any social movement. But she did walk the walk. One might say that like many other courageous women of her day and before, Phyllis was a feminist before the fact (and without the label). She married, had a child, left a husband, built a home, remarried, trained, and went into private clinical practice. The year after her daughter left New York in 1969 for medical school in Wisconsin, Phyllis Meadow joined in founding her first of several psychoanalytic institutes, the Center for Modern Psychoanalysis on West Tenth Street in New York, just blocks from where she had worked with Mills. She was at the time already in her fifties, an age when others are planning to retire.

From there she went on to found and lead two other graduate institutes in the field, one in Boston in 1973, another a quarter century later in Vermont. Both are fully certified to offer clinical certification and doctoral-level degrees in psychoanalysis, and both are research-based training centers. As a nod, perhaps, to her beginnings as a sociologist, one of the advanced-degree programs in the Boston Graduate School of Psychoanalysis is the Institute for the Study of Violence, a program she founded, along with the Vermont center, when she was well into her seventies. Approaching her eightieth birthday, she took up the study of the notoriously obscure French analyst Jacques Lacan, whose thinking she incorporated in her most important book, *The New Psychoanalysis* (2003). And at the same time she took up the study of neuroscience, which she required as one of the elements in the training of students in the Institute for the Study of Violence. All the while, she continued to treat patients in New York City and Boston, to edit an academic journal she also founded, to push all of her centers and their students toward developing their research skills, to lecture, and to travel the world.

We will never know what C. Wright Mills would have been like had he lived a long life, but Phyllis Meadow at eighty and mortally ill would have given a much younger Mills a run for his money. Many describe her as a force of nature. The physician who diagnosed her cancer could not believe it when, after he examined her physically, she told him how old she was; nor over the years could her students and patients. Her most urgent clinical work in the last months of her life was to help her patients and students work through their feelings about *her* pending death. She kept no secrets. She was willing to hear or say anything, including talk of her own death. She was, thus, a woman who faced squarely the dangers of the deadly and violent worlds, reflexively to take them on and in—thus to reinvent the local worlds about her. One of the more puzzling statements she would often make when people tried to tell her she could not do what she set about doing was, "Of course not. Life is impossible. Don't try to change me." Then she would do the impossible.

How is such an individual possible? As one could say that biology may have contributed to Mills's early death, so one could say that the luck of the draw of her early life may have stood behind Phyllis's astonishing personal qualities. When she was seven, her parents separated. Her mother moved to Maine. Phyllis chose to remain with her father in Massachusetts, largely because she could not bear to leave her grandmother, who, though prim and proper in appearance, was a woman who talked about anything, saying whatever needed to be said. There began Phyllis's childhood appreciation for the most important work of psychoanalysis—the skill to support the patient's courage to say everything about his feelings. Then, too, the separation she suffered from her mother had its effect. As a child she longed for the absent mother, whom she saw mostly in the summers until she moved to Washington, D.C., when Phyllis was ready to join her (which led, of course, to the meeting with Mills at the University of Maryland). Late in life Phyllis attributed her ability to feel and talk about these longings for both parents, and the anger at the loss of her primal family, as important emotional elements in her interest in psychoanalysis. But, at an age when she could not have spelled the word, it would seem a stretch to suggest that her adult life was already determined by childhood experiences; far from it.

There are many children separated from parents at a young age who go nowhere in particular, some even who suffer lifelong disorders that block their energy and frustrate their lives. This happens as often as there are young men who may or may not have congenital heart disease but who find a way to manage the disease and live to old age. Neither family circumstances nor biology is destiny. They can help or hurt, to be sure, but the question of survival is one of how one plays the hand dealt at birth.

There is one word that Phyllis Meadow used to describe her own ability to survive full of creative energy to live a long life: *aggression!* This may seem odd, especially in a culture where aggression does not have a good reputation. But if one stops to think about it, aggression may well be the key to survival. It certainly is with the animals that face natural worlds ever more deadly than the ones humanoids have created over time. If alpha wolves could think, they would surely know that their day of death and defeat will come. Yet, they rise, perhaps as much by instinct as by physical prowess, to conquer the males that would kill them for the status of head of the pack with all the sex you could want. Somehow, over the same cultural history of the modern world that has led to more and more social violence, the culture itself has lost the ability to think of aggression as a natural human virtue. Perhaps we have lost or neglected the instinct for aggression as a key to the survival of the human animal in large part because we have witnessed, on the social scale, the terrible effects of aggression in world affairs.

There is, however, a difference between the aggression that leads to violence and the kind that leads to rich and powerful living. Even the alpha wolf does not kill when he is not threatened. Curiously, behind the timid moralities of modern culture, the only places one can find positive ideas of aggression are in the cases of a just war against an evil enemy like Hitler and in the face of violence against oneself or one's family. The self-defense argument seems, however, to stand alone in the meager debates over aggression, especially in a world where it is attributed to the male of the species, who is said to be more inclined than the female to be the alpha killer and rapist.

Never, however, have we heard of anyone who thought of Phyllis Meadow as having masculine qualities. She was, if any one personal thing, mostly sexual and seductive (and this until her last days of life). People did call her, as she would have agreed, a killer, meant mostly but not entirely metaphorically. She was a woman filled with available sexual energy, who focused her career always on building groups and motivating individuals. But her way with people was not unrelated to her status as a killer—that is, as a woman who would not tolerate anyone trying to change her or to stand in her way. More than a few times people would storm away from her or her institutes outraged at her aggression. Charles personally knows of at least four senior leaders of her institutes (himself included) who quit in disgust because she was willing to run over them to get her way. Some never came back; some did

(Charles included). She was more than glad to embrace the prodigals. But she refused to be swayed by their resistance, even when she may or may not have been right in the actions to which they objected.

This, we should say right off, is a very unusual kind of aggression—a killer instinct that arises not so much from self-knowledge, or even self-confidence (though surely that is part of it). Phyllis's aggression was rooted in her willingness to know the worlds for what they so messily are—impossible and aggressive and violent. It is one thing to be ambitious or brilliant as Mills was. It is another to have these traits of character and to pursue them against those who wish to kill to protect the comforts of their (usually) bourgeois positions. Mills refused to let the academic establishment rein him in. Nor did he allow the prevailing norms of political liberalism to dissuade him from speaking out in favor of Castro's Cuba. Yet, we know that he suffered under the exclusion and criticisms to which he was exposed in his intellectual worlds, as he seemed to have been affected by the challenges to his radicalism in *Listen Yankee!* The title is bold and aggressive, but his first heart attack came just when he risked embarrassment and exposure before the nation.

Risks are everywhere, more so today than ever. Ulrich Beck and the British thinkers are right on this score, even if they fall a bit short of describing the violent nature of a globalized world. In this sense they are closer in their understanding of human nature to Mills than to Phyllis Meadow. Mills's famous slogan of the sociological imagination put all the hope for power in knowledge—the ability of the individual to study the sociology of social structures. There can be no doubt that he, like many intellectuals, put a good deal of his personal faith in knowledge. "I tried to be objective." If objectivity is the standard for truth, however much one tries to overcome detachment, there is a point beyond which facts will not carry you. In a somewhat similar way, thinkers like Anthony Giddens and Ulrich Beck, and certainly ones like Richard Sennett in the tradition of lament over the isolated individual, are closer in spirit to Mills. They may not suppose that sociological knowledge is the answer to the risk society. But they do seem to write about the reflexive self as if the reflexive coming to terms with global risk were a naturally available, if traditionally ignored, human quality.

To face risks, when the risks are real, is to face the possibility of real dangers, even violence. We will never come to terms as individuals with the new global realities if we begin with any sort of innocence about just how deadly these new worlds are. We certainly respect the now long history of men and women who have attempted to salvage their inner sense of integrity as individuals while living against and in an inhospitable world. We respect also every bit as much the social critics from Adorno to Giddens who have sought to account for the transformations, even fundamental ones, in the social structures affecting and very often limiting the individual's capacity to survive and flourish. We even (and obviously) agree with them that there is a new kind of individualism abroad on the planet—a necessary one, and one that can be thought to hold a promise of new possibilities for human kind.

Where we hold reservations is on the point of assessing the risks before individuals in the globalizing worlds, in respect to which we propose that a more seriously critical theory of the new individualism is required. If we live in a risk society, then we live with danger. If the dangers are real, they put individuals at risk of violence. If the violence in the social order is real, then how will the new individuals ever be able to survive if they do not develop their own inner capacity for aggression? Aggression on the inside of the individual is not an idea but a feeling—a feeling that some say is due to the residual of the animal within us; and it is not (at least not first and foremost) a theory or a concept. Try to *think* of yourself as aggressive in a culture that teaches the contrary and you will draw a blank. Try, however, to *feel* the aggression within you—those impulses to speak an angry word, those actions that could lead to the breaking of a relationship, those fantasies to murder or otherwise silence an enemy. So far as is known, there has not yet been an individual without feelings of this kind. The difference between us and the wolves, however, is that, though some do, we humanoids do not, in the normal course of events, need to kill in order to survive. We can use words. But to use the words or take the actions that allow us to *be* aggressive, we must be willing and able to experience our own personal feelings of aggression. The talk does no good if you do not feel the aggression—and accept the hard truth that in the worlds in which we live there will be aggression, aggression not unrelated to that within us all. Nor, on the other hand, does it serve the individual if he can only act on the feeling without first experiencing it and coming to a conclusion whether talk (or silence) or action might be the way to achieve the goal at hand in the situation.

Phyllis Meadow lived by her feelings but not by feelings alone. She was a genius as a thinker and a therapist and a powerhouse as an organizer. Without question she was a risk taker and one who could reflect on herself, thus to invent her unique and individual self as she went along. But she could not have done any of what she accomplished *just* by being aggressive. The aggression was always balanced against the love of others and the constructive desire to join them in working to build a better world. She had her psychoanalytic theories for the way she lived. Anyone interested in them can consult her books and articles. But we do not tell her story here, as we do not tell any of the stories of others in this book, to set up anyone as a paragon of virtuous accomplishment or of disgracing failure. If the costs of the new individualism are real, thus more than mere risks, then some will fail and some survive, while most will make do with both.

The issue at hand today is, how do individuals survive and thrive amid and against deadly worlds that would take it all away? The question may be more acute on the plains of Darfur or in the *bidonvilles* on the margins of economic progress. But it is a universal human question. Phyllis Meadow would not have thought of herself as a universal hero, a model for the new individualism. She was much too occupied with the local and human work to which she devoted her life, not to mention with enjoying what pleasure could be had along the way. For her the key was joining the aggression with pleasures, to lead a whole and honest life.

If her story rings less true as an example available to all, then at the other end of the social and economic scale keep in mind Norman Bishop. He has little education, no money, no particularly acknowledged training or skill—beyond, that is, his acquired capacity to focus his life on living and helping others to survive. Remember him as one who had lost his life to drugs, disease, and the poverty that follows therefrom. But he is also the most self-reflexive individual you could hope to meet, and this because he faced the risks before him. Anyone suffering HIV, not to mention poverty, in his part of the world has a chance that millions in Africa will not. But Norman's survival is far from an accident of his birth. He survived to thrive in life *only* because he was able to look at his life *and* his world (call it reflexivity if you want, or not).

In his own surprising way, Norman is aggressive. Just as Phyllis Meadow's aggression was always mixed with her drive to form creative relations with others, so Norman Bishop's was displaced into a powerful energy that serves his own desire to shape a better life for the ill and poor. Though not a man who confronts, Norman is one who persists. Though his manner toward others is quiet, even saintly, he does not let go of a good idea. Though he respects others, he does not let them go until they've agreed to do something to help. This remarkable brand of positive aggression did not come easily. There was a day when Norman's life could not possibly have been more miserable, and miserable because he was unable to focus his aggressions, which, with the aid of drugs, he turned against himself—until that day when he had to turn his life around. Such a day is the one addicts call hitting bottom—the day when they must decide whether to continue the risk-taking life that leads to death or to take the very different risk of giving up the worlds of addiction for a new life impossible at the time to imagine. Addicts cannot take the steps they must to be free of the addictions until and unless they take the step away from the old life. When and if they do, then the only way they can live is by, first, giving themselves the experience of living, as it is said, one day at a time. Each day they must remember who they are (a drunk or a junkie who had ruined his previous life). Every day they must several times over decide *not* to use or drink, or whatever it is. They must, in a word, live in continuous reflection on themselves, while always looking at the worlds about. This they must do until they come to believe that the risks of this life are deadly, which in fact they are for them in the most personal and emotional ways. For those suffering any form of addiction—whether Norman or Kelly or Ruth or Larry—"deadly worlds" is not a throwaway line, unless of course they refuse to embrace the risks and costs of their ways of life. Only when men and women refuse to ignore the realities can they hope to live without lapsing back into the grip of a violent life. And even then one is still an addict in recovery, never without risks, even after years of accepting the costs. Hitting bottom, strictly speaking, means falling just precisely to that point where one more instant of it means certain, if not immediate, death; surviving the deadly worlds means remaining constantly vigilant that one could give in to the deadly life with no more than a single misstep. Life in these deadly worlds may not be quite the same as life recovering from an addictive disease, but how different is it? The practical work the worlds demand of us all is to watch out always for the costs in the risks.

If the globalized social worlds are risk societies, then the risks must be real enough to be deadly. And if there is *a* model for surviving the new individualism, it could be (though cautiously so) the lives of those who survive a real encounter with the deadly worlds and live to tell the story. The death before them may be their own, or that of a marriage, or war, or neighborhood violence, or a child lost to street wars, or a criminal past, or any number of things that, being enumerated, we realize are all too commonplace in these worlds today. The new individual may well be a woman of culture and means like Phyllis Meadow. But, more often than not, as Hegel once taught, it may be better to look at the slaves and their heirs, at those who suffer on the margins of the fast worlds—that is, those who have little choice but to feel and experience the suffering of life as they look in their own ways for the new individualism. However one thinks of the new individualism—and it *is* necessary to think about it—one must think of it as hard and aggressive work whose accomplishments are ever exposed to the aggressions of others who would take it all away.

Yet, the remarkable thing is that those who try and fail, or those who come through it awkwardly, and those who seem to have succeeded, know very well that there are millions the world over for whom life is not a mere adjustment and culture not so powerful as to reduce them to one narrow dimension. They are men and women, and more children than you would suppose, who see and feel the self within, accept it for what it is, and use its aggressions and drives for attachment to others with whom they remake themselves and what corners of the world they can.

NOTES AND
SOURCES
~

ON THE SELECTION OF INDIVIDUALS
FOR *DEADLY WORLDS*

Much of the research for this project, both the review of existing theoretical standpoints and empirical work, was funded by the British Academy in the form of a Large Research Grant (award no. LRG-37286). We wish to thank the fellows of the academy for their extended support, as well as for the excellent research guidance that came from several anonymous referees. Additional funding for the project was secured through the Centre for Critical Theory at the University of the West of England, Bristol, which facilitated both the review of the extent to which globalization is transforming the emotional textures of individualism and interpretation of interview material.

The need to disguise individual identities has been extended, we believe, into novel territory through our use of fictionalized characters. While this is not true of all the lives and individualisms discussed in the book (for example, our discussions of Norman in chapter 5 and of Phyllis Meadow and C. Wright Mills in chapter 6 are drawn from both the recollections of these individuals and our experiences of them), many of the lives we develop here are in fact fictionalized. In fictionalizing these stories, we have drawn from Susie Orbach's pioneering work, *The Impossibility of Sex* (Penguin, 1999). "There are inevitable emotional truths," writes Orbach, "that transcend the characters I am writing about. . . . The actual situations on the page might not have happened but the relationship between emotional truth, biography and narrative truth is one of current interest to both psychoanalysis and literary studies. What many writers involved in both autobiographical and fictional pursuits are search-ing to express is an authentic representation of feeling states rather than a strict adherence to narrative truth" (pp. 196–97). It is our hope that our extension of this method of retelling the stories of the new individ-ualism we have heard people tell us will similarly affect the broader con-cerns of sociology and social theory.

Introduction

Kelly's story was reported in Morag McKinnon, "The Plastic Generation," *Daily Mail*, 18 November 2004, pp. 51–55. The report covered the experi-ences of approximately ten young women, all of whom had undergone plastic surgery in the search for a new self. Moreover, almost all—both those satisfied and those unsatisfied with the transformations effected by the surgery—had decided to undergo further cosmetic surgery. McKinnon concludes her article by noting that the stories of these young women "illustrate all too starkly a society which has become obsessed with achieving a physical perfection that can never be attained." This apparent contradiction between the search for perfection and the lack of its attainment lies at the core of societal processes of the new indi-vidualism as we define and explore it throughout this book.

Chapter 1: Individualism for Beginners

The occasion for the Bristol meeting of Caoimhe and Annie in November 2001 was Charles Lemert's visit to the Centre for Critical Theory at the University of the West of England as Distinguished Visiting Professor.

Chapter 3: Living in a Privatized World

The story we tell of Larry's life derives as a composite from the follow-ing sources. First, Thomas Ogden's incisive psychological portrait of Dr. L in his captivating book *The Primitive Edge of Experience* (Jason Aronson, 1989) provided the initial inspiration. Second, the missing or only latent social and cultural contexts affecting Ogden's Dr. L were examined in depth in Anthony Elliott, *Subject to Ourselves: Social Theory, Psychoanalysis, and Postmodernity*, 2nd ed. (Paradigm Publishers, 2004), and again we have drawn in detail from this work. Finally, Larry emerges as an example of the invented, fictionalized case-study method we mention above.

The narratives of Joe and Xavier derive from a chance encounter and discussion in Paris. Exploring the daily life of hyperglobalists such as these two, much in the spirit of an anthropologist, meant listening to various stories about their present circumstances as well as their deeper hopes and fears. We have necessarily had to condense the stories we heard into a more linear, focused narrative, and we have also changed aspects of personal and professional details in order to protect identities. Notwithstanding these modifications, we have sought to reflect the key elements of the stories we were told.

CHAPTER 4: On the Individualist Arts of Sex

The stories of Simon and Ruth are condensed composites derived from interviews conducted early in 2004 and informed by various psychoanalytic case histories published in the mainstream journals. The initial inspiration for these characters came from Arlene Kramer Richard's article "A Romance with Pain: A Telephone Perversion in a Woman?" *International Journal of Psychoanalysis* 70 (1989):153–64. The final versions of Simon and Ruth owe a great deal to the fictionalized case method detailed in the introduction.

CHAPTER 5: The Self and Other Ethical Troubles

Norman Bishop's story is based on numerous conversations and interviews between him and Charles Lemert, many over early breakfasts or late at night after the day's work. Bishop is president and founder of Positive Solutions Inc. in Middletown, Connecticut. Among other of his creative insistences, Norman has involved Charles in the work of the organization, as a teacher and organizer of the parenting program and chair of the board of directors. More information on Positive Solutions can be found at www.positivesolutionsinc.org/.

CHAPTER 6: Surviving the New Individualism

The biographical material on C. Wright Mills is cobbled from several available, if flawed, sources. One is the only available full-length biography, Irving Louis Horowitz's now dated and in any case tendentious *C. Wright Mills: An American Utopian* (Free Press, 1983). Another is the somewhat overedited and all-too-glowing collection of his letters, Kathryn Mills with Pamela Mills, eds., *C. Wright Mills, Letters and Autobiographical Writings* (University of California Press, 2000). Naturally, Mills's recollections of his own life in this collection are especially valuable. To be a sociologist in America today is to have heard endless stories of the legendary figure, some second- or thirdhand. Among them, Dan Wakefield's introduction to the letters, as well as the memoirs of his daughters included in the edited letters, are helpful. Among those from whom Charles remembers hearing stories over the years are Dick Flacks, Herb Hyman, Phyllis Meadow, and Al Gouldner. Otherwise, it cannot be certified which of the impressions owing to legend may have influenced the telling of Mills's story here. We should note that a fresh and well-researched biography by John Summers is in the works; it should be a valuable addition to our knowledge of Mills's life. Summers has confirmed the appealing, if unproved, idea that Mills's heart troubles were aggravated by the pressures of public attention. Also Tom Hayden's shorter biography written as an MA thesis at the University of Michigan early in the 1960s will appear in 2006 as *Radical Nomad: C. Wright Mills and His Times,* with new essays by Hayden, Dick Flacks, Stanley Aronowitz, and Charles Lemert.

The story of Phyllis Meadow is based largely on a personal interview on October 29, 2004, by her granddaughter, Rebecca Reed, and Charles Lemert. That interview, along with other biographical information, will appear in a festschrift to be published by Paradigm Publishers, hopefully in 2006. Like Mills, Meadow was a legend among those who worked with her, including Charles, who, among countless other relations over the years, has taught in her Institute for Study of Violence and was for a while chair of the board of trustees of the Boston Graduate School for Psychoanalysis (BGSP), until he stomped out one fine day. Other members of the BGSP group have provided a wealth of stories, none of which is betrayed by the direct experience. More information on Meadow can be found through the Web site of the Boston Graduate School for Psychoanalysis in Brookline, Massachusetts, www.bgsp.edu, which provides links to information on her other two centers in Vermont and New York City. For the Center for Modern Psychoanalysis in the West Village, go to: /www.cmps.edu. Her principal and most current book is *The New Psychoanalysis* (Rowman & Littlefield, 2003). Other of her writings can be found in *Modern Psychoanalysis,* an academic journal associated with the Center for Modern Psychoanalytic Studies.

ON REFERENCES AND OTHER SOURCES AND NOTES

Introduction

The quotation from Ulf Hannerz is taken from his stimulating *Transnational Connections: Cultures, Peoples, Places* (Routledge, 1996), pp. 88–89.

CHAPTER 1: Individualism for Beginners

The survey conducted by ChildWise was reported in the UK by Denis Campbell, "Mobiles, MP3s, DVDs: Raising a Generation of Techno-kids," *Observer*, 13 February 2005, p. 14.

Some useful guides to Baudrillard's work include Mark Poster's edited collection, *Jean Baudrillard: Selected Writings* (Stanford University Press, 1988), and Douglas Kellner's *Baudrillard: A Critical Reader* (Blackwell, 1990). See also Charles Lemert, *Postmodernism Is Not What You Think* (Blackwell, 1997).

For Erik Erikson, we consulted his classic *Identity: Youth and Crisis* (Faber and Faber, 1974). The quotes are from pp. 17–19. For William James, we used his *Principles of Psychology* (Dover Publications, 1955). For Goffman, see his *Presentation of Self in Everyday* Life (Doubleday, 1959) and *Stigma* (Prentice Hall, 1963). See also Charles Lemert and Ann Branaman, *The Goffman Reader* (Blackwell, 1997).

The final section, "The Individualist Imagination," raises issues concerning sociostructural transformations sweeping the globe that we discuss in detail throughout the book, and to which we return from the angle of political history in the final chapter. The article detailing the new American social contract is Jackie Calmes, "In Bush's 'Ownership Society,' Citizens Would Take More Risk," *Wall Street Journal*, 28 February 2005, p. 1. Our discussion of privatization here is substantially indebted to the works of Zygmunt Bauman, specifically *Postmodern Ethics* (Blackwell, 1993), *Postmodernity and Its Discontents* (Polity Press, 1997), and *The Individualized Society* (Polity Press, 2001).

CHAPTER 2: Was the Free Individual Just a Dream?

Recent social theory has identified pressures for individualism, identity politics, and individualization, as well as a more thoroughgoing privatized culture where we are increasingly "subject to ourselves," as key processes of global social change. For a summary of these trends in recent social science research, see Anthony Elliott, *Subject to Ourselves: Social Theory, Psychoanalysis, and Postmodernity*, 2nd ed. (Paradigm Publishers, 2004). Today, a breakdown of traditional stable identities based on social-class hierarchies is said to give rise to multiple, fragmented, and more liquidized identity practices, which in turn unleash new possibilities and risks for personal and social life. The best starting point for grasping changes to the fabric of individualism within the broader context of the polished, expensive cities of the West is Zygmunt Bauman's various contributions to this debate, most notably *Postmodernity and Its Discontents* (Polity Press, 1997), *Liquid Modernity* (Polity Press, 2000), *The Individualized Society* (Polity Press, 2001), and *Liquid Love* (Polity Press, 2003). See also Anthony J. Cascardi, *The Subject of Modernity* (Cambridge University Press, 1996); Anthony Giddens, *Modernity and Self-Identity* (Polity Press, 1991); Anthony Elliott, *Concepts of the Self* (Polity Press, 2001); and Charles Lemert, *Postmodernism Is Not What You Think* (Paradigm, 2005).

Many works looking at changes in the area of identity, identity politics, and the study of individualism more generally have drawn attention to the personal and cultural significance of global organizations, networks, and flows in the reshaping of everyday life. A seminal contribution is Manuel Castells's three-volume series, *The Information Age: The Rise of the Network Society* (Blackwell, 1996), *The Power of Identity* (Blackwell, 1998), and *End of Millennium* (Blackwell, 2000). The crisis of individualism today has its roots in a range of transboundary or global phenomena, which include, among others, the spread of new information technologies, the development of multinational culture industry and multinational telecommunication corporations, the organization of intensive transnational networks of production and distribution, the integration of finance systems in the world economy, and the formation of transnational political alliances and lobbies. This takes us directly to the contested terrain of globalization—a debate that is looked at in some detail in the next chapter.

The theoretical backdrop to this chapter can be summarized as follows. Much recent social and political writing about the reshaping of identity arising as a consequence of globalization hinges on an apparent increase in individualism in contemporary culture. One highly influential theoretical perspective has explored broad cultural shifts and identity tensions in relation to definitions of "national character," especially American political culture. In a different theoretical fashion, and at a more transnational or global level, problems in identity construction and cohesion have also been tied to wide-reaching transformations associated with capitalism, modernity, and processes of postmodernization. We discuss these different theoretical perspectives in this chapter under three broad headings: manipulated individualism, isolated privatism, and reflexive individualization. All of these theoretical orientations, we argue, have tended to ignore or isolate elements of emotional or psychic investment in the production and reproduction of the practices of individualism in contemporary society. That this is an important omission is apparent from recent research concerning debates over the homogenization of national identities and local cultures in conditions of globalization. As several influential studies in this field have stressed, the homogenization thesis rests upon a passive view of individuals and their capacity to make and remake their identities in alternative and unexpected ways. See, among others, Daniel Miller, *Modernity: An Ethnographic Approach* (Berg, 1994); and John B. Thompson, *The Media and Modernity* (Polity Press, 1995). In stressing that cultural globalization is always individually consumed, locally read, and regionally transformed, these studies have advanced new understandings of the self-society nexus in contemporary advanced society. Our thesis of an emergent "new individualism" arises against the backdrop of these theories, tensions, and omissions in the debate over individualism and seeks to develop further conceptualizations of the extent to which global forces at once increase and decrease the "affective density of social relations," paying particular attention to the emotional investments of individuals in global processes, flows, and organizations.

MANIPULATED INDIVIDUALISM   For Simmel, we consulted his essay "The Metropolis and Mental Life" in Mike Featherstone and David Frisby's edited collection *Simmel on Culture* (Sage, 1997) and the collection by Donald N. Levine, ed., *Georg Simmel, On Individuality and Social Forms* (University of Chicago, 1971), where the several references to his idea of the new individualism are to be found. Also useful are David Frisby's studies *Fragments of Modernity* (Polity Press, 1985) and *Georg Simmel* (Routledge, 2002). For the Frankfurt school, some helpful overviews are Martin Jay, *The Dialectical Imagination: A History of the Frankfurt School and the Institute of Social Research, 1923–1950* (Heinemann, 1973); David Held, *Introduction to Critical Theory* (Polity Press, 1990); Douglas Kellner, *Critical Theory, Marxism, and Modernity* (Johns Hopkins

University Press, 1989); and Rolf Wiggershaus, *The Frankfurt School: Its History, Theories, and Political Significance* (Polity Press, 1994). On the culture industry, see Theodor Adorno, *The Culture Industry*, ed. Jay Bernstein (Routledge, 1991). Some good overviews of Jürgen Habermas's social theory include Thomas McCarthy, *The Critical Theory of Jürgen Habermas* (MIT Press, 1978); and William Outhwaite's edited collection *The Habermas Reader* (Polity Press, 1994). We have drawn here mostly from the early work of Habermas, notably *The Structural Transformation of the Public Sphere* (Polity Press, 1989). For Habermas's account of the colonization of the lifeworld, see *The Theory of Communicative Action* (Polity Press, 1986).

ISOLATED PRIVATISM We consulted the following texts: Richard Sennett, *The Fall of Public Man* (Norton, 1992); Christopher Lasch, *The Minimal Self: Psychic Survival in Troubled Times* (Norton, 1985); Robert Bellah, Richard Madsen, William Sullivan, Ann Swidler, and Steven Tipton, *Habits of the Heart: Individualism and Commitment in American Life* (University of California Press, 1996); Robert D. Putnam, *Bowling Alone: The Collapse and Revival of American Community* (Simon & Schuster, 2001); and Arlie Hochschild, *The Commercialization of Intimate Life* (University of California Press, 2003).

REFLEXIVE INDIVIDUALIZATION Ulrich Beck's ideas on reflexivity and individualization are set out in his books *The Risk Society* (Sage, 1992), *The Reinvention of Politics* (Polity Press, 1997), and *What Is Globalization?* (Polity Press, 2000). (The long quote is from *Reinvention*, p. 95.) The link between reflexive individualization and globalization is developed in Ulrich Beck and Elizabeth Beck-Gernsheim, *Individualization* (Sage, 2002). One among many critical responses to Beck's sociological writings is Anthony Elliott, *Critical Visions: New Directions in Social Theory* (Rowman & Littlefield, 2003), chap. 2.

THE INTERIORS OF THE NEW INDIVIDUALISM The quote from Marshall Berman is from *All That Is Solid Melts into Air* (Verso, 1982); the quote from Perry Anderson is from *The Origins of Postmodernity* (Verso, 1998). Our outline of an imaginary domain that shapes, and is shaped by, the new individualism is substantially informed by Anthony Elliott's *Social Theory and Psychoanalysis in Transition: Self and Society from Freud to Kristeva* (Free Association Books, 1999) and *Social Theory since Freud: Traversing Social*

Imaginaries (Routledge, 2004). Other writings in this tradition that inform our conceptualization of both an imaginary domain and the interior of the new individualism include Jacques Lacan, *Ecrits* (Routledge, 1977); Jean Laplanche, *Essays on Otherness* (Routledge, 2000); Julia Kristeva, *The Sense and Non-Sense of Revolt* (Columbia University Press, 2002); Cornelius Castoriadis, *The Imaginary Institution of Society* (Polity Press, 1987); Thomas Ogden, *The Primitive Edge of Experience* (Jason Aronson, 1989); and Phyllis Meadow, *The New Psychoanalysis* (Rowman & Littlefield, 2003).

CHAPTER 3: Living in a Privatized World

Self-Therapy: A Guide to Becoming Your Own Therapist, by Janette Rainwater, was published in London by Crucible, 1989. The quotation is from p. 9. For an interesting use of Rainwater's ideas in the context of a social-theoretical critique of therapy, see Anthony Giddens, *Modernity and Self-Identity* (Polity Press, 1991), chap. 3.

The literature on globalization is huge. Much of the debate over globalization has emanated from the academy, yet it is equally true that the topic has been central to current political debate as well as economic and social policy dialogues. Useful guides to the various controversies about globalization are Malcolm Water, *Globalization* (Routledge, 1995); Martin Albrow, *The Global Age* (Polity Press, 1997); Robert Holton, *Globalization and the Nation State* (Macmillan, 1998); Zygmunt Bauman; *Globalization: The Human Consequences* (Polity Press, 1998); Ullrich Beck, *What Is Globalization?* (Polity Press, 2000); Jean Aart Scholte, *Globalization: A Critical Introduction* (Macmillan, 2000); and Leslie Sklair, *Globalization: Capitalism and Its Alternatives*, 3rd ed. (Oxford University Press, 2002).

Concerning the Globalization I debate, the case of the skeptics was most forcefully advanced by Paul Hirst and Graeme Thompson, *Globalization in Question* (Polity Press, 1996). On the antiglobalization discourse, see David Held and Anthony McGrew, *Globalization/Anti-Globalization* (Polity Press, 2002).

Roland Robinson's *Globalization: Social Theory in Global Culture* (Sage, 1992) was one of the first systematic works to contextualize globalization in relation to a growing consciousness of the world as a single place, a "global consciousness." His approach directs us to issues of types of social agency, relationships, networks, and communities within the broader global frame of multidimensionality. In addition to Robinson's important research, we also have found the following books on the personal, political, and cultural aspects of globalization useful: Arjun Appadurai, *Modernity at Large: Cultural Dimensions of Globalization* (University of Minnesota Press, 1996); Ulf Hannerz, *The Transnational Connection* (Routledge, 1996); John Urry, *Global Complexity* (Polity Press, 2003); and John Keane, *Global Civil Society* (Cambridge University Press, 2003).

Important liberal presences in the globalization debates include Joseph Stiglitz, *Globalization and Its Discontents* (Penguin, 2002); Jagdish Bhagwati, *In Defence of Globalization* (Oxford University Press, 2004); and Martin Wolf, *Why Globalization Works* (Yale University Press, 2004).

David Held's research, which powerfully contextualizes globalization in the frame of social and political theory, is set out most recently in *Global Covenant* (Polity Press, 2004). But we have also drawn from the work of Held and his associates for contextualizing the "diffused globalism" of Larry's world and the "thick globalism" of Joe and Xavier's worlds. See David Held et al., *Global Transformations: Politics, Economics and Culture* (Polity Press, 1999). Held and his associates examine global flows, networks, and relations in terms of their possible consequences for extensity, intensity, velocity, and impact propensity. From this analytical baseline, four potential shapes of globalization are identified: "thick globalization," "diffused globalization," "expansive globalization," and "thin globalization." In reviewing and interpreting the interviews of Larry and of Joe and Xavier, we have drawn from this model for identifying the "deep drivers" of globalism, with particular reference to how its contemporary shape might affect practices of identity and the emotions. This is an extension of the model elaborated by Held and his associates beyond the institutional political field of their research to the individualized emotional field of our research, and one that we believe is highly fruitful for connecting contemporary forms of globalism to what people say in interviews about emotional transformations occurring in their lives.

The quotations from Beck are from *Individualization* (Sage, 2002), pp. 38, 49. The quotation from Bauman is from *Wasted Lives* (Polity Press, 2004), p. 128.

CHAPTER 4: On the Individualist Arts of Sex

The best general discussion of the many forms of intersection between globalization and sexuality is Dennis Altman, *Global Sex* (University of Chicago Press, 2001).

Freud's analysis of the polymorphous plasticity of sex is in "Three Essays on Sexuality," in *The Standard Edition of the Complete Psychological Works of Sigmund Freud*, edited by John Strachey and Alex Strachey (Hogarth Press, 1973). For a discussion of how Freud's theory of sexuality connects to wider social and political forces of change, see Anthony Elliott, *Psychoanalytic Theory: An Introduction* (Duke University Press, 2002).

For Giddens, we draw upon his books *The Consequences of Modernity* (Polity Press, 1990) and *Modernity and Self-Identity* (Polity Press, 1991). See also Ulrich Beck, Anthony Giddens, and Scott Lash, *Reflexive Modernisation* (Polity Press, 1994). For Giddens's theorization of sexuality as reflexive, see his book *The Transformation of Intimacy* (Polity Press, 1992). There is now an extensive literature on the sociological powers and limits of Giddens's theory of reflexivity; among others, see Charles Lemert, *Sociology after the Crisis*, 2nd ed. (Paradigm Publishers, 2004); and Anthony Elliott, *Critical Visions: New Directions in Social Theory* (Rowman & Littlefield, 2003), chap. 2. See also Dennis Altman, *Global Sex* (University of Chicago, 2001).

Janice Radway's provocative analysis of why women read, and what they are doing psychologically when reading, is outlined in her *Reading the Romance: Women, Patriarchy, and Popular Culture* (University of North Carolina Press, 1984). John B. Thompson's critique of new media and information technologies as related to the "relevance structure" of personal and social experience is developed in his book *The Media and Modernity* (Polity Press, 1995). Richard Lanham's excellent work on the creativity of computational text is *The Electronic Word* (University of Chicago Press, 1993). Sherry Turkle's *Life on the Screen* (Simon & Schuster, 1995) is one of the best psychosocial studies of the relationship between computers and emotional life available, with many references to online love.

Regarding the politics of therapy, we consulted Phillip Rieff's classic *The Triumph of the Therapeutic* (University of Chicago Press, 1987) as well as Stephen Frosh's *For and Against Psychoanalysis* (Routledge, 1997). Our discussion here foregrounds Michel Foucault's *History of Sexuality* (Penguin, 1980) and Eva Moskowitz's *In Therapy We Trust: America's Obsession with Self-Fulfillment* (Johns Hopkins University Press, 2001). Another recent study of the topic, Frank Furedi's *Therapy Culture* (Routledge, 2003), casts the contemporary dominance of the therapeutic imperative as an outcome of a new emotionalism, in which the boundaries of private and public life are significantly redrawn. Furedi's argument is that therapy culture seeks to repress and exclude the challenges and conflicts that individuals and groups necessarily deal with in daily life, shifting the management of people's emotions to the terrain of political blueprints and professional experts. Therapy culture for Furedi inaugurates a new order of emotional vulnerability, in which people are incited to feel powerless and helpless, a social order in which the politics of daily life becomes centered on issues of personal resilience and on an individualized capacity to cope with risks, hazards, and dangers.

In our view, it might be more fruitful to contrast, not therapy and therapeutics as Furedi does, but emancipatory and commercial uses of these terms. Criticisms of therapy are now as multiple as the therapies on offer to individuals, and so it would seem evident that any cultural agreement or consensus on the powers and limits of therapy is unlikely to emerge. Of course the critique of therapeutics initiated by writers like Moskowitz and Furedi is important, especially where the private and therapeutic are recast as part of processes of social regulation or personal demoralization. But the new individualism suggests that the reverse lining of this argument needs to be taken into account too. It's not just that insidious forces of social power or ideological domination are at stake here, but rather that oppressive rewritings of therapeutic practices render imaginative space too restrictive and insufficiently our own. Another way of putting this would be to say that we should consider using Freud's fundamental psychoanalytic insight—namely, that we are not transparent to ourselves—to question the knowingness of the therapeutic imperative and especially the transmission of what passes for therapeutic insight across organizations and institutions.

Therapy culture, in its more functionalist or instrumental modes, is the product of a relentless postmodern drive for self-fulfillment and self-expression. The therapeutic imagination is, in this sense, essentially devoted to simple, fast, and final solutions, compressing complex individual and collective problems down to the point of psychologism—to a belief that focusing attention on private life is all that is needed for coming to terms with the riddles of being-in-the-world. The utopianism in all this is almost appealing. Not only will therapeutic confession lead to better, and indeed happier, lives, but also the outcomes from psychological diagnosis will produce a complete eradication of disorders, addictions, and syndromes. Instead of human ambivalence and productive psychic conflict (as conceptualized and recommended by Freud), therapy will put an end to the dynamic unconscious, to repressed desire, to depression and the death drive.

Such demand for psychological certitude, at once craved and reproduced by the more instrumentalist forms of today's therapy culture, is fortunately not everywhere supreme. Modernist demands for a designed, managed, and conformist therapeutic authority are increasingly brought low by our fast-globalizing world, in which a proliferation of knowledge systems and knowledge capital means that dependence on professional authority can no longer take the form of either passive acceptance or blind trust. What this suggests, in a nutshell, is that claims to specialized knowledge advanced by therapists enter into direct competition and conflict with the claims of other professional experts in the fields of health, medicine, psychology, and so on, with the result that the client or consumer has no choice but to engage with an endless menu of possible choices regarding matters of emotional health and psychological well-being. From this angle, therapy culture becomes squeezed between modernist dreams of psychological certitude and uncertainty-free solutions on the one hand and late modern or postmodern aspirations for polytherapeutic or multicultural engagements with the emotional dilemmas of the age on the other. This revaluation of personal choice and individual decision making in our increasingly consumer-orientated society is manifested in a rapidly proliferating distrust of "experts" (witness the explosion of litigation against therapists in the United States especially), and particularly in an increasing rejection of the tendency of the "psy" professions to recast emotional dilemmas as forms of illness.

Debates about forms of therapy and their efficacy are not simply the preserve of experts and intellectuals, however, but also draw in those who have most to gain or lose from such psychological exploration—namely, the clients or subjects of therapy. Nearly everyone entering therapy today is aware, at however minimal a level, that there is no authoritative version of psychotherapy. To enter the therapeutic domain today is to enter a field comprising an almost inexhaustible variety of approaches, orientations, practices, theories, and philosophies. By choosing a therapist, people implicitly make a choice regarding which of the competing schools and approaches best suits them and their strivings for human autonomy. Yet, in exercising choice in this way, people are engaging in much more than mere consumer selection. For just as therapists are viewed less and less as "professional authorities" and more as "coworkers" in revising narratives of the self, so clients themselves are demonstrating an increasingly sophisticated understanding of the competing claims, counterclaims, and aims of therapeutic traditions and trends, not only initiating self-reflexive investigations of how the therapeutic process relates to the broader contours of their emotional lives but also engaging in discussion and debate with their therapists over the value of therapeutics more generally. The prime value of therapy from this angle is that it provides people with—to use British sociologist Anthony Giddens's phrase—"a methodology of life-planning."

Of course, in actuality, things may not appear so plural or reflexive for subjects of therapy as they go about the daily business of reflecting on the apparent jumble of their emotional lives. And while it is also true that psychotherapy as a profession has been notably inward-looking and reclusive, the diversity of therapeutic imaginaries is increasingly evident— for anyone who cares to look—at the level of theory and clinical practice. Classical psychoanalysis, it is true, retains a considerable degree of intellectual superiority here, especially for academics, but also for those with the time and money to pursue "a methodology of life-planning" in such exquisite detail. Yet it is in the marketplace that one can find the strongest indication of the ever-growing diversity of therapeutics, from counseling and survivor groups to psychotherapeutic mysticism and postmodern psychodynamic approaches. Perhaps the best indication of such pluralism is to be found by looking at one particular version of therapy, namely, psychoanalysis. It may be that, as the so-called culture wars have it, the fascination with Freud is over—but, then again, look at the sheer diversity of psychoanalytic theories and treatments on offer today. Classical psychoanalysts, post-Freudians, Kleinians, the interpersonal school, Lacanians, neo-Lacanians, Jungians, Winnicottians, relational analysts: such is the diversity of therapists that confronts anyone contemplating psychoanalysis today. What might such analytic differentiation within psychoanalysis mean in broader terms? We might, for one thing, expect to find diverse cultural emphases and psychological expectations operating within such approaches and theories. For example, Kleinian therapies might be subtitled "Portrait of the child overwhelmed by her mother," or "How to keep Mommy and beat back Daddy"; classical Freudian therapies might be cast as psychocultural imaginaries locked on exclusions, denials, displacements, and repressions; Lacanian therapies can be understood as fascinated by the early self's relation to loss, lack, and language. When competing versions of psychoanalysis are pictured in this way, a different understanding of therapeutics opens out, one in which a concern with open-mindedness, difference, and diversity comes into view.

If therapy is complex, contradictory, and diverse at the level of clinical practice, why might this not also be true within the broader field of culture? That is, why shouldn't therapy culture participate in a mixture of opportunity and risk similar to that characteristic of modernity itself? The short answer is that it does. Only a more refined psychosocial analysis, we argue, based on careful appraisal of the cultural consequences of the new individualism, can succeed in addressing the powers and limits of therapeutics. What is required now is the kind of social critique capable of addressing the ways in which therapeutics infiltrates and frames diverse aspects of personal and organizational life—from the use of self-help manuals to the directives handed down from management therapists acting as consultants to various global conglomerates—and of how such social practices often bring with them gains in personal and social autonomy. Equally, what is also needed is a guiding framework that can trace and map the complex ways in which therapeutics often becomes degraded, that is, comes to be deployed oppressively and exploitatively. In a world of advanced globalization, in which media sound bites fuel political reaction and counterreaction, this is clearly a pressing public issue. The rise of confessional culture and mediated scandal—from the Clinton-Lewinsky scandal to the sexual rumors surrounding soccer icon David Beckham and the state of his marriage—highlights only too well the growing place of therapy-centered politics in our time. Sociologies of all kinds must try to grasp both these enabling and constraining features of therapeutics—in the worlds of individual selves certainly, but also culturally and across the globe.

CHAPTER 5: The Self and Other Ethical Troubles

The issues addressed in this chapter are discussed at great length and detail in Charles Lemert, *Dark Thoughts: Race and the Eclipse of Society* (Routledge, 2002). The general argument on multicultural ethics is in Charles Lemert, "Can the Worlds Be Changed? On Ethics and the Multicultural Dream," *Thesis Eleven* 78 (August 2004): 46-60. The references to Zygmunt Bauman's concept of liquidity are from his *Liquid Modernity* (Polity Press, 2000). Ulrich Beck's second modernity is from *Reinvention of Politics* (Polity Press, 1997), among other places. Anthony Giddens's radical modernization appears in several of his many writings, notably *The Consequences of Modernity* (Polity Press, 1990). Scott Lash's version of reflexivity modernity is in *Reflexive Modernization*

(Polity Press, 1994), a collection of essays on the subject by Giddens and Beck as well as Lash.

CHAPTER 6: Surviving The New Individualism

In the reprise of the social history of the three types of new individualism the references to authors of various theories can be found in the original presentation of the ideas in chapter 2. Those few that are mentioned here but not there are assumed to be so well known as to be recognizable. Still if they are not, try Charles Lemert, *Social Theory: The Multicultural and Classical Readings*, 3rd ed. (Westview Press/Perseus, 2004), where the reader can find short selections as well as biographical information on the authors. Lemert's long introduction to the historical periods covered in *Social Theory* provides more information on the history of the times from the 1920s on. Otherwise sources for the social history of the various periods are too numerous to mention, but some of the more notable are Eric Hobsbawm, *The Age of Extremes: A History of the World, 1914–1991* (Vintage Books, 1994); Howard Zinn, *A People's History of the United States: 1492 to the Present* (HarperCollins, 2003); Martin Jay, *The Dialectical Imagination: A History of the Frankfurt School and the Institute of Social Research, 1923–1950* (Little, Brown, 1973); Ann Douglas, *Terrible Honesty: Mongrel Manhattan in the 1920s* (Farrar, Strauss & Giroux, 1995); Elaine Tyler May, *Homeward Bounder: American Families in the Cold War Era* (Basic Books, 1988); Wini Breines, *Young, White, and Miserable: Growing Up Female in the Fifties* (Beacon, 1992); Walter Russell Mead, *Moral Splendor: The American Empire in Transition* (Houghton Mifflin, 1987); David Halberstam, *The Fifties* (Fawcett, 1994); John D'Emilio, *Sexual Politics, Sexual Communities: The Making of a Homosexual Minority in the United States, 1940–1970* (University of Chicago Press, 1983); Godfrey Hodgson, *America in Our Time: From World War II to Nixon—What Happened and Why* (Vintage, 1976); and Immanuel Wallerstein, *After Liberalism* (New Press, 1995), and *The Decline of American Power* (New Press, 2003).

INDEX

~

ABOUT THE
AUTHORS

~

CHARLES LEMERT was born in Cincinnati, Ohio, which in an earlier time was a stop on the Underground Railroad to freedom for runaway slaves—thus ever after a well-worn path to the North and one that allowed his black virtual mother, Florence, to find him and, no doubt, for him to find his black daughter, Annie. He teaches sociology at Wesleyan University in Connecticut and lives in New Haven, where he, Geri, and Annie walk the family dog, Yogi. His wife, Geri, is a literary agent in New York City, and his oldest son, Noah, is an outdoor educator in Connecticut. Otherwise, Lemert works with HIV-positive people at Positive Solutions in Middletown, Connecticut, and teaches occasionally at the Institute for the Study of Violence at the Boston Graduate School of Psychoanalysis.

Among his recent books are *Muhammad Ali: Trickster in the Culture of Irony*; *Dark Thoughts: Race and the Eclipse of Society*; *Postmodernism Is Not What You Think: Why Globalization Threatens Modernity*; and *Durkheim's Ghosts: Cultural Logics and Social Things*. The third edition of his best-selling *Social Things: An Introduction to the Sociological Life* is published by Rowman & Littlefield (2005).

ANTHONY ELLIOTT was born in Australia and came to the UK on a Commonwealth Scholarship in the late 1980s to undertake doctoral studies at the University of Cambridge. Since that time he has held academic positions in the UK and Australia, most recently as professor and chair of sociology at the University of Kent at Canterbury.

Dividing his time between the UK, Ireland, and Australia, Elliott is married to Nicola Geraghty. Their daughter Caoimhe, one of the subjects of this book, is now in regular school and loves, above all else, playing with her younger brother, Oscar.

Since the early 1990s Elliott has been a regular reviewer and commentator for newspapers and magazines around the world. Among his recent books are *The Mourning of John Lennon; Psychoanalytic Theory: An Introduction; Critical Visions; Subject to Ourselves;* and *Social Theory since Freud.*